Israel Horovitz: Three Gloucester Plays

Three Gloucester Plays

by
Israel Horovitz

Garden City, NY

Design by Maria Chiarino
Photographs of "Park Your Car in Harvard Yard" by Joan Marcus
Photographs of "Henry Lumper" by Clark Linehan and Carol Rosegg/Martha Swope Associates
Photographs of "North Shore Fish" by David Benoit and Martha Swope
Manufactured in the United States of America

INTRODUCTION

Gloucester, Massachusetts, is thirty-eight miles north of Boston and precisely marathon distance from my birthplace, Wakefield, Massachusetts. Gloucester was where my parents took my sister and me on special days.

My first play (with a devilishly ironic title: "The Comeback") opened in Boston when I was nineteen. Some years and several plays later, after I'd found the courage to actually leave New York City, summers, without fear that my "New York Playwright" logo would be passed to a younger, fresher out-of-towner, I thought to myself, "Why not put my life down where special days are spent?" I bought my first (and last) Gloucester house, a tiny wood-framed Victorian with slightly Gothic pretensions.

I thought that I'd bought a house for summers and for the odd warm weekend. And then I noticed that I'd stayed in Gloucester for sixteen consecutive months. In 1985, my twin children, Hannah and Oliver, were born at the Addison-Gilbert Hospital in Gloucester. They are Gloucester kids.

Gloucester is a place of great natural beauty. Majestic cliffs overlook a Kodak-perfect coastline. Every Gloucester kid knows a half-dozen secret sandy beaches. Every Gloucester kid knows a dozen secret swimmable granite quarries. Tourists in search of cheap lobsters and/or early Americana usually bypass Gloucester, opting for the calendar-cute village of Rockport, five miles up the road. And as Brackish says in "Park Your Car in Harvard Yard", come Labor Day . . . "the tourists all pack up their dreadful, greasy, hot-dog colored bodies and their God–awful charcoal sketches of Motif #1" . . . and we locals smile, because we locals know that September and October are simply the best months. . . .

Gloucester's heroes are carpenters and fishermen, not playwrights. The more time I spent in Gloucester, the more I felt the need to have a theatre in town, a place to see plays . . . a place to try my new work first. In 1980, I helped found The Gloucester Stage Company. We started out as a summer theatre, producing one-act plays in the back room at the Blackburn Tavern. From day one, we had an audience.

Although Gloucester has always boasted a tradition of High Art

(Winslow Homer, Edward Hopper, Milton Avery, T.S. Eliot, Charles Olson, etc. all lived and worked in Gloucester), Gloucester is and was and always will be essentially blue collar . . . a home to "fish people" . . . fishermen, lobstermen, lumpers, cutters. Once a bustling, world-class seaport, Gloucester's best days are either past or deeply-buried in secret years ahead. At the moment, Gloucester is in trouble. The fish business has all but gone away. The economy is floating belly-up. Drug traffic is unthinkably high. Gloucester people are, in a word, worried.

My first Gloucester play, "Mackerel," was whimsical . . . a sort of Nixon/Bush parable about a Gloucester man, Ed Lemon, who has a 250,000-lb. mackerel crash through the wall of his house. As I settled into actually living life in Gloucester, my notion to write more plays that were actually set in Gloucester became more serious. As did the plays themselves.

"Park Your Car in Harvard Yard" was first done at the Los Angeles Actors Theatre in collaboration with Gloucester Stage. Bill Bushnell came to Gloucester to work with me on the script and to direct "The Widow's Blind Date" at Gloucester Stage. "Park Your Car in Harvard Yard" was clearly a success in Los Angeles, but it was a *triumph* in Gloucester. Local people identified with the people and with the place of the play . . . and with the play's politics. They were deeply moved by the play. And I was deeply moved by my play's audience.

"Henry Lumper" was by far the most sensational of the Gloucester plays to premiere at Gloucester Stage. "Henry Lumper" retells Shakespeare's "Henry IV—Parts One and Two," sort of. The play is set on the Gloucester waterfront. I used this particular play to dramatize Gloucester's terrible drug problem. Heroin was being run through Gloucester, much of it arriving by boat, hidden in the bellies of frozen fish. Local people were dealing drugs. Local boats were "running heavy." A lobsterman could make more money carrying one cigar-box filled with cocaine than he could in a month of hauling traps. But worst of all, local people, in great number, were using drugs themselves. Such was the frustration of a community that hadn't just lost its jobs, but had also lost its primary industry, its primary way of life.

A local woman, Gail Randazza, helped me research "North Shore Fish," a play specifically about the quantum relationship of loss-of-work to loss-of-hope. Gail was "fish people." She was a fish-packer, as had been several generations of women in her family before her. While Gail and I were visiting fish plants together, Gail told me a great deal about the inner workings of Gloucester's drug scene. She knew a lot. I asked her why she knew a lot. She said she had "a junkie in the family." Less then a year later, I was stunned to learn of Gail's death . . . from an overdose of heroin. Gail turned out to be her family's junkie. I modeled Florence, one of the central characters of "North Shore Fish," on Gail, sort of. After losing her job, Florence ends the play in tears with a simple, plaintive "I've got nothing left to teach my children!"

I dedicated "North Shore Fish" to Gail's memory and returned to writing plays set in Gloucester with renewed enthusiasm.

"Henry Lumper" shocked Gloucester. Because of this play, I made many new friends in town, but I made an even greater number of new enemies, many of whom thought the "dirty laundry" I'd aired in this particular play was simply "private stuff." After seeing a performance of "Henry Lumper," the then-Mayor of Gloucester told me he learned of his city's drug problem from my play. Ultimately, so did the Boston *Globe*. Gloucester's drug problem was out in the open, ready finally for a cure. It was a thrilling time in my life. To be a playwright and to actually have impact on a community! To be . . . timely!

"North Shore Fish" was the first production in Gloucester Stage's present performance space. We'd been forced out of the Blackburn Tavern by a greedy new owner/landlord. Gorton's of Gloucester came to our rescue with an 175'×175' abandoned warehouse space overlooking the harbor at Rocky Neck. The warehouse was filled with obsolete fish-processing equipment . . . exactly what we needed for the set of "North Shore Fish." To open the theatre and the play, we "arranged" the equipment, cleaned the space of its twenty years of accumulation (wharf rats included!), brought in 100–plus seats. And "North Shore Fish" opened to a world. The play ran for six consecutive months, only closing at Gloucester Stage in order to re-open at the WPA Theatre in New York. "North Shore Fish" was nominated for that season's Drama Desk Award. Neal Simon won it, of course, but Gloucester Stage and still another of my Gloucester plays had had a great outing in New York City . . .

Several years ago, I wrote another cycle of plays, "The Wakefield Plays." I was fresh out of CUNY's Ph.D. Program in English Lit and "The Wakefield Plays" were brimful of complex, arcane literary allusion. Martin Esslin called the work "an American Orestia." Thornton Wilder had something else to say.

I had dinner with Mr. Wilder, from time to time. He was eighty-six years old and not able to get around easily. When we met together, we talked about playwriting and about life. He read my "Wakefield Plays" and was extremely flattering in his praise . . . but, at the end of it all, Thornton Wilder spoke one sentence that would alter the course of my playwriting for years and years to come. He ended his praise of "The Wakefield Plays" with ". . . of course, there isn't very much Wakefield in those plays."

Spoken by Thornton Wilder, who had created Grovers Corners, New England's best-known, best-loved small town, that ten-word sentence had, for me, great meaning and great impact. If my Gloucester-based plays would be nothing else, they would be brimful of Gloucester.

Mr. Wilder often talked about a notion that "all knowledge flowed through the trunk of the tree." If one thing could be learned to its fullest, then all things would be at the same time learned. Consider that a carpenter who is truly a master . . . the ultimate genius-joiner . . . could easily do skillful brain surgery . . . because the essential theories of great carpentry and of great brain surgery are essentially the same.

For the past several years, I've been writing about life as it is lived on a tiny dot on the planet Earth: Gloucester, Massachusetts. No more, no less. It seemed to me that if I could get it right for Gloucester—really and truly get it right—I wouldn't ever have to write about The World . . . about Life . . . because, in a substantial way, I would have already gotten it right . . . about The World . . . about Life.

To date, I've written eight Gloucester-based plays. Three are collected in this volume: "Park Your Car in Harvard Yard," "Henry Lumper," and "North Shore Fish." The other extant Gloucester Plays are "Strong-Man's Weak Child," "Year Of The Duck," "Firebird At Dogtown," "Sunday Runners in The Rain" and the yet-unfinished "Fighting Over Beverly." I may stop now, move on. I may not.

While yes, it is thrilling to watch Broadway audiences stand and cheer "Park Your Car in Harvard Yard," quite honestly, among the few unthinkable thrills of my life was my being able to watch "Park Your Car in Harvard Yard" have its great success in Paris, in French . . . my hearing the laughter, my seeing the tears . . . my watching a very French audience find my play to be . . . well . . . very French.

—Israel Horovitz
New York City
February 1992

Park Your Car
in
Harvard Yard

PARK YOUR CAR IN HARVARD YARD was originally produced by Los Angeles Actors' Theatre, Bill Bushnell and Diane White, Producers. The production featured Barbara Babcock as Kathleen Hogan and Stefan Gerash as Jacob Brackish. The production was directed by Bill Bushnell.

The Gloucester Stage company (Israel Horovitz, Artistic Director) production of PARK YOUR CAR IN HARVARD YARD featured Dossy Peabody as Kathleen Hogan and Thomas Celli as Jacob Brackish. The production was directed by Richard Hughes.

Subsequently, the play was workshopped at the Manhattan Theatre Club featuring Ellen Burstyn as Kathleen Hogan and Burgess Meredith as Jacob Brackish. Michael McNamara was the radio voice of Byron Weld. The MTC production was directed by Lynne Meadow. The Manhattan Theatre Club presented the New York premiere of the play on February 28, 1984.

The French premiere of PARK YOUR CAR IN HARVARD YARD featured Jane Birkin as Kathleen Hogan and Pierre Dux as Jacob Brackish. The production was directed by Jean-Loup Dabadie.

PARK YOUR CAR IN HARVARD YARD opened on Broadway at The Music Box Theatre on November 7, 1991, in a production produced by Robert Whitehead, Roger L. Stevens and Kathy Levin; set design by Ben Edwards; costume design by Jane Greenwood; lighting design by Thomas R. Skelton; sound design by John Gromada; directed by Zoe Caldwell.

KATHLEEN HOGAN . . . . Judith Ivey
JACOB BRACKISH . . . . Jason Robards
BYRON WELD . . . . Christopher Plummer

For
Gillian

The People of the Play

JACOB BRACKISH: eighty-ish, a Yankee Jew, Gloucester native.

KATHLEEN HOGAN: forty-ish, an Irish Catholic Yankee, Gloucester native.

The Place of the Play

The action of the play is set in the upstairs and downstairs rooms of the home of Jacob Brackish, East Gloucester, Massachusetts: a small 1850s wooden-framed, two-story Victorian house with slightly Gothic pretensions.

The Time of the Play

From one winter to the next: the final year of Jacob Brackish's life.

The Sequence of the Scenes of the Play

Sequence One—End of winter.
Sequence Two—Spring/summer (tourists in town)
Sequence Three—Autumn (tourists gone from town)
Sequence Four—Start of winter.

ONE

The end of winter

The audience is seated. House lights remain up in auditorium. We hear Vivaldi, "Concerto in A Minor," played over auditorium loudspeaker.

The voice of BYRON WELD *interrupts the music to make a small announcement—a plea for money for his one-man* FM-*radio station. As* WELD *speaks, Vivaldi fades under.*

BYRON WELD's *voice has the quintessential sound of North Shore Massachusetts. It is the very essence of "wicked awful" . . . it hems and it haws. It is a veritable symphony of upper nasal croak and squeal, combined with splintery timbres of remarkably old age: years of poverty, a lifetime of frustration.*

BYRON WELD *(over loudspeaker):* This is Byron Weld, WGLO-FM, Gloucester, Massachusetts on Cape Ann. If you think wint'ah's rough where you're sittin', try comin' 'round here by the transmitt'ah! You'll know what *rough* is! I got so many air leaks around the windows, every time the wind blows, the curtains shoot out straight, parallel to the floor and the ceilin' which, by the way, stopped leakin' finally 'cause it's so cold in here, the water that was pouring through the holes *actually froze up* . . . buttt, you'll never hear *me* complain! *(New, solicitous attitude)* Donations can be addressed to me, Byron Weld, WGLO-FM, Gloucester, Massachusetts 01930. Don't hold back 'cause you think what you're sendin' is too small. I'll take anything . . . *(The auditorium lights are black by now and we begin to hear the sounds of a winter's storm)* Antonio Vivaldi lived from 1678 to 1741. He wrote five gorgeous cello concerti. This one is his *"Concerto in A Minor,"* RV422, on an RCA Red Seal Recording featuring Ofra Hanroy on the cello with Paul Robinson conducting.

(We again hear the agonizing sound of the Andante of Vivaldi's "Concerto in A Minor," soft, Baroque. Additionally, we hear the storm sounds, now increased. Music to full.)

7

The season is winter. Any exterior foliage on set is without greenery: absolutely bare.

Lights up in rooms of late nineteenth century woodframed "Gothic Victorian" house. Upstairs, two bedrooms visible, but dimly lit in this first scene of play. Downstairs, we see living room, dining area and kitchen alcove. Overstuffed chair at center, sofa, bookshelves crammed with books, stereo and speakers (prominent), substantial collection of records, CDs and cassettes on bookcase.

It is night in February, deadly cold. In the distance, the wind howls, the odd hound bays, the copious buoys sway, causing their warning bells to chime, the lighthouse foghorn bleets its endless caution, a seagull screeches out in hunger. A seasonal thunderclap claps.

JACOB BRACKISH and KATHLEEN HOGAN stand near the door. BRACKISH is ancient and frail of frame, but he is powerful and immeasurably authoritative. By contrast, KATHLEEN is quiet and mousey. She is a strong–backed woman, around the age of forty. Both are quite tweedy. BRACKISH wears baggy trousers, dress shirt, necktie and baggy wool coat–sweater. Hearing aid in BRACKISH's right ear prominent. KATHLEEN wears wool skirt, black tights and wool sweater. A swatch of black fabric is in evidence, pinned to KATHLEEN's sweater. She is in mourning. BRACKISH holds KATHLEEN's dripping wet raincoat and is about to find a hook on which to hang it. She clutches dripping wet boots.

KATHLEEN stares at BRACKISH each time he looks away. When he looks at her, she stares downward, frightened. He is animated. She is paralyzed. They are both intensely anxious. He goes to radio, turns off music)

BRACKISH: Kathleen I . . . I'm very happy you're here.

KATHLEEN: I . . . I'm very happy to be here, Mr. Brackish.

BRACKISH: I'm very pleased that it was a person like you who answered my advertisement. *(Notices boots hugged in her arms)* You wouldn't believe how few people replied. You'd think nobody needed work around these parts. Not that you wouldn't have landed the job if dozens had replied. I mean . . . you would have . . . *(Pause)* it's

not like I'll live forever, you know. . . . You'll still be young when
this is over, Kathleen. I can promise you *that*.

KATHLEEN: I'm not complaining.

BRACKISH: No, no, you're not . . .

KATHLEEN (*Laughs nervously; sees puddle on carpet caused by her boots*):
Gawd! I made a wicked big puddle on your carpet! (KATHLEEN *bends
down quickly, tries to rub out the wetness with corner of her scarf. She
looks up at* BRACKISH, *laughs again nervously*)

KATHLEEN: Just rubbin' it up . . .

BRACKISH: Could you please let me take your *boots*, Kathleen? (KATHLEEN
*removes a wadded packet of letters and money from her boot, pockets
it*) Ohh, I see. Valuables . . .

KATHLEEN: Here. I'm really wicked sorry about yo'r carpet . . .

(BRACKISH *goes to the doorway, hangs up coat and drops her boots.* KATH-
LEEN *stares about the room intently. Her suitcase is near the door.* BRACK-
ISH *lifts it, returns to her proximity, smiles at her nervously.* KATHLEEN
averts her eyes)

BRACKISH: I imagine that your stomach's in knots, too, Kathleen . . .
this isn't an everyday sort of occurrence.

KATHLEEN: I'm not complaining, Mr. Brackish . . .

BRACKISH: Oh, I know you're not. . . . *(Pauses)* I've resisted having a
housekeeper, but this last spell I had was a pip . . . I saw Doctor
Chandler, up Addison–Gilbert. He was my student, two thousand
years ago. He gives me six months to a year, if I turn myself into the
hospital for total bed rest. But I prefer to live it out in luxury, thank
you very much, right here in my own house. So you've got yourself a
job and I've got myself an employee.

KATHLEEN: I'm not complaining, really . . . what with my husband
passin' on so sudden and leavin' me with next ta nothin', I mean,

really, I'm happy ta be here . . . ta be your housekeeper 'n all.
Happy. *(Pauses nervously)* Six months to a year is fine with me . . .

BRACKISH: Yes. I see . . . *(Hands suitcase to her)* You're probably tired.
You should go on up . . . I hope the room's not gonna be too tiny for
you . . .

KATHLEEN: Oh Gawd, no! First time I ever had a room on my own! I
always hadda share with my sistahs kinda thing. . . . Afta' I got
married, a' course, I shared with my husbin. *(Smiles, nervously)* This'll
be my first room. My first bed, too . . .

BRACKISH: You never had a *bed*?

KATHLEEN: On my *own!* I always hadda share beds . . . before here.

BRACKISH: Ah yes. I see what you mean . . . I think. . . . Well now
. . . the things you dropped off yesterday are up there already . . .
I cleaned out four drawers for you. If you need more storage space, I
can find the room, I'm sure.

KATHLEEN: Gawd, look at that! You've got about a million records. *(Smiles
timidly, then looks directly at BRACKISH)* I personally never saw the
need for accumulation. It'll be fine.

BRACKISH *(looks up at her; confused)*: Accumulation of my records'll be
"fine"? Your antecedent is unclear.

KATHLEEN: Oh gosh, no! Not y'or records. I just meant my *stuff!* Four
drawers will be more than enough for my *stuff!*

BRACKISH *(sensing KATHLEEN's deep discomfort)*: We'll both be more
relaxed with each other in short order. I know you're not complaining,
Kathleen. It's just that the intimacy of the thing never occurred to me.
These rooms have been mine alone for, well . . . (BRACKISH *pauses
uncomfortably, crosses to his chair)* This chair has been my closest
friend . . . my comfort and my company . . . my sole *confidant.* It's
a hell of a thing when a man comes to depend on his chair not only to
hold up his backside, but also to hold up the other side of the
conversation. . . . *(He pats chair, lovingly)* I've come to love my

chair, Kathleen . . . me and my chair . . . the two of us . . .
against the world!

*(He sits in chair, picks up a writing-board, slots writing-board across
arms of chair: a perfect fit.* BRACKISH *now pauses. His eyes turn in. He is
still and silent, totally lost in a memory.* KATHLEEN *turns away, looks up
staircase or at records. When she looks at* BRACKISH *again, she thinks he's
dead)*

KATHLEEN: Mr. Brackish? . . . Mr. Brackish? . . . *Mr. Brackish!*

BRACKISH *(jostled out of his reverie):* Hmmm?

KATHLEEN: I was just afraid maybe the doctor, you know,
underestimated. I can bring the most wicked awful bad luck ta
people! I gotta tell you: I have personally had all the death I can take
for a while . . . *(Painfully embarrassed by what she's just said)* I'd
better go on up.

*(*KATHLEEN *exits up the stairs.* BRACKISH *sits in his chair, looks out front,
extremely worried.*

We see KATHLEEN *in her room above. She goes to window, looks outside.
She, too, is extremely worried.*

Lights crossfade to BRACKISH *downstairs. He goes to the radio, turns it on.
Bach emanates from the radio, filling the house. He then executes his
morning routine, compulsively tidying living room . . . straightening
papers and furniture, precisely etc.*

Bach is now interrupted by BYRON WELD *who makes a second small plea
for public funding)*

BYRON WELD *(over lightly playing music):* This is Byron Weld, WGLO-FM,
Gloucester, Massachusetts on Cape Ann. You are listening to Johann
Sebastian Bach, music that's been played continuously by music
lovers ever since it was first written in 1725. Imagine! Music that's
held up more than 250 years, when this music station won't hold up
another twenty-five *days* if you don't send in some hard cold cash.
This is a final warning!

BRACKISH (*calls out loudly to* KATHLEEN): Kathleen? Hullooo?

KATHLEEN (*off*): I'm in the pantry, Mr. Brackish!

BRACKISH: *Still?*

KATHLEEN (*enters*): I've got about a half dozen more to go.

BRACKISH: Isn't it cold out there?

KATHLEEN: Oh yuh, wicked . . . it's freezing.

BRACKISH: I don't want you to freeze to death on your first day! Finish up in here!

KATHLEEN: That'll be alright?

BRACKISH: What'll be alright? Freezing to death on your first day or finishing up in here?

KATHLEEN: To iron . . . in with you!

BRACKISH: It'll be fine.

KATHLEEN: I'll get my stuff. (KATHLEEN *disappears, and quickly re-appears, carrying ironing board. She knocks into furniture with ironing board, knocks pots off stove. She attempts to collapse ironing board. It won't. And then refuses to open. Finally, it explodes open. She sets up ironing board near desk in living room*) Sorry for bangin' inta everything . . . a strange ironing board can kill a woman. (*She giggles, nervously*) No problem . . . (*Giggles again*) I'll get the iron . . . I'll plug in here . . . (*She plugs it in under desk, stands, touches iron, burns fingers*) Oh gawd! It's still hot! . . . no problem. (*She runs off again, re-appears with laundry basket filled with white shirts about to be ironed, plus an armload of freshly-ironed shirts, holds up shirts she plans to iron*) These are the ones to do . . . (*She now holds up armload of freshly ironed shirts on wire hangers*) These are the done ones . . . they'll be much better over here by the grate where it's wa'm . . . (*Begins to hang the shirts from bookshelves, above the fireplace grate*) They're still slightly dampish . . . the heat comin' outta the grate here will dry 'em nice. *(She now hangs freshly-ironed white shirts everywhere . . . the effect should be such that* KATHLEEN*'s enthusiastic labor—and her boundless energy—change the look of the room absolutely.* BRACKISH *watches* KATHLEEN, *bewildered)* Are you ready for another cuppa tea yet?

BRACKISH: No more tea, Kathleen, please! I don't want to hurt your feelings, but I don't want to drown in my own living room either! *(Suddenly, he whacks his hearing aid, yells at* KATHLEEN*) What?*

KATHLEEN *(startled):* What?

BRACKISH: My hearing aid died out! *(Points to his ear)* I can't hear you. I'm deaf as a haddock without this thing! *(He taps hearing aid twice)* Just a minute . . . *(He crosses to small writing desk and rummages through drawers)* I gotta change my battery. I went dead on you . . . *(Searches for and finds a new battery)* Wicked awful thing, to hav' ta depend on the likes of the Radio Shack to make the difference between hearing and not hearing. *(Changes battery)* Ahhh . . . that fixed it. *(Suddenly, he is aware of the music)* Ahhhh . . . Bach . . . "Concerto #2 in E Major."

BYRON WELD *(On radio):* Bach "Concerto #3 in D Major" played by the English Concert of London, under the direction of Trevor Pinnock. . . . This is Byron Weld, your host at radio station . . .

BRACKISH *(overlapping the last words):* Goddammit, Byron, that was Number 2, E Major!

BRACKISH *(switches radio off, angrily, turns to* KATHLEEN*):* Number 2 in E Major! You can take my word for it, Kathleen. The man knows *nothing!*

(He goes to his chair, sits. The moment his bottom touches down, KATH-LEEN *screams out)*

KATHLEEN: Whoa!

BRACKISH: Somethin' wrong?

KATHLEEN: Iron's a little leaky. No problem.

BRACKISH *(looks at shirts everywhere. Looks at* KATHLEEN *ironing more shirts):* You're not overdoing it, are you? I mean, there's no need to iron *all my shirts* the first day . . . I don't have any active *plan* for dressing-up . . .

KATHLEEN: I don't mind, really. I like ironing.

BRACKISH: Okay. Well then. Iron. (BRACKISH *starts reading his newspaper: obituary page)* Oh, dear . . . Porker Watson died. Scares me to open the paper these days. 'Course, at my age, I'm runnin' out of possibilities. *(Reads a moment, looks up again)* Look at that! Crispy Franklin's son died. I'm so old now I've not only outlived my friends, I've outlived their *children! (Makes a noise.)* Fffhhh . . . *(Puts down the newspaper: enough awfulness. Speaks to* KATHLEEN) You've seen some tragedy yourself? I don't mean to pry, but you did mention your husband's death . . .

KATHLEEN: Oh, well . . . no point in complaining, is there?

BRACKISH: Oh well, I dunno . . . I complain all the *time!*

KATHLEEN: I mean, nothin's bringing him back, right? Once you're dead, you're dead . . .

BRACKISH: I suppose . . .

KATHLEEN: The worms crawl in, the worms crawl out kinda thing . . . *(He looks away disgusted)* My Da used ta say that . . . he also used ta say that "all the complainin' in the world wasn't worth two-bits for a box'a clams, down Woodman's . . ."

BRACKISH: Woodman's . . . you grow up local? On the North Shore, I mean? I thought you were living down the line in Woburn? Didn't you say you grew up in Woburn? *(Pronounced "Wooobin")*

KATHLEEN: Oh noo. I was just staying up my husband's cousin's . . . she's married to a Woburn boy . . . McGrath . . . *(Suddenly) Gosh darn it!*

BRACKISH (*Stands, goes to* KATHLEEN, *inspects her labor*): What now?

KATHLEEN: Leaked on the shirts again . . . it's been doin' that on me all mornin' . . .

BRACKISH: Don't worry if you spoil a couple . . . I've got a lifetime of white shirts. (*Looks around room*) Looks like the Marblehead Regatta in here. (*He sees her fiddling about with the leaky iron*) You can't fill it all the way. If you drain off some of the water, you'll be fine . . . (*Makes small joke*) I think I bought that iron off President Taft . . .

KATHLEEN: Mmm . . . (*Thinks about* BRACKISH'*s small joke*) Oh . . . gotcha!

(*She* doesn't *drain off any water. She continues to iron.* BRACKISH *watches her*)

BRACKISH: Say, aren't you gonna . . . (*She looks up*) . . . drain it off?

KATHLEEN: No point in drainin' it off with just a couple of shirts to go . . .

BRACKISH: It'll only leak . . .

KATHLEEN: It's goin' better . . .

BRACKISH: Suit yourself. (BRACKISH *returns to his chair, sits.* KATHLEEN *completes ironing another shirt, buttons it on to a wire clothes hanger walks it past* BRACKISH *into living room, hangs it in an inappropriate place in living room. She manages to move furniture and papers, somehow undoing* BRACKISH'*s compulsive morning routine.* BRACKISH'*s space is clearly invaded. And he is clearly not happy. He pauses, sighs deeply*) This first day is probably the most difficult we'll ever have . . . together, I mean . . .

KATHLEEN: Oh well, I guess, yuh . . . (*She crosses to get another shirt*)

BRACKISH (*His most practiced, most charming smile*): You mentioned you had sisters.

KATHLEEN *(relieved, she chirps her answer):* Oh yuh . . . two, plus me, for three. Irish triplets. All three of us sistahs born in less than four years. . . . They both went to Catholic school. I'm the only one got to go to public school. I'm the baby. *(Laughs)* We're all "eens."

BRACKISH: I beg your pardon?

KATHLEEN *(steps forward to tell what is, possibly, the best joke she knows):* Me and my sistahs . . . we're all "eens" . . . Maureen, Doreen and Kathleen. (BRACKISH *doesn't laugh.* KATHLEEN's *courage withers)* I guess they didn't have a lot of time for thinkin' up imaginative names or nothin'. . . .

BRACKISH: It's quite difficult for me to follow the complexity of your sentences, Kathleen . . . the twistings and the turnings, so to speak. *"We're* all "eens" . . . *"they* didn't have a lot of time for thinkin' up names" . . . the antecedents to many of your pronouns are not precisely clear . . . not as clear as they should be . . . *(Sees he's hurt her feelings)*

KATHLEEN: I guess I should finish . . . up. *(She goes to ironing board. She picks up iron. Water gushes out onto shirt and onto floor)* Goddam it!

BRACKISH: What?

KATHLEEN: Oh Lord! Sorry to be swearin' in the house!

BRACKISH: What happened?

KATHLEEN *(lifts the arm of the white shirt that she has been ironing. It is brown, stained, ruined):* The iron leaks brown rusty water . . . it's all over the floor . . . I can bleach this out . . . *(She puts shirt into laundry basket, starts to iron another)*

BRACKISH: Aren't you gonna mop it up? . . . the rusty water!

KATHLEEN: I'll get to it, later. No point in moppin' it up and havin' it leak again . . . moppin' it up, havin' it leak, moppin' it up, havin' it leak . . . over and over. I'll get to it later . . .

BRACKISH: It's your decision . . .

KATHLEEN *(After a few moments of thoughtful ironing):* I don't speak well, do I, Mr. Brackish? From a point of view of bein' understood quickly or, you know, bein' a natural conversationalist kinda thing . . . from a language point of view, I mean. *(Pauses; thinks)* My husband cooked short order. He never had much of a mind for long sentences. Just quick little ideas. "Hi. How's it goin'?" kinda thing. "I'm hot, I'm cold, I'm tired" . . . those kinda little quick ideas . . . I mean, the only thing he said to let me know the heart attack was comin' on was "Heart!"

BRACKISH: "Heart!"?

KATHLEEN: That was *it!*

BRACKISH: Certainly not much warning there.

KATHLEEN: He was dead inside a minute. *(Irons, thinks)* Coulda be'n worse, I guess . . .

BRACKISH: I guess . . .

KATHLEEN *(she stares a moment, lost in a memory):* He hated music.

BRACKISH: I actually *taught* music. Music Appreciation and English Literature . . .

KATHLEEN: 'Course, you did! You taught my husband.

BRACKISH: I didn't know your *husband* was local . . . his name was . . . ?

KATHLEEN: Otto . . . Otto Hogan.

BRACKISH: Possibly . . . there were so many . . . possibly . . .

KATHLEEN: Definitely! His name was Otto Hogan . . . we called him Princie . . .

BRACKISH *(Sincerely):* I'm afraid I don't remember your Princie, Kathleen. I hope that doesn't hurt your feelings any . . .

KATHLEEN: Oh no, Mr. Brackish, really . . . it don't matter . . .

BRACKISH: Strictly speaking, I suppose it really doesn't.

KATHLEEN: I don't have any kinda wicked serious regrets . . . if you get my message . . .

BRACKISH: I certainly do.

KATHLEEN: He was good to me.

BRACKISH: I'm sure of it . . .

KATHLEEN: We had our fun.

BRACKISH: No doubt of that . . .

KATHLEEN *(pauses, has a memory):* He wore a bright orange shirt every day. Day and night. I don't even think they required it.

BRACKISH: I really don't get your message this time, Kathleen. *Syntactical! Who* required the orange shirt?

KATHLEEN: Bob's Clam Shack. Princie cooked short order for 'em.

BRACKISH *(he's had enough, he rolls his eyes to heaven):* Why should I want to remember this Princie person? *(Realizes his gaffe)* Your *husband,* I mean . . . was there anything unusual about him . . . ?

KATHLEEN: He saved your life.

BRACKISH: In what sense, Kathleen?

KATHLEEN: It was years back when you used ta work summers givin' lectures on the tourist boat in the harbor . . . the Dixie Bell. . . . Princie was havin' a cigarette out back a' Bob's and he saw ya flip over and he swam out . . .

BRACKISH: My God!

KATHLEEN: You were trapped under the boat with three tourists.

BRACKISH: Labor Day Weekend . . . *YES!* I was in a stupor from their endless questions about cheap lobsters and early Americana. A former student . . . swam out . . . saved us . . . and thank the Lord he did, they woulda buried me with *tourists!* . . . I remember that he wore an odd uniform . . . orange . . .

KATHLEEN: That's what I've be'n tellin' ya!

BRACKISH: . . . He wasn't one of the good ones . . . students . . . I remember that. He wasn't one of the good students.

KATHLEEN: You flunked him in English and gave him a D+ in Music Appreciation.

BRACKISH: Really? I suppose I had to . . .

KATHLEEN *(moves to collect shirts from shelves):* It wasn't like he was dumb . . . retarded or nothin' . . .

BRACKISH: Some were, Kathleen . . . some of them actually *were* . . . dumb, retarded. My memory system has set up a kind of magical defense against remembering the failures: they fail, I forget. If "To err is human," then "to forget is *divine*" . . . forgiving is forgetting! . . . *Je ne me souviens pas, donc je suis! Non momento ergo sum!* (BRACKISH *laughs heartily at his own arcane joke. On hearing his laugh,* KATHLEEN *wheels about and—accidently?—drops armload of Brackish's freshly-ironed white shirts into the rusty water. An instant of shocked silence)* You've dropped them in the muddy water! Oh Kathleen! I told you six times to mop it up! Oh Kathleen! What a shame! What a waste of effort! Oh dear . . . Oh dear . . . (BRACKISH *turns and goes to the radio, switches it on.* KATHLEEN *swishes stack of shirts around on wet floor, mops up water.* BRACKISH, *satisfied that he's found Byron's station, goes to chair, finds newspaper, opens same, sits, reads.* KATHLEEN, *in the meantime, has placed the soiled shirts in a saucepan to which she adds some bleach.* BRACKISH *sniffs the air, looks over at* KATHLEEN *smugly)* Brahms. Notice the contrapuntal shading . . . (*Hums along with music)* Dah dee dah dummm . . . *(Calls to* KATHLEEN) A composer of great sobriety. Don't you agree?

KATHLEEN *(nervously bleaching out the shirts, she fakes paying attention with false admiration for Brahms):* Me? Oh yuh . . . marvelous.

BRACKISH: What the hell's that smell?

KATHLEEN: Bleach water. I could do it outside.

BRACKISH: In the snow?

KATHLEEN: I guess I won't . . . *(Nervous giggle)* I forgot about the snow . . .

BRACKISH: It smells, like more than just bleach . . .

KATHLEEN *(suddenly realizes that pan on stove is on open flame, empty, burnt):* Ah, shoot! The pot's burnt! *(She leaps to stove, burns her hand, screams out. She tries to pretend that she hasn't burned her hand)* No problem! *(She does a little dance around kitchen after chucking hot pot loudly into sink and running cold water on to the thing, causing steam and sizzling sound in room.* BRACKISH *watches the entire sketch in astonishment)*

BRACKISH: You okay?

KATHLEEN: Oh yuh, perfect.

BRACKISH: It was an old pot. Not to worry . . .

KATHLEEN: Oh no . . . pot's okay. It was only bleach water . . .

BRACKISH: In the pot?

KATHLEEN: Mmmm . . .

BRACKISH: In the pot that boiled away?

KATHLEEN: That's all. Nothin' black . . .

BRACKISH: Bleach was boiling away all that time . . . evaporating into the air we breath?

KATHLEEN: I s'pose. Yuh . . .

BRACKISH: That's chlorine . . .

KATHLEEN *(corrects* BRACKISH, *lightly):* Chlorox . . .

BRACKISH: When chlorine evaporates into the air, it is deadly, Kathleen, *deadly* . . .

KATHLEEN: I'll crack the window . . . *(She opens kitchen window)* There. That should be better . . .

BRACKISH: The German nation was censured by the entire *world* for using chlorine gas in World War I . . .

KATHLEEN: You can hardly smell it now . . .

BRACKISH: Chlorine gas causes a slow, devastatingly painful death.

KATHLEEN: I'll crack open the back door, too . . . *(She does and smiles)* Smell's all gone in here. Really . . . (BRACKISH *coughs.* KATHLEEN *begins to scrub pot enthusiastically)* I'll have this shining like a baby's *bee*-hind in no time at all.

(BRACKISH *rolls his eyes to heaven. He re-opens his* Boston Globe, *reads.*

The Brahms piece has concluded and now Bach's "Chaconne" fills the world brilliantly.

BRACKISH *listens to the music a moment. He is embarrassed by his behavior toward* KATHLEEN. *He looks over at her, watches her labor a moment silently. He tries to make calming small talk, speaks)*

BRACKISH: I don't know why the *Globe* gives so much attention to the marathon runners. The sport requires no brains at all. It's just left, right, left, right. I mean what *is* the big deal, I ask you?

KATHLEEN *(absently, barely looking up):* Hmmm?

BRACKISH: The Boston Marathon . . .

KATHLEEN: Mmm?

BRACKISH: It's weeks off and they're already startin' to tout the thing . . .

KATHLEEN *(displays clean pot):* See? Good as new.

BRACKISH: Why don't you take a break now, Kathleen. . . . *(Pauses)* You don't hav'ta work day and night . . . it isn't as if we're goin' against any kind of *deadline* here. . . . *(Pauses)* Sit down, Kathleen . . . take a break . . . (KATHLEEN *smiles. She enters the living room nervously. She takes her quilting basket, sits on sofa, in corner of seat at furthermost possible distance from* BRACKISH. *Bach's "Chaconne" plays on, in spite of all.* BRACKISH *looks over at* KATHLEEN, *who is now intently working on a patchwork quilt. She is deciding among various patches which to appliqué and which to discard)* You hear this piece, Kathleen?

KATHLEEN *(intent on choosing quilting patches, doesn't look up. She fakes an interest, smiles and grunts lightly):* Mm.

BRACKISH: Bach. The "Chaconne."

KATHLEEN: Mmmmmm.

BRACKISH: The same few notes are repeated in different variations. Twenty-nine of them in all: variations. The untrained ear would never hear the repetition, but I do. I hear 'em all. And they scare me silly . . .

KATHLEEN: Mmm.

BRACKISH: Over and over, nothing changes, sometimes faster, sometimes slower, sometimes broken into bits and pieces that accumulate in the memory and one day shock you with the realization, "I've heard all this before!" . . . It honestly does scare me silly . . .

(Following speeches overlap)

KATHLEEN: That's what scares me, too . . . the repetition . . . *(Pauses.* BRACKISH *barely looks at her)* The waking up one morning and the realizing, "I've done all this before" . . . over and over again . . .

BRACKISH: Even the beautiful parts of it irk and irritate . . . irk and irritate.

KATHLEEN: The seagulls screaming and screeching . . . the bed getting made and unmade . . . the food shopped, cooked, eaten, shopped, cooked, eaten . . .

BRACKISH: Twenty-nine variations in all . . . twenty-nine variations.

KATHLEEN *(looks at* BRACKISH *absently):* Huh?

BRACKISH: The "Chaconne," Kathleen . . . *(Annoyed)* This Bach piece . . . *(Shakes head in schoolteacherish fashion, scolds her)* Don't you *ever* pay attention, Kathleen?

*(*KATHLEEN *is devastated. She takes her quilting basket, runs upstairs to her room and sits on her bed.*

Downstairs, BRACKISH *is thoughtful after* KATHLEEN's *exit from the room. He feels guilty.*

The "Chaconne" concludes. BRACKISH *goes from his chair to the staircase. He pauses a while, as though looking upstairs. He listens, as well. He goes to bookcase and removes hearing aid batteries from where he hid them earlier, depositing same in wastebasket beside desk. He then covers them with waste paper.* BRACKISH *goes to the radio, carrying hearing aid in his hand. On the radio, we hear Beethoven's "Diabelli Variations." He turns the volume up full blast deliberately.* KATHLEEN *hears the change, perks up her ears)*

BRACKISH: Dammit, dammit, dammit! *(He moves to foot of stairs, screams up to* KATHLEEN*)* Could you come down here? Hello? Helloooo?

(He now crosses to writing desk, begins fishing through drawers. He continues to call KATHLEEN *as he searches for fresh batteries.* KATHLEEN *appears at top of stairs)*

KATHLEEN: Did you call me? *(No response. She screams over Beethoven blasting from radio)* Did . . . you . . . call . . . me, Mr. Brackish? *(No response)* MR. BRACKISH!

BRACKISH: I'll have to ask you to go out and buy some batteries for me . . .

KATHLEEN: *Now?* It's freezing out there!

BRACKISH: *What?*

KATHLEEN: Yuh, sure, why not . . .

BRACKISH: Be an angel, will you, and fire down to Radio Shack . . . better still, try Tru-Value . . . yes, Tru-Value . . . *(Reaches into pocket, produces wallet)* Better buy two.

KATHLEEN *(Makes an okay sign):* Fine. I'll buy two . . . right away . . .

(KATHLEEN takes overcoat from clothes tree, puts it on. Takes hat from hook)

BRACKISH: Bundle up now, young lady . . . I wouldn't want your catching your death on my conscience . . . *(KATHLEEN smiles.* BRACKISH *thinks she has spoken to him.)* What?

(KATHLEEN puts her cap atop her head; en route to door, sneaks to radio, switches the station. We hear jazz station, Miles Davis being played.

KATHLEEN *allows the music to play for a moment, checks* BRACKISH. *He doesn't hear: no reaction. She switches station again, settling now on a raucous, caustic rap song . . . MC Hammer or Ice T.* BRACKISH *does not seem to hear the music, thus does not at all react to it.*

KATHLEEN *smiles, exits quickly, never looking back.*

BRACKISH, *alone, engulfed in the dreaded music, sinks low in his seat.*

Dreaded music swells and then concludes. The lights fade out.)

TWO

Spring/summer

In darkness, we hear BYRON WELD's *voice on radio.*

BYRON WELD: This is Byron Weld, WGLO-FM, Gloucester, Massachusetts on Cape Ann. You're in your wa'm house with your heat turned back on again against this Memorial Day cold snap . . . no doubt toasty-warm, while I'm sittin' here on a metal stool by the transmitt'ah, half-frozen ta death for the want of heat. If you don't send in your contributions, this station's closin' down. No ifs, ands or buts. This next selection is on a Musical Heritage Society recording, "Symphony #40 in G Minor," K550, Wolfgang Amadeus Mozart . . .

*(*BRACKISH *is at the stove, fussing with a hot pot of soup, bowls, cooking utensils. We hear* KATHLEEN *coughing upstairs . . . three substantial coughs)*

BRACKISH *(calls upstairs to* KATHLEEN*)*: Are the vapors helping?

KATHERINE *(calls from bathroom, off):* I'm just now fillin' the bowl with hot water. *(She coughs, then sneezes)*

(Lights up in KATHLEEN's *bedroom. Season is now spring/summer. Exterior foliage now lush green.* KATHLEEN *enters bedroom, sits atop bed. She is bundled in gathering of bathrobes, towels, scarves; wears heavy stockings on her feet over which are jammed slippers of the "mule" variety. She is a veritable symphony of pastels. Her head is swathed in terry cloth pastel toweling. There is a large steaming pot on her lap, producing vapors, which she inhales from time to time by means of an intricate system of toweling connecting the pot to her headdress. Chutes of toweling are employed to convey the vapors from pot to nostril. She coughs, six times.)*

BRACKISH *(calls upstairs):* A Memorial Day cold snap is just God's way of telling us that the tourists are coming and that makes everybody sick. And that's no doubt why the good Lord invented chickens. So there'd be a cure. *(Burns his hand, screams out) Owwwwwwww!* I burned my hand!

26

KATHLEEN *(calling downstairs, worried):* Oh God! Are you okay?

BRACKISH *(he does a little dance, whisking his hand, flailing his arm. He calls out in a new voice: gentlemanly):* You'll have to excuse this, Kathleen . . . *(He throws back his head, bellows)* HO'SSSSSSSSSSSSSSSSSSS-SHHHHHHHHHHHHIIIIIIIITTTTT!

KATHLEEN *(after a short silence):* Is your hand better?

BRACKISH *(calls upstairs):* It feels just fine now. "There's nothing so far gone that a little ho'ss-shit can't make it better." *(He walks upstairs to her room carrying tray with soup, etc. He calls out, whilst on staircase)* My father used ta say that. My father used ta say lots more than that, too. *(Enters* KATHLEEN's *room)* If this old house could talk. What it's seen, huh? *(Pours chicken soup into cup, crosses to* KATHLEEN. *She coughs)* My mother's secret potion. Many a chicken died so that you might live, Kathleen. I suggest that you drink this slowly and reverentially . . . it tastes like what it is.

KATHLEEN *(samples soup):* Ugggggggggghhh! . . . dead chickens.

BRACKISH *(smiling his agreement):* Dead chickens . . . even honey tastes like medicine when it's medicine. . . . My mother used to say that . . . *(Looks around room)* This was my room. *(Smiles)* This house was built by a stevedore . . . a lumper. It's a poor house. I imagine the original owner spent his life workin' the docks . . .

KATHLEEN: My father was a lumper . . .

BRACKISH: Hmmm?

KATHLEEN: Nothin' . . . not important, really, go on . . . this house, built by a lumper . . .

BRACKISH: It's tiny, really, but me bein' an only child and all . . . it was spacious . . . a perfection. Imagine . . . living an entire life in one house. . . . My father bought this house when he was twenty-two years old with money he earned, sellin' door-to-door off a horse and buggy. He was born over in Plum Cove—God!—over a hundred years ago! He was a Yankee Jew. Quite a rare breed. He spent his last cent educating me . . . wanted the best for me. *(Pauses)* I always figured I'd move from here one day, when I married and had children, but I didn't: none of those things. *(Pauses: another memory)* Forgive me if you've told me this, before, Kathleen, but did you and your husband have children?

KATHLEEN: Us? No. We never did.

BRACKISH: Understandable. It's already such a crowded planet.

KATHLEEN: I guess. All my friends were havin' em . . . used ta trouble me at first, worryin' why we were, you know, bein' *passed over*.

BRACKISH: I myself never wanted any . . .

KATHLEEN: Yuh, well, you weren't *married,* were you?

BRACKISH: Still and all, the choice is a basic human right.

KATHLEEN: Yuh, well, life's a lot different for Catholics.

BRACKISH: I suppose.

KATHLEEN: Princie was never bothered. He said he was glad to never bring any kid of his inta *this* mess.

BRACKISH: My sentiments, precisely . . .

KATHLEEN: Sittin' with his body down ta Pike's, I couldn't help but wonder if it mighta be'n different if we'd had 'em: kids . . .

BRACKISH: Only natural to wonder.

KATHLEEN: He was laid out four extra days, on accounta the ground froze up solid and they couldn't get a bite with the bulldozer ta get his grave dug. I had a lot of time alone with him ta think.

BRACKISH: Must've been grim.

KATHLEEN: Wasn't so bad. It was kinda like havin' him asleep in front of the TV, only there was no TV. *(She shrugs)* This cold is getting me mentally depressed. *(She smiles. Silence.)*

BRACKISH: I regret, Kathleen, that we have this odd coincidence between us . . . that your late husband was my student and that he . . . failed . . .

KATHLEEN: It wasn't like he was dumb or nuthin' . . . he was wicked unhappy when he found out he'd flunked English. He was supposed ta repeat, in order ta graduate, but he didn't . . . he dropped out. Since he didn't finish high school, college was outta the question . . .

BRACKISH: And you?

KATHLEEN *(looks up)*: College? Me? No.

BRACKISH: What held you back?

KATHLEEN *(stares* BRACKISH *straight in the shoes)*: I'd have to say, more than anything, it was the grades.

BRACKISH: "The grades" in what sense, Kathleen? Antecedents.

KATHLEEN *(screws up her courage, as best she can)*: The grades you gave me in Music and English. They ruined any chance I had for a scholarship.

BRACKISH: You were my *student?*

KATHLEEN: Both subjects, yuh . . .

BRACKISH: But I . . . My God, Kathleen! Why didn't you mention this *before!?*

KATHLEEN: No point . . .

BRACKISH: Of course, there was a *point!* I . . . I had no idea! *(He is shaken by this news)* It's so *perverse*, Kathleen . . . *really!* You should have mentioned this to me specifically . . . during our interview. . . . You just let me ramble on and on and you never once mentioned this to me . . . my God!

KATHLEEN: I guess my feelin's got hurt, 'cause you forgot me kinda thing . . .

BRACKISH: Kathleen, *really*. Do you have any idea of how many students passed through my life in fifty years of teaching two completely different subjects?

KATHLEEN: Lots, I guess . . .

BRACKISH: "Lots," you *guess?* Tens of thousands, Kathleen. Tens of thousands . . . *(Pauses)* Did you fail?

KATHLEEN: Fail? Me? Oh, I wouldn't so much say I failed as I would say I was failed. Object versus subject kinda thing. . . . You gave me a C in English IV and a D-plus in Music Appreciation which, a' course, pulled my senior average down too low for a scholarship anywhere. I didn't even bother applyin', finally . . .

BRACKISH: Oh, Kathleen . . . I *am* sorry . . .

KATHLEEN: Doesn't bother me, Mr. Brackish, really. No sweat . . .

BRACKISH: Oh no, really, I am sorry. . . . I don't really remember: that's the worst: I don't really remember. I'm sure I had my reasons . . . I was fair. I was *demanding* . . . hard, strict, but I was fair! . . .

KATHLEEN: I said that it didn't bother me, okay?

BRACKISH: There were so many . . .

KATHLEEN: Yuh. There were. In my family alone, there was a number. You might even say an *astonishin'* number . . . mother, father, husbin' . . .

BRACKISH: That I taught?

KATHLEEN: That you failed. Good thing Maureen and Doreen went to Sistah school! You probably woulda nailed them, too! *(She smiles at an astonished* BRACKISH*)* You were the toughest teacher in Gloucester, Mr. Brackish. Practically no one got away . . . from *you.*

BRACKISH: I was strict. It's true.

KATHLEEN: Listen, it's really no bother to me at all. Really. I hardly think about it. And I do understand. There are tests and kids either flunk or they don't. It just happens that most of the people in Gloucester that I was connected to did: flunk. That's just the way it happened . . . the past is the past, right? Nothin's gonna change it.

BRACKISH: What was your maiden name, Kathleen?

KATHLEEN: O'Hara.

BRACKISH *(Stands, stunned):* Was it?

KATHLEEN: My father was Jebbie O'Hara and my mother was Francine Flynn. . . . I'm in the Flicker with the green cover, tenth from the end, second shelf down, if you ever wanna check it out . . . (BRACKISH *moves to window, bends forward, terribly upset.* KATHLEEN *is suddenly aware of his upset. Foghorn sounds)* Mr. Brackish . . .

BRACKISH *(turns to her, suddenly):* You lied to me! . . . what are you doing in my house? *(She turns away, terrified)* Don't you turn away from me, Francine Flynn! . . .

KATHLEEN: *What?*

(Foghorn sounds again)

BRACKISH: . . . Lying to me about who you are . . . tricking me into pleasant chat . . . *(He shivers)* I feel cold. *(Tries to calm himself down)* I will not have this terrible upset in my house! I never have and I never will . . . not here . . . not in this house. I simply will *not!* I'm going to my room. I want to be alone now. I should like to regain the sanctity of my home . . . I'm going to my room.

(A distant foghorn groans.

BRACKISH *moves quickly to his room, sits atop his bed, facing front sadly.*

Foghorn groans in distance, again.

BRACKISH *and* KATHLEEN *sit in their separate rooms, each facing front, each alone, but inexorably connected to one another by their similar pride, similar guilts, their similar anger, their similar regrets.*

Light fades down to spotlights on both . . . one moment . . . then, lights to black. In Black, tea kettle whistles.

Lights fade up again in BRACKISH's *room. He is looking out of the window. He moves to his bedside chair, sits, reads. His hearing aid sits atop bedside table, out of use. He has a headache.*

Lights fade up in kitchen . . . and KATHLEEN *is there, removing kettle from flame.* KATHLEEN *puts tea pot and aspirin bottle on a tray, along with cup and saucer, glass, silver, etc. She sticks dust rags and feather duster under her arm, calls up stairs to* BRACKISH)

KATHLEEN: I'm bringin' your tea up! . . . *(No reply)* Hullo? *(She climbs the stairs to* BRACKISH's *room, pauses at the door, seemingly unnoticed by* BRACKISH, *who continues reading, his back to* KATHLEEN. *She tests his deafness)* Hullo? Your hearin' aid in or out or what? Hullo? *(No reply)* Hullooooo! (KATHLEEN *enters* BRACKISH's *room. She slams door closed to test his hearing. He doesn't respond at all. She pauses, directly behind him, out of his line of vision. She stares at him, silently, five count. Satisfied that he cannot hear her,* KATHLEEN *speaks into his deafness)* Sometimes I am just amazed to think that I'm standing here and you're just there, within striking distance and all. You're like a legend to me, really. . . . If my father could see me now. Wouldn't he'd a' b'en the jealous one, huh? I mean, he used ta dream a' bein' this close ta you . . . and havin' a rock in his hand, a' course! . . . He was interested in marine biology, my father. He loved the sea and the boats and all. He always loved ta point out the different kindsa' weeds and name the fish and all . . . especially down the marshes. You'd think you were listenin' to some kinda *Ha'vid professor* or somesuch. It really pisses me off ta think that he spent his life, workin' the docks, lumpin', as he did. It killed him young, carryin' crates in wintah and all. Deadhead stupid labor. Stupid, stupid useless! . . . He used ta get tanked up wicked down ta Sherm's . . . he'd come home and beat my mother . . . I know he woulda loved to have beaten *you*, Brackish, but the closest he could ever come was ta beat my mother. The three of us girls cowerin' in the corner . . . like mice, scared shit so wicked bad. . . . Nobody havin' a life worth livin'. . . . Every time I heard your name out loud, Brackish, it was in connection with somebody like my father gettin' their hearts broken, gettin' flunked, gettin' creamed. Nobody was ever good enough . . . smart enough . . . worth sendin' on inta the world. . . . You musta hated passin' the ones you had ta pass: the John Connors and the Annie Bells . . . the naturally-smart-student-types. Mosta' us scared little bastids, us poor lumpers' kids, we didn't stand a chance, did we? Not a chance!

BRACKISH (*whirls around, faces her, suddenly aware of her presence in his room*): There you are! I was wonderin' if you'd taken a walk . . . forgotten me . . . my aspirin . . .

KATHLEEN: I didn't forget nothin' . . .

BRACKISH (*points to hearing aid on table*): I'm keepin' my hearing aid out . . . better for my headache.

KATHLEEN (*mouths the words broadly*): Fresh tea . . . your aspirin . . .

(*She starts to pour a fresh cup of tea for* BRACKISH. *He pulls back, frightened*)

BRACKISH: Careful! You're gonna scald me!

KATHLEEN: Wouldn't I love ta, huh?

BRACKISH: Excuse me, are you saying something?

KATHLEEN (*startled; stiffens*): Me? Nope . . .

(BRACKISH *returns to his reading, deliberately ignoring* KATHLEEN. *Hostility abounds.*

KATHLEEN *straightens* BRACKISH's *bed. He glances at her, returns to reading. She resumes talking to his back . . . to his deafness)*

KATHLEEN: I'm gonna keep you alive until you apologize to us all . . . me, mother, father, husbin. . . . And after you do . . . then you can kick off . . . and I can kick off, too . . . 'cause there won't be any reason for us two pathetic bastids not to . . . *(She goes to* BRACKISH, *touches his arm, gesticulates widely as she talks)* I'm goin' back downstairs . . .

BRACKISH: Fine.

*(*KATHLEEN *turns and exits his room, carrying tea kettle, tray, etc. She walks downstairs and into kitchen, begins chopping vegetables for a soup.* BRACKISH *sits alone awhile, worried. He puts down his reading and, curiosity having gotten the best of him, replaces his hearing aid in his ear, goes downstairs. He stops at radio, finds* BYRON WELD's *station. A Bach cantata fills the room. Satisfied,* BRACKISH *goes to his chair, sits. He looks over at* KATHLEEN, *who is busying herself with the cutting and slicing of soup vegetables.* BRACKISH *listens to the music a moment, smiles, takes his book again, reads. Suddenly,* BRACKISH *looks up startled.)*

BRACKISH: *Oh, my God!* I just went completely dead! It was cracklin' with static when I put it in. Now, there's *nothin'! (He whacks his battery pack)* I'm taking this machine out of my ear, once and for all. *(Pops the hearing aid out of ear, places battery pack on table, looks at* KATHLEEN) Much better. *(Suddenly, yells out) What?*

KATHLEEN *(rolls eyes heavenward):* Oh, sweet Jesus! *(Yells to* BRACKISH, *pantomiming her message.)* I'll go downtown and getcha some new batteries as soon as I finish my soup! *(*BRACKISH *stares dumbly)* As soon as I finish my soup! *(Panto, with screams)* As soon as I finish . . . the soup . . . *(Whacks pot with wooden spoon) The soup!* Lemme finish the soup *first!*

BRACKISH: No, no, dammit! You finish your soup *first* and *then* head downtown for the batteries. No trouble ta me ta wait a couple a' extra minutes. *(Looks at* KATHLEEN; *sees her frustration)* I'm a hard man to please, aren't I, KATHLEEN?

KATHLEEN: Sayin' you're "a hard man ta please" is kinda like sayin' "a rattlesnake's a hard animal ta *hug*"!

BRACKISH *(Looks up, suddenly, feelings hurt. Has he heard her?):* I beg your pardon, young lady?

KATHLEEN *(alarmed):* I didn't say nothin' . . . *(Mouths the words carefully)* I didn't say nothin', Mr. Brackish . . .

BRACKISH: Gotcha!

*(*KATHLEEN *smiles.* BRACKISH *smiles.*

KATHLEEN *chops the final vegetables and adds them to the soup stock. She smiles again.* BRACKISH *smiles again.*

She will now speak to him, into his deafness, simply, clearly, perversely . . . and without fear or hesitation)

KATHLEEN: Well, that's it! Add some . . . fire and water . . . and, by magic, in three hours we shall have . . . *seagull shit!* (She smiles at him again, as though she's just said something expected, such as "soup") I love it when you're stone deaf, Jake!

BRACKISH: It's no use, Kathleen.

KATHLEEN *(smiling deeply, sweetly):* That's probably the hot roasted goat shit . . . we're talkin' hot roasted goat shit on a bed of clam shells, seasoned with the seagull dung that I just mentioned, and topped off, Mister stone-deaf-and-dumb Brackish, with hound's pubic hair! *(She pats the pot atop the stove)* . . . *That* is lunch, dearie!

BRACKISH: What's that you've got cookin'? Smells good . . . *looks* good, too!

KATHLEEN *(smiles and nods):* I live for these moments, Mr. Bricklips, I truly do . . .

BRACKISH *(samples soup): Tastes* even better! *(Sees and returns* KATHLEEN*'s smile and nod)*

BRACKISH: I'm delighted by your mood, Kathleen. Your spirits have lifted, haven't they?

KATHLEEN *(nods and smiles again):* Goat shit, rat shit and my grandfather's leather boot up you arse, Brackish . . .

BRACKISH *(returns smile and nod again):* This does my old heart good.

KATHLEEN *(returning his nod and smile with still another nod and a smile):* Oh, you are a foolish-lookin' turd, you are!

BRACKISH: While you're in such a jolly mood . . . could I take up your offer to fire on down to Tru-Value?

KATHLEEN: I'll fire on down, alright. An hour away from you is worth more ta me than a whole fuckin' day at the beach!

BRACKISH: Yes? Or no?

KATHLEEN *(nodding affirmatively, broadly):* Oh yes . . . Oh yes . . . ohhhh *yesssssss!*

BRACKISH: Oh, that's good of you! I'll be waiting right here.

*(*BRACKISH *faces front, smiling.* KATHLEEN *seems to be leaving. She goes behind his back to the radio and switches the station. This time, she settles on Beastie Boys' "Hey, Ladies")*

KATHLEEN: Yuh, right, Mr. Backlash . . . you wait. I'll be back.

*(*KATHLEEN *stops at the door, gloats.* BRACKISH *looks across room to* KATHLEEN. *She smiles, blows a kiss to him. He smiles, returns the blown kiss. She exits.* BRACKISH *sits a moment, not reacting to the music, which is loud and frenzied. He now rises from his chair and crosses to the radio. He picks up his hearing aid from the table, tosses it in the air a few times, sets it back down on the tabletop in easy view of the audience.*

A moment passes. He wipes his forehead, bringing his palm over his eyes, which he covers for a moment, masking his face. He switches dial . . . "Hey, Ladies!" magically changes to Bach "Jesu Meine Freude." We hear male singer singing sweetly. After listening a moment, BRACKISH *sings along with the recording in perfect German, word for word.*

We are now certain that BRACKISH *is not at all deaf. He has heard everything we have heard.)*

(SINGER *and* BRACKISH: "Duld ich schon hier Spott und Hohn, dennoch Bleibst du auch im Leide, Jesu, meine Freude . . ."

(BRACKISH *has sung in perfect harmony with recording. The motet ends, music fades. After a brief silence,* BRACKISH *bows his head. The lights fade to black.)*

THREE
Autumn

The auditorium is dark. BYRON WELD's *voice is heard in darkness.*

BYRON WELD: It's just gorgeous out there, isn't it? . . . Could you ask for a better autumn weekend? 'Course not. Perfect football weather. Or perfect for just takin' a brisk walk along the Back Shore. But a' course, I'm locked up here alone at the transmitt'ah . . .

(LIGHTS UP now in downstairs rooms. KATHLEEN *is in the kitchen, cooking jelly. Fruit baskets and jelly pots, all around. Two huge corn pots steam away on the stove.*

Foliage blazing with color: reds, yellow, browns, oranges. Some leaves already on ground.)

BYRON WELD *(continues):* . . . I'm cooped up here like a man in prison, so's I can play for you the work of composers who are all deeply gifted . . . and this station better be gifted, too, and quick, 'cause without your gifts, we're gonna fold faster than you can say "Wolfgang Amadeus Mozart" . . . speaking of which [*sic*], this is a Columbia Masterworks recording, K172 . . . Mozart "Quartet in E Flat" . . .

(Music up. BRACKISH *appears outside of kitchen window, presses nose against glass, peers inside, sees* KATHLEEN, *smiles. He disappears momentarily, then enters house through kitchen door.*

He is a symphony of fall colors, plaids and tweeds. His trouser-cuffs are tucked into his argyle socks, creating the effect of plus fours. There is a pith helmet atop his head, for private reasons. He carries a basket of beach plums and rose hips in one arm and a fat, neutered male cat in the other. Cat should be absurdly fat, friendly: no question of safety near the beast wanted)

BRACKISH *(chirping gaily):* There isn't a tourist left on the entire beach. It is a marvelous, marvelous, *marvelous* thing, the way the seasons change. It restores faith in the Deity. *(Smiles)* March: the snow melts.

38

April: the cellar floods. June, July and August: the cars all sport New York and New Jersey plates and they weave from side to side, takin' in all the sights, threatening life and limb. *(Smiles and pontificates)* But then, by God, Labor Day comes and the tourists all pack up their dreadful, greasy, hot-dog colored bodies and their God–awful charcoal sketches of Motif #1 . . . and they vanish . . . like greenheads and mosquitoes: mystically, magically, they are . . . simply . . . *gone* . . . and it is a marvelous, *marvelous* thing . . . *(Nuzzles cat, sighs)* Ah, it does please me: autumn. I don't know why people insist on calling autumn "fall" . . . autumn is autumn . . . fall is what you do from grace!

KATHLEEN: Who's your friend?

BRACKISH: Ohhh. The cat's name is Nathaniel Hawthorne. Say hello, Nathaniel. The girl's name is Kathleen Hogan. *(Pretends to be the cat's voice)* "Hello, Kathleen . . ." *(Laughs)* Oh, did I get a phone call while I was out?

KATHLEEN: This phone? *Ring?* Uh uh.

BRACKISH: I thought maybe Nobby Ellis called. Nathaniel's Nobby's cat. I bumped into him . . . Nathaniel . . . back of Good Harbor Beach, near where Nobby and I used ta pitch our ho'ss-shoes . . . so, I thought maybe Nobby was back home, seein' the cat and all . . . *(pauses)* We took a walk up to Nobby's house, up Brier Neck, but it was still boarded up. *(Pauses)* Kinda a worrisome thing . . . *(Smiles, nuzzles Nathaniel absently)* He'll be callin' me. . . . If it were bad news, I would have heard it by now. Nothin' spreads faster than bad news and cheap oleomargarine . . .

KATHLEEN *(offering* BRACKISH *a saucer of milk for the cat):* Are we gonna' boil Nathaniel down, too? Or are we just gonna eat him in the rough?

(NATHANIEL *squirms*)

BRACKISH: Oh, dear, I think Nathaniel heard you, Kathleen. *(Strokes cat)* Easy, easy, easy, Nathaniel! Kathleen was just joking. She would never boil a wonderful cat like you. The girl just has a warped sense of humor! *(Nuzzles cat)* I've known this beast for fourteen years . . .

each human year is worth eight cat years . . . eight fourteens is a hundred and two . . . Nathaniel's a hundred and two, Kathleen. I'm just a kid, next to this old codger . . .

(BRACKISH *first sets down milk, then cat. Cat knows exactly what to do with milk.*)

KATHLEEN: A hundred and twelve . . .

BRACKISH: What's that?

KATHLEEN: A hundred and twelve. You said Nathaniel was a hundred and two . . . eight fourteens is a hundred and twelve. You got it wrong . . .

BRACKISH *(after a long pause):* Well, my God! . . . you're quite right, Kathleen . . .

KATHLEEN: Yuh, I guess I am, yuh . . .

(BRACKISH *(harumphs.* KATHLEEN *turns away, giggles.* BRACKISH *flashes an over-acted look of annoyance at* KATHLEEN *who giggles again)*

BRACKISH *(stops, worries):* Where was I?

KATHLEEN: We'd both counted up Nathaniel's age. You got it wrong and I got it right.

BRACKISH: C'mon, Nathaniel, walk me to the mailbox. I'm gonna get my paper. (BRACKISH *exits.* KATHLEEN *goes immediately to radio, switches it on, tries a few stations before settling on "Never, My Love." She lip-syncs and dances to music.* BRACKISH *re-enters without* NATHANIEL, *carrying newspaper. He catches her dancing. She blushes, runs into kitchen, mortified)* Weather's changin'. I think we're in for it . . . *(Goes to the radio)* What an odor comin' from the fish plant. Hard to believe the stuff they're bakin' is gonna' *be* food, instead a' havin' already *been* food!

KATHLEEN *(shrugs):* Makes a lot of jobs.

BRACKISH: I s'pose.

(He switches station, finding BYRON WELD's *WGLO*-FM. BYRON *has caught the cold of his life!)*

BYRON WELD: . . . and it'll be yo'r fault, not mine. *(Coughs)* This is Johann Pachelbel . . . *(Coughs)* . . . "Canon in D Major" with Jean-Francois Paillard conducting his Chamber Orchestra . . . *(Coughs)* . . . recorded in 1972 at Albert Hall. . . . *(Coughs)* I've got a wicked cold . . . coughin' . . . the chills.

(The music begins. BRACKISH *sits in chair, reading* Gloucester Daily Times. *He suddenly yells aloud, middle of a thought, height of a rage)*

BRACKISH: *Scabrous–son–of–a–bitch!* I knew when I saw his cat on the beach, he'd pull something like this! Nobby Ellis was a scabrous son of a bitch from the day I met him! I was five years old, Kathleen . . . five years old . . . and I could tell! He was competitive! To the point of somethin' very nearly illegal! *competitive!* I would get an A, he would get an A+! I would buy a bike, he would buy a red bike. 'Course, as I knew he was *pathologically competitive,* it didn't really bother me when he beat me out for valedictorian . . . 'cause I understood the psychology of the situation: He, being from a broken home and all, and me, bein' from a wonderful family-oriented family. . . . But when he went into *graduate* school . . . *graduate school* . . . well . . . I knew he was directly competing with me. I mean, I got my B.A. from the finest, right? As did he. Two Gloucester boys goin' off to Cambridge like we did? Hell, as far as I was concerned, the competition was finished: dead tie. Dead tie . . . But no, not Nobby Ellis . . . he hadda keep competin' . . . M.A. from Yale in English Literature. Isn't that just the most goddam absurd thing you ever heard of? I pick up the *Gloucester Daily Times* and I cannot believe my eyes! "Norbert Alvin Ellis II will leave tomorrow for New Haven, Connecticut where he will begin his studies for a Masters Degree in English Literature . . ." (KATHLEEN *tries to pour his tea)* I didn't ask for that, did I? (KATHLEEN *backs off)* I shoulda let it go. I shouldn't a' got down to his sick level and competed . . . BUT . . . I went back ta Harvard . . . two miserable years of takin' the heart and soul outta the likes a' Byron and Keats and Shelley . . . learnin' lists of what Dr. Johnson had for breakfast on his two–hundred–mile

walk with Boswell . . . makin' maps of goddam Wordsworth's
goddam walks around the Lake District . . . I mean, really, is this
the stuff that's gonna get the fire lit on a cold winter's morning?
(Pauses, disgusted) No sooner do I get back ta Gloucester and back ta
teachin' . . . bang! I pick up the *Times* and there's Nobby . . . off
to Trinity College, Toronto, Canada for a Ph.D. in guess what? Right!
English goddam Literature. . . . This still gets my nipples up,
Kathleen, if you'll pardon my anatomical reference. . . . Ph.D. in
E.L. . . . Great! Off I go into Cambridge. You'd think I was working
for the M.T.A., I rode it so often. . . . Back I come ta Gloucester
. . . four years older, carryin' more letters after my name than a
postman could fit in his goddam sack! A Jewish Ph.D. teachin' high
school Music and English in Gloucester, Massachusetts. What I was
was something that happens every *two hundred* or *three hundred
million* years! And Nobby Ellis goes off ta England, to Oxford
University, to teach English to the English. . . . Isn't that a kettle of
fish you'd call "just fine"? . . . It never ended, Kathleen! . . .
Never! They retire the son-of-a-bitch at age sixty-five, same as they
retired me, but where does he come for his twilight years? Does he
stay in Merry Olde You-know-where? You know he doesn't! Right
back ta Merry Olde Gloucester, where I have ta pitch horseshoes
against him at Good Harbor Beach every wa'm day and play Gin
Rummy against him every cold day, right here in my own dining room
. . . for eighteen years, until they take the stupid bastid away ta
Rattray's Old Age Home down Wakefield because Nobby ain't got the
brains, nor the guts, ta simply say, "No, I ain't goin' ta any old age
home, anywhere, under any condition!" His half-wit son-in-law speaks
and he obeys, like he was still in goddam graduate school. I begged
the pencil-brain ta move in here with me . . . I offered free rent, the
works. . . . We were practically even in gin games and I was way,
way up pitchin' horseshoes . . . but he went. He goddam went . . .
(He is desolate now) Over a year and not a single word . . . until this
. . . *(He picks up* Gloucester Daily Times *and slams it down)* First-ta-
Die Award. Nobody wins it, huh? The stupid bastid, leavin' me like
this. He was two months and a week older'n me, Kathleen, so, you
know what that makes me now, huh? I am officially the oldest livin'
man in Gloucester, Massachusetts, U.S. of A. Nobby was it, but now
it's me. I outlasted him. I took the title. I . . . win.

(KATHLEEN *offers cup of tea to* BRACKISH *again. This time, he picks up cup, sips.* NOTE: *Pachelbel piece must be timed out to conclude precisely as speech concludes. The lights fade to black.*

Lights up in kitchen. KATHLEEN *has prepared a tray with "vapours"* . . . *bowl, toweling, etc.* BRACKISH *pulls on bathrobe, puts thermometer under tongue. She calls over to* BRACKISH, *softly, gently)*

KATHLEEN: We're ready for you . . . *(She sets vapours-bowl and toweling at table)*

BRACKISH: You'd better check on Nathaniel. Make sure he's peeing in his box instead of in my bed.

KATHLEEN: Don't talk with the thermometer in your mouth . . .

BRACKISH: What the hell's the difference? We know I've got a fever! A thermometer's a waste of time, if you ask me! (BRACKISH *goes to calendar)* Same damn thing as a calendar! If you don't know what date it is already, a calendar's no use at all! I mean, really, try starin' at one when you really don't know the date! All a calendar will give you is 365 guesses! *(Turns on radio, flips through stations, finds* BYRON WELD, *who is also ill)*

BYRON WELD *(coughs twice):* Robert Schumann lived from 1810 to 1856 . . . *(Coughs twice again)* Excuse me, I'm sweatin'. I'm wicked sick . . .

BRACKISH: You hear that? Byron's sick, too . . . *(To* KATHLEEN) This sickness you caused is goin' through the town like wild fire! I'm one foot in the grave . . . Nathaniel's up there half-dead . . . sweating away, incontinent . . . *(Music in: Schumann's "Bach—Op. 60."* BRACKISH *walks slowly to the dining table under* KATHLEEN's *watchful eye, overacting his illness badly, as might a child. He stops en route to the table and sticks a finger in the orange frosting of a partly-eaten Halloween cake, doesn't respond to the taste. He hands thermometer to* KATHLEEN, *sits.* KATHLEEN *moves the vapours-bowl in front of him.)* We'd better use the blackboard. Last time I took the vapours with my hearing aid in, the steam rusted the damn thing brown. . . . Get the blackboard . . . (BRACKISH *takes hearing aid out of ear, places it on table*) What? *(Music continues under)*

KATHLEEN *(fetches a largish blackboard from kitchen, sets it up, propping same against stack of books):* Get under the towels.

BRACKISH: What?

KATHLEEN *(pantomimes his getting under toweling):* Go under . . . towels.

BRACKISH: What's my temp?

KATHLEEN *(under her breath):* I thought you weren't interested. *(Reads thermometer)* Ninety-nine-one . . .

BRACKISH: I can't hear you, dammit. Write it!

KATHLEEN *(writes same on blackboard):* Ninety-nine-point-one . . .

BRACKISH: Ninety-nine-one? That's *nothing!* I'm burning up! I'm way over a hundred! Goddam thermometer's useless!

KATHLEEN: Go under the towels . . .

BRACKISH: That s'pose ta be *funny?* . . . talkin' ta me when I can't hear?

KATHLEEN *(exasperated, pantomimes):* Go under . . . the *towels!* . . .

BRACKISH *(goes under and comes right back up, glasses steamed opaque):* Great! My glasses steamed up! Now, I can't see what I can't hear . . . *(Rubs glasses, puts them on)* Did you say something?

KATHLEEN: Nothin'. I didn't say nothin' . . .

BRACKISH *(from under towel):* I cannot bear this.

KATHLEEN: Yuh, well, tough luck.

(KATHLEEN *walks to radio and switches it off, pops in cassette of Phoebe Snow singing Paul Simon's "Something So Right." She allows music to play in room softly. She returns to kitchen and work.* BRACKISH *continues his complaint,* sans fin)

BRACKISH *(pops out from under towel):* Philosophically speaking, the ultimate danger for a deaf man in not hearing a tree fall in the forest isn't that the sound doesn't *exist!* It's that the goddam tree will fall on your *head! (Goes under the towels again, pops out again.)* Where the *hell* is United Parcel with my records? Did you call them?

KATHLEEN *(nods an enormous nod):* Yes, I did . . . *(Holds up three fingers)* Three times, three . . . one, two, three times . . . (KATHLEEN *writes "3 TIMES" on the blackboard*)

BRACKISH: There's no need to write *that!* I counted your fingers, dammit! I'm not blind, ya know! I'm *deaf! (Sneezes, coughs)*

KATHLEEN *(exaggerated bowing and scraping):* Sorry, sorry, sorry . . . SORRRY! *(Writes word on blackboard)*

BRACKISH: Don't act mousey with me, Kathleen. *(She shoves him under the towels)* I hate this. Dammit! I am an educated man! I don't want to die face-down in a bowl of Vick's Vapo-Rub! *(Pops out from under)* This is your fault, really. All that damned opening and closing of the door for trick-or-treaters. That's what did me in . . . one of the horrid little killer snot-noses brought us the trick and the treat of this virus, that's what. *(Sips tea)* Encouraging them with *cupcakes!* Gimme one of those! . . . (KATHLEEN *places cupcakes on table. He tastes frosting)* Why's this frosting orange? What did you use to color it? It tastes weird.

KATHLEEN: Carrot juice.

BRACKISH: What?

KATHLEEN: Carrot juice!

BRACKISH: I can't hear you. You forget?

KATHLEEN *(Writes "CARROT JUICE" on blackboard): Carr . . . ott*
fucking *jooooosss! (Picks up hearing aid)* Will you please put yo'r
goddam hearing aid back in!

BRACKISH: Carrot juice? Carrots are vegetables! *(He shoves cupcake aside
in disgust)* You feed 'em carrots, they'll be able to see in the dark!
They'll be comin' around every night! *(Coughs, listens to music a
moment, forgetting his alleged deafness.)* Is this your idea of music?
This isn't music!

(BRACKISH stands, walks to cassette deck, switches music off.

KATHLEEN *stares at hearing aid in her hand and then at* BRACKISH. *She is
amazed to catch him hearing without his hearing aid)*

KATHLEEN *(a voiceless whisper):* Oh . . . my . . . God . . .

BRACKISH *(snaps at her, meanly):* I'm talking to you, young lady!
*(*KATHLEEN *turns and faces him)* I need some tea. What you put in front
of me is cold. . . . You have a simple job to do here, young lady . . .
to keep things hot . . . *(*KATHLEEN *doesn't move)* I must insist that you
keep your half of the bargain. I provide wages and a place for you to
hang your hat and you provide *assistance* . . . as I need it . . . *and
I need it now, please! (Yells, full voice) Now, please! (There is a silence)*

KATHLEEN: Lemme just put a record on first, Mr Brackish . . . one a'
your favorites . . . a' course, you won't be able to hear nothin', what
with your hearin' aid outta your ear and on the table . . . right? *(She
walks to phonograph, pulls out an album at random)* Pablo Casals . . .
Bach . . . "Suite For Unaccompanied Cello" . . . 1936 to
1939 . . ."

*(*KATHLEEN *puts phonograph record on turntable, starts the music lightly.
We hear the gentle sound of Casals' cello . . . until . . .* KATHLEEN *pulls
the arm of the record player and needle across the record. A terrible
scratching sound is produced.* BRACKISH *looks away. Another pull, another
scratch. Another and another.* BRACKISH *finally talks to* KATHLEEN *through
clenched teeth)*

BRACKISH: Stop it! . . . STOP! . . . STOP! . . . *STOP THAT!*

KATHLEEN *(after a long, pregnant pause):* It's kinda a miracle your hearin' improved so much, ain't it? *Ain't it???* (KATHLEEN *throws hearing aid into wastebasket. A moment's silence)*

BRACKISH *(mortified):* I'd better check on Nathaniel.

(He stands, gets away from KATHLEEN *as quickly as he can. He switches radio back on, defiantly, childishly . . . then switches on light on stairs. He then runs up the stairs into his room. He picks up* NATHANIEL, *rolls his eyes to heaven, places cat on his lap as he sits, smiles. He is beyond embarrassment: mortified.*

We hear: Beethoven's "Symphony #1 in C Major, Opus 21."

KATHLEEN *goes to kitchen, sits at table, begins writing a letter.*

The music stops suddenly. The lighting dims. We hear BYRON WELD. *His voice is incredibly weak, near death)*

BYRON WELD: I'm sorry ta hav'ta shut down shop for a while . . . *(Coughs)* . . . I'm sick as a dog . . . *(Coughs)* . . . I'm just gonna hop up ta Addison-Gilbert and get myself looked at . . . *(Coughs. Coughs again)* . . . This is Byron Weld, signin' off . . . *(Coughs)* . . . WGLO-FM, Gloucester, Massachusetts on Cape Ann . . .

(Suddenly, dead air: silence. In his room, BRACKISH *hears this, sits erect, alarmed. We now hear voice of young man replace* BYRON)

NEW VOICE: This is Arnold Weld, Byron Weld's nephew. Uncle Byron died last night, up Addison-Gilbert. Before he died, he told me to tell ya's that he thanks none of ya's. I'm takin' over the station for the moment and WGLO-FM, Gloucester, Mass. is gonna be playin' more Sixties, Seventies, Eighties and Nineties rock'n'roll than any other station north of Boston. From the Seventies, here come the Buzzcocks . . . *(Music in: Buzzcocks "Mad, Mad Judy")*

BRACKISH *(without cat, rushes down stairs, shuts off radio. Sits):* I sent the bastid six dollars a week, fifty-two weeks a year for forty-one years in a row, you know that? And do you think he ever once mentioned my name on the radio?! Even just *once?!* I cannot tolerate his ingratitude!

. . . I cannot tolerate the ingratitude of my former students, either! Not a one of them calls, comes around. Not a one of them. I never married because of my students, you know . . . I mean, did I have need for children? I had . . . thousands, right? (KATHLEEN *ignores him, doesn't answer. Instead, she sits at kitchen table, writing letter, intently*) Don't you know that non-verbal non-communication reveals an *ignorance?* If you have a thought to express, express it in language . . . speak English words! (KATHLEEN *ignores him, continues writing letter*) So? Here I sit alone, except for the likes of you, Kathleen O'Hara, and Nathaniel Hawthorne, a fat, half-blind, half-dead, neutered male housecat! So? What added up? What *accumulated?* What . . . mattered? (*With self-pity, but aimed at* KATHLEEN) A lifetime of teaching in Gloucester High School. A *lifetime!* Thousands of students and not a single one of 'em can come around and say a "Hello." *Not a single one of 'em!*

KATHLEEN (*speaks without looking up*): You oughta be thankful nobody come around and stuck a knife in your heart. You oughta be thankful. Thankkkfulll.

BRACKISH: I might remind you that my hearing is working just fine, young lady. Your obscenities are coming in loud and clear. *Loud and clear!*

KATHLEEN: Really?

BRACKISH: Really.

KATHLEEN: Kathleen O'Hara shoulda gone ta college and be'n somebody, but you crapped it up!

BRACKISH: Jacob Brackish shoulda stayed at Ha'vid and taught some real students . . . but you crapped it up! (*Screams*) Who are you writing to, Goddam it! Sittin' in that mousey way, scratchin' . . . scratchin' . . . who? Who? WHO?

KATHLEEN: None of your damn business!

BRACKISH: I don't wanna sit in this chair! (BRACKISH *throws his lap robe onto floor, leaps up, enraged*) I don't want these terrible flashing pains

inside my head . . . under my arms . . . I don't want my gums
pulling back and my teeth falling out in the sink! And I don't want you
sitting there in that mousey way, scratching those letters in my house.
(He moves to her and raises his hand, strikes her)

KATHLEEN *(pulls back from him, stunned)*: Oh my God! You hit me. You
old bastid! You hit meee! *(Leaps up)* I'm writing to my mother and
father!

BRACKISH: They're dead!

KATHLEEN: I'm still writin' to them! I'm writin' to my husband, Princie,
too . . . all of 'em, Brackish! I'm tellin' all a' them!

BRACKISH: You're squealin' on me, Kathleen???

KATHLEEN: I am! I'm tellin' 'em everything I know . . . every goddam
thing about you I've picked up . . . and I seen it all, Brackish, *I seen
it all!* (KATHLEEN *runs upstairs and into her room)*

BRACKISH: You don't know a thing about me!

KATHLEEN *(screams to him, downstairs)*: Lonely, miserable old fuck!
Lives alone with a half-dead cat and a Scrooge–voice that drops dead
on the radio! They're all leavin' you, Brackish! Every last one of 'em!
Same way I'm gonna be cuttin' outta here myself!

BRACKISH: Ungrateful little bitch! You deserve to flunk!

KATHLEEN: Yuh, sure! I deserve ta flunk and so did Mama and Da and
Princie and Josie Evangelista and Floey Rizzo and Fast Eddie Ryan
and Ruthie Flynn! . . . You wanna hear the whole list? I got it all
written down! Every last one of us you ruined!

BRACKISH: You know what a sick waste of your time it's been makin' a list
like that?

KATHLEEN *(runs downstairs, confronts* BRACKISH): Ohhh, you're really
somebody ta be talkin' ta *me* about a "sick waste a' time"! How's about
the sick waste a' yo'r time never marryin', huh? Nobody in this town

was never good enough for you, Brackish? You were too *smart*, too *sophisticated*, too *worldly* for any of the local crop, right? So, you coop yo'rself up in this pathetic hovel for fifty-sixty-seventy years! You coop yo'rself up, pissed off and gutless and you flunk the whole goddam town of Gloucester . . . and *you* talk to *meee* about "a sick waste of time"? What are you? *Crazy?*

BRACKISH: I did not, young lady, flunk the "whole town of Gloucester." I did nothing of the kind!

KATHLEEN (*counting on her fingers*): Mother, Father, husbin, me . . .

BRACKISH: *You failed! Your family failed!* I may not be proud of much else in my life, but I am pretty goddam proud of my teachin' record, so don't you attack it! And don't you attack the way I lived my life, either! I've got no regrets! Not *one!* All's I hate is the bein'-old part of it . . . bein' trapped inside a body that doesn't work. *I hate it!* But most of all, I hate bein' trapped inside a house with the likes of you! *I just hate it!*

KATHLEEN: Then what did ya beg me ta come here for?

BRACKISH: You answered an ad . . . for *money!* I have never begged anybody for anything in my life!

KATHLEEN: *THEN TRY IT! IT'LL DO YA SOME GOOD!* Try sayin', "Thank you" and "You're welcome" and "You ain't so smart, but you ain't *nothin'* . . . you ain't a piece a' tossed-out goddam lobstah shell on the beach"! *TRY SAYIN' THAT, BRACKISH!* Try sayin', "You ain't Einstein, but you certainly do deserve a pat on the back for gettin' through the wintah, 'cause it's miserable wicked awful cold and lonely . . . and it's *tough* . . . It's *TOUGH*"! (*Chokes back her tears*) I ain't gonna cry I ain't gonna cry I ain't gonna cry! I ain't gonna *mouse outta this!* (*Looks up at* BRACKISH. *Square in the eye now, no tears*) I may've be'n a D-plus dodo in Music Appreciation, Mr. Brackish, but I knew how ta give a hug and a kiss and I knew how to get a hug and a kiss . . . and you didn't! Now look at you! You got no friends at all. Cooped up alone with the goddam radio and this half–blind neutered cat who, by the way, ain't fakin' his blindness, Brackish. He ain't fakin' a handicap like some *SICKOS* I know, tryin' to win sympathy 'steada' love, hidin' behind fake deafness, spyin'! Pretty fuckin' pathetic, if ya ask me! I'll give you another dose of the truth: I came here to watch you die. I came here to enjoy your death. I open the paper ta see the obituary I phoned in for my Princie and it ain't there, Brackish. It ain't in the paper! I call Nan Cobbey who I've known since Girl Scouts and she's now some kinda deal down the *Times* and she don't know and she calls back an hour later and says the *Times* is ". . . sorry they left it out . . . that the little blank hole on the page is where it was s'pose ta be, but after the paper was pasted up, Princie's ahhhticle fell off, somehow. . . ." Princie fell off the goddam page! She asks me did I know "A white hole on a newspaper page is called a "widow"? And isn't this a "gross irony"? And then she gives me her "sympathy". . . . The next thing I see in the paper is your ad, which stuck ta the page like God himself glued it down. And I knew I hadda take your job. I knew I hadda do it. . . . There was nobody at Princie's wake down Pike's Funeral Home, Mr. Brackish. Just me and nutso Buster Sheehan, who'll sit with anybody's body overnight, so long as you give him the Guinea Red. . . . I felt relief when Princie died, Mr. Brackish. I did. I felt relief. He wasn't very nice ta me. *(Sobs openly)* They start you out in fifth grade with a nickname like "Titmouse" and it don't do a whole lot for your spine. They tell you when you're seven that "you'd better learn ta typewrite, K.O., 'cause you ain't goin' ta no college or endin' up intellectual or even hopeful"! *(Ruefully)* K.O. Great little set of initials ta start out with, huh? K.O.'d at birth! K.O.'d right at the first round *bell!*

BRACKISH: I've never heard such self-pitying paranoic ho'ss-shit in my entire life! The world was out to get Kathleen O'Hara, right? Even me: outta getcha, right? I gave you a D-plus, not because it was what you earned, but because I was perverse . . . vindictive . . . whimsical! It had nothin' whatsoever to do with your actual achievement, right? (KATHLEEN *starts to run upstairs.* BRACKISH *stops her with his voice)* Am I correct? Am I correct? AM I CORRECT???

KATHLEEN *(covers her ears, as might a child. She turns, screams at* BRACKISH *and to the world):* I did it all ta myself: *me! (She slaps her own face three times powerfully)* I did it myself, okay? *(She now punches her own hip to punctuate her guilt)* I only got myself ta blame. Okayyy? *(Punch)* I been my own worst enemy. Okayyyy? *(Punch)* Okay? Okay? OKAYY??? *(Final punch)*

(KATHLEEN *weeps, turning her face away from* BRACKISH. *She leaps into chair and buries her face in pillow on the back, so as to muffle her sobs.* BRACKISH *chokes back his own tears now. He speaks to her compassionately*)

BRACKISH: Oh Kathleen . . . Kathleen, please . . . tell me what I can do for you. I want very much to help you. I want to know that this time you've spent with me was *worthwhile.* Please . . . tell me what I can do . . . for you.

KATHLEEN *(looks up at him, turns front):* A make-up test in Music Appreciation. I want private tutoring and I want another chance . . . to raise my grade. A make-up test in Music Appreciation. That's what I want.

(Lights suddenly bump up to day lighting: hot, bright, alive. Music in. Lights build as music by Strauss fades in . . . swells.

KATHLEEN *runs upstairs. She appears in bedroom wearing Walkman earphones, studying sheet music.* BRACKISH *goes to desk, gets his bluebook, crosses to bookcase, arranges albums for test, then puts one record onto turntable. The Strauss piece is the first of a medley of Bach, Debussy, Brahms, Chopin selections, ending with Mendelssohn's "Symphony No. 4 in A Major."*

KATHLEEN *runs downstairs carrying bluebook and pencil. She goes to coffee table, writes her answers in bluebook.*

When final piece in medley has played, BRACKISH *drops the needle arm of the phonograph onto the record. The lights come up to scene level. Schubert's "Unfinished Symphony" is heard. The make-up test is underway)*

BRACKISH: There's a time limit.

KATHLEEN: I know, I know . . .

BRACKISH: Enough?

KATHLEEN *(panicked):* One sec, one sec . . . Oh God . . . *(Yells, relieved)* okay! Okay! Got it!

BRACKISH: Three to go . . . (BRACKISH *plays a snippet of Mozart.* KATHLEEN *bites her pencil and suddenly remembers. She writes an answer, stops, thinks better of it, punches fist down on tabletop, three sharp blows)*

BRACKISH: Ready?

KATHLEEN: One sec, one sec . . . Oh God, oh God, oh God . . . *(She writes her answer into her notebook)* Okay. Ready . . .

BRACKISH: The final pair . . . here's the penultimate . . . (BRACKISH *places arm of record player into groove and Bach's "Chaconne," played by Nathaniel Milstein, plays in room. After a few moments, during which* KATHLEEN *smiles and writes her answer,* BRACKISH *switches the record and plays a final piece)* Last one. (BRACKISH *puts the arm of the phonograph onto the record and Rachmaninov's "Symphony No. 2 in E Minor" fills the room)*

KATHLEEN *(worried):* Oh God, oh God, oh God, God, God . . . *(She thinks she's got it. She writes her answer into her book)* Done.

BRACKISH *(turns from stereo and faces her):* Done.

KATHLEEN: My brain's inside out . . .

BRACKISH: You wanna check over any of 'em?

KATHLEEN: I heard 'em once. Fair's fair . . .

BRACKISH: Would you like a cup of tea before you turn 'em in?

KATHLEEN: What are you so nervous about?

BRACKISH: Ready when you are, Mrs. Hogan . . .

KATHLEEN: Number one was Strauss . . . definitely . . . late Romantic period . . . Strauss. . . . Number two is Bach . . . Baroque . . . G Major . . . the Brandenberg concertos. . . . Number three was hard . . . impressionistic. Debussy. My guess is one of the "Nocturnes" . . . I'll go with that: Debussy "Nocturnes." Number four was Romantic . . . Brahms . . . fairly easy. Number five was a gift, thank you very much for the birthday present, Chopin "Ballade in F Minor". . . . Six was Romantic, I'll have ta say Mendelssohn. . . . Number seven was another piece of cake, thank you for the birthday present, Schubert "Unfinished Synhony". . . . Number eight was sneaky, but I'm gonna go with Mozart and I think it was "No. 40 in G Minor". . . . I dunno, but I'm relatively certain it was Mozart, so that's my answer: Classical period, Mozart . . . number eight. And number nine was Baroque: Bach's "Chaconne." No doubt about it. And number ten was a wicked awful, sneaky thing for you to pull on me, 'cause you know I don't really know much about Rachmaninov, I would say Rachmaninov . . . maybe not, but my hunch is Rachmaninov . . . "No. 2 in E Minor" . . . and that's it. Oh, and I'm wicked awful sorry I scratched your Casals record . . . how'd I do?

BRACKISH: That was precisely the I.D. section of my freshman General Music "drop the needle" midterm at Harvard. I got six out of ten, which was good enough to pass, but just. I saved my bluebook. Here . . . *(He opens a dog-eared bluebook, reads)* I missed Rachmaninov. I also missed Mendelssohn, Bach's "Chaconne," and that piece of cake: Chopin "Ballade in F Minor," thank you very much. . . . You didn't miss anything. You went ten for ten.

KATHLEEN: I did. Yuh. I knew I did.

BRACKISH: The I.D. section counted only fifty per cent.

KATHLEEN: What?

BRACKISH: The other fifty per cent is all on Section Two, which I have decided to make oral: one question. You ready?

KATHLEEN: I am. Yuh.

BRACKISH: Here goes then. Final question . . . worth fifty per cent. This is probably the most important question you'll ever have ta answer in your entire life about classical music! . . . Ready?

KATHLEEN: Yes. I'm ready.

BRACKISH: Did you enjoy the music, Kathleen?

KATHLEEN: I did. Very much, Mr. Brackish. I did.

BRACKISH *(pause):* Congratulations. A perfect score.

KATHLEEN: Oh my God! That was the *question?!*

BRACKISH: Oh yes, as you suggested, I listened to your Miss Phoebe Snow singing the Paul Simon song "Something So Right" and I do see what you mean . . . homophonic . . . romantic . . . reminiscent of English court ballads . . . in the sonata form . . . lyrically quite sound, really. *(Smiles, simply)* I . . . liked . . . it.

(The lights fade.)

FOUR
The start of winter

Music in: Albinoni "Adagio for flute and strings" plays under entire scene. The season has returned to winter; foliage is again barren. Snow is falling heavily.

Lights fade up in downstairs rooms again. It is Christmastime. Christmas lights, hidden in bookshelves around room, around window frames, etc., now twinkle gaily.

KATHLEEN *hangs a string of Christmas lights over the mantel.*

BRACKISH *reclines on the sofa. At his feet are stacks of papers that have come from a storage trunk, old-fashioned variety, that has probably been in evidence throughout the play, upstage. There is also a large wastebasket overflowing with papers near the trunk.*

BRACKISH *takes sheet music and book written in Greek from trunk, considers them.*

BRACKISH: I regret never having the vision, the talent or the discipline to compose beautiful music. I also regret never learning to read Ancient Greek . . . this is Euripides . . . *(He tosses sheet music and book into wastebasket. He finds Chinese primer)* Or Chinese . . . *(He tosses primer in wastebasket. He finds a small oil painting kit and palette)* I also regret never having an ounce of talent as a painter. Winslow Homer's paintings of Niles Pond and Brace's Cove still thrill me silly! *(He tosses kit and palette into wastebasket)*

KATHLEEN: I was conceived on the Niles Pond sandbar . . . I'm blushin' . . . I must be beet red . . .

BRACKISH: No need to be embarrassed . . . not with me.

KATHLEEN: My mother told me that towards the end, just before she passed on . . . I was dozin' off beside her bed . . . she was sleepin' all the time . . . all's a' sudden I hears her say, "Kathy, you were

56

started inta life on the Niles Pond sandbar. Your father and I lay together there and I knew a child would come of it and you did." . . . I had a lotta trouble goin' over there after I found out . . . took me maybe a year, but I went there. . . . Two big dogs, Labrador Retrievers, were, uh, well, they were . . .

BRACKISH: . . . doin' it?

KATHLEEN: *Doin' it!* They *were!* Right there on the same spot . . . well, *relatively* the same spot! It made me laugh! Oh God, it made me feel good! *(She chortles, then suddenly she sobs)*

BRACKISH *(watches her weep for a moment, then he speaks to her soothingly):* It's the worst thing in life, Kathleen . . . outlivin' the ones you love. It's the worst thing. It strikes a terrible loneliness and a terrible fear of dyin'. . . . I always loved takin' morning walks across the Niles Pond sandbar . . . especially in summer . . . wearing shorts . . . feeling the tall wet goldenrod and angelica against my naked legs . . . smellin' the wild roses, the honeysuckle . . . nuns and priests from the Catholic Retreat on their dreamlike prayer walks, scarin' the piss outta the birds and the berries with all that spooky holiness . . . *(Watches* KATHLEEN *regain her composure)* Let your memories make you happy, girl . . . otherwise, they'll cripple you . . . turn you to stone.

KATHLEEN *(wipes eyes dry, looks up at* BRACKISH, *smiles):* Any other regrets to chuck out?

BRACKISH *(pauses, thinks):* Yup. I regret never sleeping with certain women.

KATHLEEN: Which women, specifically?

BRACKISH: Oh, uh, well, Grace Kelly, the movie actress. I've seen "High Society" nine times. And Agnes Virgilio from the bread store. She married Cosmo who'sis . . .

KATHLEEN: She's about eighty!

BRACKISH: This is not a recent regret, Kathleen. We're talking about a *lifetime* of regret! Agnes Virgilio had eyes that stopped you from thinkin' . . . deep, happy, full of promise . . . and breasts that stopped your breath. Agnes would walk into my class and I would turn, look at her and, within the countin' from one to six, I would suffer the loss of vision, of logic, of all pulmonary functions!

KATHLEEN: You ever sleep with her? . . . oh no, right. This is a regret list.

BRACKISH: And right at the top of my list, Princess Grace Kelly and Agnes Virgilio.

KATHLEEN: What held you back? From sleepin' with her?

BRACKISH: She married Rainier!

KATHLEEN: I mean Agnes Virgilio.

BRACKISH: She saw through my hearing aid, same as you. . . . *Both* my mother and my father went deaf early on. . . . I was so sure *I* was going deaf, I started to wear my father's hearing aid. I started wearing it to school. I could hear a pin drop! . . . One day, in front of my sophomore English class, it fell out. I said, "I'm deaf without my hearing aid, class. I can't hear a thing!" and one of the little sons-a'-bitches up the back of the room yells, "You're a wicked arsehole, Brackish!" . . . From that day forward, I had my own secret way of knowin' exactly what was on my students' minds . . . they told me themselves . . . same as *you!*

KATHLEEN: Oh God, I'm sorry about my swearin' and my sayin' bad things about you and all . . . *(Remembers things she said)* Oh, Godddddd!

BRACKISH: Don't apologize. I deserved every word of it. Any man who peeks through a keyhole deserves ta get a key in his eye . . . *(He laughs, she laughs. There is a pause)*

KATHLEEN: I have a regret. I regret never asking my mother about something before she died. I remember bein' home alone and getting a call from Sherm's, the bar down by the head of the harbor. . . . My father had caused a commotion . . . a fight . . .

BRACKISH: He'd . . . struck somebody?

KATHLEEN: Opposite. He'd got himself creamed by some big "mukka."

BRACKISH: Oh.

KATHLEEN: They called for Mama to come get him . . . Mama wasn't in the house and I felt panicked somethin' wicked. I rode my bike down there in about a minute flat . . . down over your hill. We were living top of Mt. Pleasant, just near here . . .

BRACKISH: Yes . . .

KATHLEEN: Papa was layin' on the floor, drunk . . . all bloody . . . singing "Red Roses for a Blue Lady" . . . I can't ever forget it . . . me comin' inta this dark pit of a barroom, seven years old, wearin' a powder blue dress with little tulips printed on it . . . findin' my Da singin' away, drippin' his blood, nobody payin' the slightest attention ta either of us. I don't think Papa knew who I was. I tried ta lift him, but I couldn't and he kept singin' the very same words over and over again. *(Sings)* "I got some red roses for a blue lady . . . I got some red roses, for a blue lady." *(Speaks)* The cops came in . . . Papa stood up and started walkin' . . . I followed him. Up Haskell Street hill here . . . he just kept singing the same words over and over 'til we got ta your yard here . . . Mama had taken our car and it was parked out at the end here . . . (KATHLEEN *screws up her courage. She will now, for the first time in her life, admit to a connection between* BRACKISH *and her mother*) Mama parked her car in yo'r yard, Mr. Brackish! (BRACKISH *looks away.* KATHLEEN *watches him, she continues speaking again softly*) Papa walked up to our car, face still all bloody, and he rubs his fingers in his own blood, after spittin' on 'em, and he takes his hands and does like finger-painting on the windshield. . . . *(Pauses)* He painted red roses . . . all in his blood . . . about a half dozen of 'em, maybe. . . . Then, Papa walked off home. I cleaned off the windshield so's Mama wouldn't get scared when she got into the car and all . . . (KATHLEEN *and* BRACKISH *allow their eyes to meet for a moment)* Mama parked her car in yo'r yard, Mr. Brackish. *(Pause)* Did you sleep with my mother a lot?

BRACKISH *(nods):* Yes, I would have to say "a lot." Francine and I began seeing each other long *after* you and your sisters were born. Your father had hit her and for some reason she came here to me. After that I was here whenever she needed me. *(Pauses)* Being with your mother was the most terrifying and exciting thing I've done in my entire life.

KATHLEEN: Poor Da . . .

BRACKISH *(pauses):* Poor Da . . . poor everybody. He was bellowing his song about the roses out by my gate . . . your mother and I went to my window, looked down and there he was . . . you, too . . . tiny little thing, off to one side, as scared as we were. . . . *(pauses)* She never came back to me after that day . . . I never saw her again. *(Sighs)* I adored your mother, Kathleen . . .

KATHLEEN *(goes to* BRACKISH, *hugs him):* So, why'd you flunk her?

BRACKISH: Why'd I flunk Francine Flynn? Are you kidding? Your mother was a terrible student, Kathleen. How could I pass a student like Francine Flynn? Just because I would choke for oxygen when she walked into my class? Just because my vision darkened and dimmed when I tried to *look at her*? These are not reasons to pass a poor student. A man's got to have some *standards! (Laughs)* Oh God! If the man I *am* met the man I *was*, there would be a fistfight! *(They share a laugh)*

KATHLEEN: If I walked into your class today, would ya' . . . you know . . . feel a little blind and dumb? Hard ta breathe kind of thing. Would ya'?

BRACKISH: Oh Kathleen . . . if I could live my life over, I would have you walk into my class and I would behave like an *animal!* I would choke for oxygen . . . you would cause a spontaneous pneumothorax . . . blindness, deafness, mental lapse . . . I would deliquesce: melt . . . *(There is a substantial silence)* Ah, Kathleen . . . Gloucester! I've got to get some rest, now. (BRACKISH *stands, bracing himself against* KATHLEEN'S *arm. He recites a schoolboy poem softly)*

Gloss-tah bo'hn . . .
Gloss-tah bred . . .
Couple a' days, I'll be
Gloss-tah dead.
(Looks at KATHLEEN. *His accent is now exactly like* KATHLEEN's *accent)* I'm
wicked awful tired. *(Starts up stairs, falters, falls)*

KATHLEEN *(runs to him):* Mr. Brackish . . . ?

BRACKISH: I went weak. I'm short of breath. (KATHLEEN *goes to him. She
helps him towards chair as lights fade out)* Yuh . . . maybe my
chair . . .

(The lights dim down. KATHLEEN *goes to* BRACKISH *and leads him slowly,
painfully, to his chair. He sits.*

*Albinoni "Adagio" swells to conclusion and Pachelbel "Canon in D Ma-
jor" begins to play softly.*

Lights swell to full. KATHLEEN *is discovered at the phone, ending conversation. She hangs up, goes to* BRACKISH. *He is incredibly weak, obviously
near death.*

KATHLEEN *chirps happily, as if to pump strength into* BRACKISH's *failing
spirit)*

KATHLEEN: I had some really great news from Mrs. Dallin down at the
high school. They're naming a prize for you. It's official: The Jacob
Brackish Prize for Outstanding Scholarship in English Literature and
Music Appreciation. Mrs. Dallin is workin' out the final details with
Mick Verga who's president of The Gloucester National Bank now.
(Do ya ba-leeeve that?) If the graduate goes ta Ha'vid, he (or she) gets
double. Great news, huh? *(She sings Paul Simon's song "Something So
Right" softly.* BRACKISH *is unresponsive. Her smile fades)* They've all
be'n callin' from ten towns around. You'd think it was the Pope himself
that was sick, honest ta God! Some of them wanted ta run right over
here now and give ya their get-well-quick wishes in person, but I told
'em all ta wait 'til you're feelin' a bit less punk. . . . *(Pause)* Maybe I
better call Dr. Chandler, huh? I won't let 'em take you to any hospital.
I'll keep my promise on that, but maybe he better come over and just

have a look, huh? *(She stands and starts to the telephone.* BRACKISH *dies with a death rattle.* KATHLEEN *turns around suddenly, looks across to him)* You say som'pin? *(She goes to* BRACKISH, *stares a while before realizing that he is dead. She crosses herself)* Oh God. Oh God. Oh God. Oh God . . . (KATHLEEN *removes his glasses, closes his eyes. She talks to* BRACKISH *as if to comfort him)* You remember Snoddy Timmons from my year? He called. They all called: August Amoré, Franny and Evvie Farina, Harry and Margaret Budd, John Sharp, the Shimmas . . . God! *Everybody!* You're really respected around these parts, Jacob. You can't imagine. *(She sits holding his hand, watching him, waiting. They are both at peace. She smiles at* BRACKISH. *She looks at him admiringly. She removes her locket)* This was Mama's locket. My baby picture's in one side. Mama herself is in the other . . . from when she was, ya know, young. I was thinkin' you might want it. I've got other stuff of hers ta keep for myself. . . . *(Presses locket into his hand)* Thanks, Mr. Brackish . . . Jacob. I'll always be grateful. (KATHLEEN *stands, listens to the music just one brief moment, speaks softly to a world)* Pachelbel . . . "Canon in D Major" . . . Eighteenth century . . . Baroque . . . beautiful. *(She walks to the telephone, dials the police station)* Hullo . . . I wanna report a death.

(The lights fade to black.

The play is over.)

Henry
Lumper

HENRY LUMPER was first presented at the Gloucester Stage Company in Gloucester, Massachusetts (Israel Horovitz, Artistic Director). The play was subsequently presented in New York by the Working Theatre (Bill Mitchellson, Artistic Director)/Gloucester Stage Company in association with Actor's Outlet Theatre on January 31, 1989. The play was directed by Grey Cattell Johnson. The set was designed by David Condino, costumes by Jose Rivera and lighting by Douglas Kirkpatrick. The Stage Managers were Elizabeth Keeden, Douglas Gettel and Elaine O'Donnell. The New York cast was as follows:

FATHER O'MALLEY, GUS, DAN . . . . Robert Arcaro
MARK LISSA . . . . Ralph Bell
PATTY PERCY. . . . . Carol Bradley
YOUNG HENRY BOLEY, HAL BOLEY . . . . Brian Delato
ENSEMBLE . . . . Michael DellaFemina
ALBERTA FUSCO, MIDGY . . . . Beverly Dretzel
FABIANO, PACKY, DR. BERKOWITZ,
MORT SHIMMA . . . . David Wolos-Fonteno
ANGELO CATALANO . . . . Randy Frazier
SCROOP, BARDOLF, BOBBY,
COOKIE, ARTIE . . . . Kilian Ganly
YOUNG LISSA, PORKER, BARRY . . . . . . Anthony J. Gentile
GUIDO VEGA. . . . . Billy Gillogly
PASTA . . . . Luis Guzman
TOM PERCY. . . . . Joseph Jamrog
ALLIE RICHARDS, FRANK PERCY . . . . Cullen Johnson
MRS. NELSON . . . . Mary Klug
DR. NAGOA, HENCHMAN II,
TOWNSPERSON . . . . Ben Lin
JACK SILVA . . . . Jordan Lund
ELLEN PERCY, ALICE QUIGLEY,
AGNES VIRGILIO . . . . Honour Molloy
YOUNG TOM PERCY, HARRY PERCY . . . . . . Paul O'Brien
MARY-ELLEN PERCY . . . . Courtney Peldon
MRS. BOLEY, EMILY FUSCO,
DOLLY . . . . Cathy Reinheimer
YOUNG ANGELO, PETEY . . . . Monte Russell
VERNON KOSKI. . . . . Rocky Santo
HENRY BOLEY. . . . . Roger Serbagi

For
Grey Johnson

The People of the Play

HENRY BOLEY: leader of the Waterfront Workers and Fishermen's Benevolent Association, seventies. (N.B. to be played in Prologue at age thirty-five by the same actor who plays HAL BOLEY)

THOMAS PERCY: retired co-leader of WWFBA, BOLEY's contemporary. (N.B. to be played in Prologue at age thirty-five by same actor who plays HARRY PERCY)

HAL BOLEY: son of Henry, thirties.

HARRY PERCY: son of Thomas, thirties.

PATTY PERCY: wife of Harry, thirties.

JACK SILVA: HAL BOLEY's closest friend, fat; small-time gangster; a/k/a TUBBY SILVA, thirties.

MARK LISSA: second in charge of WWFBA: HANK BOLEY's closest friend; seventies. (To be played in Prologue by thirty-five-year-old actor)

PETEY, DAN and FITZIE: HAL BOLEY's friends.

ANGELO CATALANO: third in charge of WWFBA; chubby and bald. (To be played in Prologue by thirty-five-year-old actor)

VERNON KOSKI: HARRY's young cousin.

DR. NAGOA: second in command of the Church of the New Way, in Glossop, Mass., a/k/a the "Lillies."

ALBERTA and EMILY FUSCO: sisters; two of HAL's many girlfriends.

GUIDO VEGA, COOKIE EVANGELISTA, MORT SHIMMA; various CAPTAINS.

MRS. NELSON: HANK BOLEY's housekeeper; kindly; old.

DOLLY: JACK SILVA's mistress.

MARY-ELLEN PERCY: HARRY's young daughter, age six.

BOBBY, GUS, MOWBRAY, HASTINGS, PASTA, PORKER: lumpers.

FABIANO: a gangster.

GADSHILL, LAZZARO, BARDOLPH: cronies of SILVA.

Various LUMPERS, FISHERMEN, TOWNSPEOPLE, SHOPKEEPERS, POLICEMEN, KOREANS, "LILLIES," DOCTORS, NURSES, etc.

NOTE: Essential that cast be racially mixed.

The Place of the Play

Various locations in Glossop, Massachusetts on Cape Ann, including Waterfront Workers and Fishermen's Benevolent Association Hall; homes of Henry Boley, Harry Percy, Thomas Percy and Jack Silva.

The Time of the Play

The play begins thirty years ago, and then leaps to the present.

The Accent of the Play

North Shore Massachusetts ("Pah'k Yo'r Ca'h in Hav'id Yah'd") accent required.

A Note From the Author

If at all possible, a turntable should be included in the scenic design. Also, weathered oil drums should be placed around the perimeter of the playing areas, to be used as live kettle drums by Actors and Crew, to "underscore" the action of the play, to punctuate scene changes, to indicate gunshots, etc. Essential scenery should be wharves, piers, gang-ways, floats, etc., with "clumps" of audience placed in and around the action of the play. Grandstands/fixed seating should be set at the outer edges, behind audience "clumps," allowing those in the grandstands a sort of overview.

Casting of the play should be a racially mixed blending of professional actors with actual waterfront workers (who have a flair for acting, of course). A few authentic Lumpers—and a few authentic Gloucester accents—will be a blessing to any cast and should be insinuated, if possible. A racially-mixed cast is recommended. *Any* of the play's characters can be cast with actors who are white-skinned, black-skinned, red-skinned, yellow-skinned, whatever. Accuracy of *age* is a factor, however. Boley should be in his seventies; Hal in his thirties; etc.

The cast enter the auditorium singing "Fish Of The Sea."* They take stage, complete their song. The Prologue begins.

PROLOGUE

Thirty years ago.

Auditorium in darkness.

Drumbeats, singly, softly, muffled, funereal. A groaner-foghorn is heard in distance.

Lights up (murky, color-filtered to support flashback) to soft glow on TOWNSPEOPLE *in semicircle, all reading newspapers with banners that feature words* Glossop Chronicle. TOWNSPEOPLE *wear tweed caps, working-man variety. Their faces are covered by their newspapers.*

Semicircle is upstage of ALLIE RICHARDS, *who is center, blindfolded, hands tied, facing into auditorium.*

Two young men, BOLEY *and* PERCY, *stand at either corner of stage, in pinspots. Both wear oversized oilskin foul weather gear and scarves pulled across their faces, masking them. Both hold pistols.*

An old man, MARK LISSA, *steps forward from among the* TOWNSPEOPLE *and speaks directly to audience as narrator: full-voiced; a storyteller.*

* Lyrics for "Fish of the Sea" appear at end of play text.

71

LISSA: Once long, long ago, there was a bustling, lively village in Massachusetts called Glossop. Glossop was on Cape Ann, not far from Gloucester, but not quite it. (RICHARDS *suddenly calls out*)

RICHARDS: Hankie . . . Tommy . . . come on, will ya's! Please, you guys! I'm beggin' ya's? Look! (RICHARDS *falls to knees*)

LISSA: Glossop was a powerful seaport, without a single condominium on its shore. It was a working port, with livings being made by a thousand lumpers and fishermen, with ships coming in from all over the world.

RICHARDS *(Pleading)*: Please, Hankie . . . there's plenty of room for all of us. We *know* each other. This is *crazy!*

LISSA: Something happened in Glossop . . .

TOWNSPEOPLE *(Whisper in unison)*: Murder.

RICHARDS: Think of yo'r kids! You guys both have kids . . . they're gonna hav'ta grow up with this! *(Suddenly, he yells his plea)* Tommy! Hankie! For God's sakes, *pleeease!*

LISSA *(Points to men as he names them)*: That man, Allie Richards, inherited leadership of the Waterfront Workers and Fishermen's Benevolent Association . . . the union for Glossop's fishermen, fish-plant workers and lumpers . . . from his father, Alfred Richards, Senior, by union law, upon the elder Richards' death . . .

DOLLY: The elder Richards was an honest man and a good leader, but his son, this younger Richards, was a racketeer and a thief . . .

LISSA: In no time, young Richards stained the Glossop waters, opening the port to drugs and easy money. Two young Glossop men . . . Henry Boley: him . . . and Thomas Percy: him . . . set out to stop him.

RICHARDS: Jesus, Hank! Listen to me!

PRIEST: They singled Richards out, cornered him, shot him dead.

RICHARDS: I got friends, ya know! I got plenty of friends! Tommy! Hankie! Come onnnnn!

DOLLY: They hid his body in an ice house . . .

RICHARDS: Your kids will hav'ta live with this!

TOWNSPEOPLE (*In a whisper; in unison*): Murder.

PRIEST: Young Henry Boley and young Tom Percy carried Allie Richards' dead body, frozen solid in the center of a block of ice, on to a lobster boat, which they sank off Bass Rocks . . . after chaining the corpse to cement blocks . . .

RICHARDS: *Jesus, Hankie, don't!*

TOWNSPEOPLE (*In a whisper*): Murder.

LISSA: A town turned its eyes and tongues inward. Jaws and front doors slammed shut. Hearts burned secretly in great gratitude to the two young men . . .

RICHARDS: *Jesus, Hankie, Tommy, please, no, no, nooooo!* (BOLEY *and* PERCY *each raise an arm now, pointing pistols at* RICHARDS)

TOWNSPEOPLE (*They turn their backs to the crime. They whisper, in unison*): Murder. (*Suddenly, four drumbeats.* BOLEY *and* PERCY *shoot* RICHARDS, *who is instantly dead, pitching forward, on his belly, legs and arms splayed.* BOLEY *and* PERCY *drag the dead* RICHARDS *by the feet, in a full circle of the lower stage, finally pulling him through the crowd of* TOWNSPEOPLE. LISSA *looks at the audience. He speaks softly*)

LISSA: The fish is fried. Long live the cooks. (*The lights fade out. End of prologue*)

ACT I

Scene One

In the darkness, we hear laughter and cheers. Uptempo popular period song is playing on record player. Lights up in Waterfront Workers and Fishermen's Benevolent Association Hall. Lighting remains color-filtered to support flashback. Turntable used to glide actors into scene, if possible.

HENRY BOLEY *and* THOMAS PERCY *are being sworn in as co-leaders of WWFBA, they will be co-Number Ones. Both men are in their early thirties. They face* MARK LISSA, *who is officiating.*

A row of men in tweed sport coats and cloth caps stretches across the edge of the stage: the footlights. Women stand in a row in front of men, children beside them.

The scene begins with a young MARK LISSA, *thirty-five, admonishing the spectators in a good-natured way.*

LISSA: I asked ya's all nicely ta quiet down, now I'm gonna hav'ta insist: quiet it down!

MAN #1: Quiet it down!   MAN #2: Shut it up!   MAN #3: We're starting!

LISSA: I'm gonna start the swearin' in ceremony . . .

MAN #1: Cover yo'r kids' ears. There's gonna' be some swearin'!

(Laughter from all. RUTH BOLEY *calls down to* BABY HAL BOLEY, *three)*

RUTH: Can you see okay, Hally?

LITTLE HAL: Uh uh, I can't! Lift me up! *(*BABY HARRY PERCY, *also three, calls out from opposite side of stage)*

HARRY: I can't see either, Mama! I can't see! Lift me up . . . *(*ELLEN PERCY *lifts her child into her arms.* RUTH BOLEY *lifts* HAL *into her arms. A young* ANGELO CATALANO, *thirty-five, points and calls out)*

ANGELO: Hey, Hank, watch out! The co-Sons-of-One are itching ta take over *already!*

HANK BOLEY: Bring 'em both up here! Give Hal to me, Ruthie. (BOLEY *reaches out and takes his son from his wife, setting* LITTLE HAL *down beside him*)

TOM PERCY: Come on. Harry, you too! Gimme him, El . . . (*Cheers and laughter as* TOM PERCY *now holds his son's hand in the air, as well*)

HANK BOLEY (*Calls out to all*)*:* You got the next hundred years of union leadership in front of ya's! (*All cheer and laugh.* LISSA *raps gavel, six sharp raps, calling the ceremony back to order*)

LISSA: This is serious stuff!

LUMPER IN BACK (*Calls out, heckling*)*:* Markie's in a hurry. He must be hungry!

LISSA: Goddam right! (*Laughter from all,* LISSA *suddenly remembers clergyman nearby; shows them his palms*) Oh, Lord, sorry, Father . . . (LISSA *raps gavel again. The gavel is small, gold, antique*) Both of ya's, touch the gavel at the same time together . . . (BOLEY *and* PERCY *try to fit their large hands on to the gavel's tiny handle*)

HANK BOLEY: Our hands don't fit. (*Laughter from all*)

LISSA: We're gonna hav'ta get ourselves a bigger gavel . . . (*Laughter from all.* LISSA *stands facing* BOLEY *and* PERCY, *awkwardly, and begins the formal ceremony. They stand awkwardly touching the gavel's handle at the same time*) For the first time in the one-hundred-year history the Waterfront Workers and Fishermen's Benevolent Association, we are swearing in a Number One who wasn't born to it: who wasn't a Son of One. (BOLEY *turns out front and smiles to his wife.* RUTHIE *waves to her husband, smiling*) This starts a new line of command for the WWFBA and a new line of leadership. . . . (*Nods to* ANGELO) Our Business Agent, Angelo Catalano, has the next thing to say here . . . (ANGELO CATALANO, *a young black man, steps forward nervously for his spot of public speaking.* PERCY *turns out front and smiles and waves discreetly to his wife.* ELLEN *waves back to* PERCY)

ANGELO: If there is any dues-paid-up member who wishes to lodge a complaint against either Thomas Percy or Henry Boley, let him do so at this particular time, 'cause these men will be in charge here for years and years to come . . . *(Applause and cheers from all after a small silence and a couple of giggles. It is all good cheer.* LISSA *raps the gavel four times officiously, bringing quiet to the room once again)* Save your applause for afta . . . *(Pauses)* Do I hear no complaints? *(Silently, each person in the line looks to the person next to him.* ANGELO *nods to* LISSA) Blessing.

LISSA: Both Father Scroop, from Our Lady of the Good Voyage Church, and Father O'Malley, from St. Ann's, have agreed to bless this swearin' in . . . bow your heads. *(Two priests step forward. Both are youngish.* O'MALLEY *is skinny;* SCROOP *is thick.* O'MALLEY *talks)*

O'MALLEY: We start here with a silent remembrance of Alfred Richards who led this waterfront, as did his father and grandfather before him, until his tragic and premature death at sea . . . *(There is a small silence.* BOLEY *looks at* PERCY, *who looks away and down.* TOWNSPEOPLE *whisper softly, a single word)*

TOWNSPEOPLE: Murder.

O'MALLEY: We ask Jesus Christ to walk beside Henry Boley and Thomas Percy to help them be gracious and thoughtful leaders . . . (O'MALLEY *nods to* FATHER SCROOP)

SCROOP: In the name of the Father, the Son and the Holy Ghost . . . on this day, March thirty-first, in the year of our Lord, Nineteen Hundred and Fifty-Nine *[N.B. Adjust date to 30 years prior to performance.]* . . . Amen.

O'MALLEY *(Overlaps):* Amen . . .

ALL: Amen . . . *(A cheer goes up from all assembled.* LISSA *hands the gavel over to the two men. There is an uncomfortable moment and each wonders who will hold the gavel.* PERCY *relinquishes his grip and hands the gavel over to* BOLEY. *The lights narrow to a spotlight on* BOLEY *and* PERCY. *Crossfade to a spotlight on* FABIANO, *a thin, mean-faced gangster backed by two stubby henchmen.* FABIANO *is enraged. He screams, loudly)*

FABIANO: What the fuck is going on here? What the fuck is goin' on here? What the fuck is goin' on here??? *(Shrieks)* I wanna see the new Number One! *Where is he? WHERE . . . IS . . . HEEE? (The lights widen now to fill the stage, changing color. We are now on State Wharf, still in flashback. The women and children have turned upstage. The men stand together in two clots; behind* PERCY *and behind* BOLEY. *Each man carries a crate on his shoulder)*

BOLEY: You're lookin' at him, Fabiano . . .

PERCY: Right over here, Fabiano . . .

BOLEY *(Softly, clearly):* You were warned not to expect Glossop lumpers to handle this load. This port is closed to you and yours, Fabiano. This is a fact of life . . .

FABIANO: Do you know who you're talkin' to?

BOLEY: Alfred Fabiano, a no-brained Palooka who ain't gonna set foot in Glossop for the rest of his life, unless he wants to float like his box of goods there . . . *(FABIANO starts to reach for a gun in his pocket)* Don't! It'd be a shitty way ta die, Fabiano. Don't. *(Every man on stage, except* BOLEY *and* PERCY, *holds a pistol pointed at* FABIANO *and* TWO HENCHMEN)*

HENCHMAN #1: Don't, Alf!

HENCHMAN #2: Hold off, Alfie.

FABIANO: That box of goods in the water's got eight to ten pounds, uncut. That's worth about $9,000 to us on the street . . . *(A sudden smile)* Listen up, you guys, huh? We can do business, yes?

BOLEY: We ain't doin' business, Fabiano. Glossop's closed to you and yours. *(*BOLEY *nods to the lumpers, who, one by one, dump their crates into the "harbor." It is the Boston Tea Party reincarnate. Possible to set wading pool offstage, filled with water, for authentic splash)*

FABIANO: You guys crazy? You know what that's worth? *(Sees guns, realizes)* Hey, what the hell are you doing, huh?

BOLEY: Swim . . . straight across. It's only fifty yards from here to the wharf in front of Sherm's, Fabiano . . . nothin' to it . . .

PERCY: Nothin' to it . . . swim!

BOLEY: What's a' matter? You ha'hd of hearin'? *(FABIANO and his HENCHMEN look at one another. BOLEY nods to LUMPERS who extend their arms, pointing their guns now directly at the gangsters)* Swim, and live to tell about it. Or don't. You got a choice. *(Suddenly, FABIANO and the TWO HENCHMEN turn and run to the "harbor." They leap into the space where the LUMPERS dumped the crates earlier. There is a splash, another, another, and then the LUMPERS cheer. BOLEY and PERCY embrace)* We did it! We goddam did it! *(Sudden silence. Tableau. LISSA, BOLEY, PERCY, ANGELO, arms around one another, frozen in place)*

Scene Two

From now on, the action will take place in the present. Thus, lighting should be brighter and less obvious colored, to support a sense of reality. Further, costumes should now be contemporary, as should all background music to individual scenes. It would be greatly helpful if some small, easily-recognizable link were found between the BOLEY and PERCY of thirty years ago and the present BOLEY and PERCY. PERCY might smoke the same pipe he did thirty years ago or wear the same distinctive garment. Or BOLEY might own a gold pocket watch, which is prominent through the play, ending up in HAL's possession at the end of the play.

OLD MARK LISSA moves to the four young men frozen in tableau. He speaks to audience, directly.

LISSA: Thirty years have passed. *(Pauses)* Lumpers grow old early, too early. And there's no turnin' back. *(An OLD HANK BOLEY and an OLD TOM PERCY now "take over" from the YOUNG HANK BOLEY and the YOUNG TOM PERCY. They are both in their sixties. BOLEY is dying of cancer. He is boney, hawklike. There is a ritual passing of the gavel from BOLEY to*

BOLEY *and a rain slicker from* PERCY *to* PERCY. *The* YOUNG BOLEY *and* YOUNG PERCY *exit, arm in arm)* Thirty years have passed. This is Henry Boley now . . . (OLD BOLEY *crosses to table where* OLD ANGELO *sits, drinking coffee)* And that's Tom Percy. (OLD PERCY, *carrying gardening tools, exits.* OLD MARK LISSA *enters, crosses to* YOUNG MARK LISSA, *who puts his arm on the old man's shoulder, smiles to audience)* This's Angelo Catalano now. And this is me: Markie Lissa. Old men: all of us. (YOUNG LISSA *exits.* OLD LISSA *walks across stage to table, joins* ANGELO *and* HANK BOLEY, *sits. The lights crossfade with* LISSA. *The place is a small pastry shop. Possible that other men might be around other tables, drinking coffee, eating pastry, talking softly. To* ANGELO) You tell him yet? (BOLEY *looks up at* LISSA) Somebody dumped a couple a' Hefty bags full a' pogies onta the Mayor's front steps . . .

BOLEY: You kiddin' me?

ANGELO: They were chucking some dead fish all over up around Haskell and Hammond, too . . .

BOLEY: How come?

LISSA: Gettin' back at some of the neighborhood people up there who got the Board of Health to close the plant down . . .

BOLEY: What's the matter with our boys? Neighborhood people didn't get any plant closed down. Nobody at the State House is listenin' to neighborhood people. It's the condo developers got Glossop Protein shut. . . . Who's gonna plunk down a quarter-of-a-million for a one-bedroom condo with a view of the harbor and the stink of the stuff Glossop Protein's producing.

LISSA: Gurry . . .

ANGELO: If that's protein, I'm stickin' with carbohydrates. Beer, bread, pasta . . . that's what Carmella says.

BOLEY: It's always the lumpers and the fishermen that lose out . . . and neighborhood people and local politicians always catchin' hell . . . takin' the blame. I'm sick of it. *(To* LISSA) Markie, I wanna set up a meeting, say Thursday, with the top ten condo developers and plant owners. Tell the plant men we wanna talk about a new contract. Tell the developers we've got some waterfront property we're thinkin' of letting go . . . they'll all be anxious to meet with us . . . *(A younger man,* GUIDO VEGA, *has entered; stands to one side waiting for* BOLEY *to acknowledge him.* ANGELO *pokes* BOLEY)

ANGELO: Hank, I think Guido's waitin' . . . (BOLEY *looks up)*

GUIDO: Hi, Hank. How goes it?

BOLEY: Yuh, sure, sit. *(Calls out to shopowner)* Hey Mike, another round of coffee. Four . . . *(To* GUIDO) you hungry? Anybody want another pastry? *(They don't)*

GUIDO: Just coffee for me, thanks, Hank.

BOLEY *(Calls out to shopowner):* Just the four coffees! *(To* GUIDO) So, how come you look nervous?

LISSA: Two guesses . . .

BOLEY: Well, I know damn well you ain't the one's been throwin' pogies around the mayor's house, so my guess is you wanna bring another cousin over.

GUIDO: I do, yuh. He's eighteen. He's speaking a little English already, too. He's a good kid. Yuh, I do.

BOLEY: You got room in the house?

GUIDO: Yuh, sure, there's room.

ANGELO: Your sister-in-law must have a good nature, huh? *(All laugh)*

GUIDO: There's room.

LISSA: Maybe she likes young cousins livin' in! *(All laugh, heartily.* GUIDO *is annoyed)*

GUIDO: I said there's room!

BOLEY *(Seeing* GUIDO's *anxiety):* Can we make him your responsibility, direct?

GUIDO *(Breaks into a smile):* I swear to God. (BOLEY *nods a "yes" to* LISSA)

LISSA: Okay. Call Sally Morella down at North Shore Fish as soon as the kid's boat gets in. He'll start him lumpin'. When do you expect him?

GUIDO: His boat left Lisbon three days ago. He should be here Saturday.

BOLEY: He left Lisbon already?

GUIDO: Yuh, well . . . *(Shrugs)*

BOLEY *(Smiles):* No wonder you were nervous . . . *(To all, smiling)* no wonder he was nervous, huh? *(To* GUIDO) How come he ain't flyin' a jet plane? It's 1989.* People don't take boats anymore . . .

GUIDO: Gettin' paid to work crew on a freighter's a hell of a lot better than buyin' tickets on a jet plane, huh?

BOLEY: Smart. It'll be good ta have another Vega lumpin' in Glossop.

ANGELO: Oh, yuh, right . . . we only got a hundred and ninety-nine Vegas on the books so far. It'll be great ta have an even two hundred!

GUIDO *(Happily pumps* BOLEY's *hand):* Thanks so much, Hank, huh? Markie, Angelo . . . thanks. (GUIDO *exits; yells to cousin awaiting him)* He said yes!

BOLEY: Good kid, Guido, huh?

LISSA: Oh, yuh, excellent. Hard-workin', family-oriented . . .

ANGELO: Family? Sure thing, Lissa . . . nothin' but family!

BOLEY: You related to Guido?

* Change to year in which play is being performed.

ANGELO: *All* the Portuguese are related! You kiddin' me?

LISSA: Yuh, well, if Portuguese don't help each other, we ain't gonna catch much help . . . (BOLEY *looks at his watch)* not around these parts, anyhow . . .

BOLEY: Whoa, I'm late. I'm s'pose ta bring Mrs. Nelson her St. Joseph roll by noon . . . (BOLEY *stands, walks to the other side of stage. Lights crossfade with him to line of people waiting for fresh bread in shop. As people see* BOLEY, *they step out of his way, usher him forward, to head of line)*

YOUNG MAN: Hey, Hank. Great day, huh?

BOLEY: It's a pip . . .

OLDER MAN: Hey, Hankie, you're lookin' good! (YOUNG MAN *and* YOUNG WOMAN *exchange a grim glance.* YOUNG WOMAN *silently mouths the word* Cancer)

BOLEY: Hey, Austin. How's the family?

OLDER MAN: Everybody's excellent, Hank. Hear Hal's home . . .

BOLEY: Yup, he's back . . . (AGNES, *an older woman, enters carrying tray of freshly-baked rolls)*

AGNES: Who's first? *(Sees* BOLEY) How many, Hank?

BOLEY: The usual. (AGNES *puts two rolls in a waxed paper bag and hands them to* BOLEY *without looking for or taking any money.* BOLEY *takes one of the rolls out of the bag, nibbles as he talks)* How's Frankie's wedding shaping up?

AGNES: Don't ask. (BOLEY *smiles)* I see Hal's livin' back home.

BOLEY: He's back in Glossop, yuh . . .

AGNES: You're lucky. Must be nice ta have him back.

BOLEY: Definitely nice, yuh.

AGNES: Frankie and his wife's gonna live down Swampscott . . . I'll never see them!

BOLEY: You'll be seein' them plenty. Don't you worry.

AGNES: I guess. See ya, Hank. (BOLEY *exits.* MAN *steps to head of line, speaks to* AGNES, *as* WOMAN *joins in*)

MAN: He looks rough . . .

WOMAN: He's getting worse . . .

AGNES: Cancer . . .

ANOTHER OLDER MAN *(Whispers):* Cancer . . . *(The lights crossfade to* MRS. NELSON, *a kindly older woman,* BOLEY's *housekeeper. She calls out to* BOLEY. *She carries a few plastic bags, filled with her belongings)*

BOLEY: You done, already?

MRS. NELSON: You didn't mess it up much this week . . .

BOLEY: That's what you said *last* week . . .

MRS. NELSON: You didn't mess it up much *last week,* either. . . . *(Smiles)* The kitchen floor's still wet. If you wanna, you could walk in that way and make a hell of a mess. . . . *(Laughs)* Guess Hal ain't stayin' home, huh? (BOLEY *looks at her. She shrugs)* His room ain't been touched.

BOLEY: Oh, yuh, no. He's stayin' with a friend . . . (BOLEY *takes remaining St. Joseph roll in its bag and hands it to* MRS. NELSON) Brought you your roll. Guess you ate something already. I got talkin' down to Mike's. I'm pretty late . . . you need a lift home?

MRS. NELSON: Kathy's on her way. . . . *(Looks at St. Joseph roll)* Sure you don't want it yourself?

BOLEY: Nope. It's yours . . .

MRS. NELSON: It'll save me goin' downtown later . . . for my supp'ah roll. Traffic's a mess, 'counta the goddam Lillie restaurant . . .

BOLEY: Yuh, I saw that just now. About fifty or so pickets . . .

MRS. NELSON: Foolishness.

BOLEY: The picketing?

MRS. NELSON: . . . The sellin' the place ta Lillies ta begin with. Imagine: the Catholic Church reads that Dr. Lill and his whole cult-following of Jesus-haters and child-kidnappers wanna buy a building in Glossop to set up their worldwide headquarters. What do they do? Do they warn their parishioners to lock their doors? No! They sell Lill a building! *Sell Lill a building!* Catholics are as crazy as bedbugs, if you ask me.

BOLEY: Catholics?

MRS. NELSON: Shoo-ahh! Now we got Lillies everywhere you turn! And who's to blame? The Catholics! Makes me want to spit! *(She makes a spitting noise) Ptwieeuu!* They're wreckin' the fish business and the whole goddam waterfront, if you ask *me!*

BOLEY: The Catholics?

MRS. NELSON: The *Lillies!* They're undercuttin' everybody's prices . . . (BOLEY *smiles.* MRS. NELSON *smiles) Ahhhhhh* . . . you're always pullin' my leg. *(Lifts one leg)* It's a wonder it ain't ten inches longer than it is . . . *(Laughs, then suddenly) Oh, God!* 'Course you're a Catholic yo'rself!!!

BOLEY *(Smiles):* Oh, yuh, well . . . not *devout* . . .

MRS. NELSON: I'm always shooting off my mouth . . . this Lillie business has everybody nuts! My nephew Gus says we oughta band together like an army and run the Lillies up 128 and right the hell outta this town!

BOLEY: Yuh, well, there's enough fish out there ta go around for everybody . . .

MRS. NELSON: Yuh, well, I guess . . .

BOLEY: And this kidnapping-of-Glossop-kids business never seemed to materialize, did it?

MRS. NELSON: Yuh, well, I just don't like the *look* of 'em! They wear funny clothes . . . and, let's face it; they're not white, are they? *(The sound of a car's horn blowing offstage in the distance)* There's Kathy. I gotta scoot . . .

BOLEY: I left your check on the table. You get it?

MRS. NELSON: I did. Thanks. Give Hal a big hug for me, okay?

BOLEY: See you next Saturday, Mrs. Nelson . . .

Scene Three

The lights crossfade to PATTY PERCY, *thirty, with her six-year-old daughter,* MARY-ELLEN. *She is frozen in place, staring across at* HAL BOLEY, *also thirty.* PATTY *and* HAL *are both extremely good-looking.*

PATTY *(Giggles):* My Goddd! *(Giggles)* Is that really you??? (HAL *walks to* PATTY *without speaking. He and* PATTY *circle each other, giggling, like highschoolers. After a few seconds,* PATTY *remembers her daughter, steps back, continuing)* This is Mary-Ellen. She's mine . . .

HAL: Hi ya, Mary-Ellen. You're nine?

MARY-ELLEN: Yuh, right. I'm a dwarf!

PATTY *(Laughs):* I didn't say she's nine, I said she's *mine* . . .

MARY-ELLEN: I'm six.

PATTY: She's six.

HAL: Hi ya Mary-Ellen. You look very tall . . . for a *dwarf!* *(He babbles a story, drunkenly, rapidly)* I knew this kid once who totally freaked when he saw his first dwarf . . . a little fat one, leaning up against a building, smoking this big cigar. The kid says to his mother, "Ma, what's that?" The mother goes, "That's a dwarf." The kid goes, "What's a *dwarf?*" Mother says, "A dwarf's an adult who never grows. Everything else is normal, except his size." After about five minutes, the kid goes, "Hey, Ma, am I a kid or am I a *dwarf?*" *(HAL smiles at PATTY and MARY-ELLEN)*

PATTY: I married Harry.

HAL: You married Harry. That's great. Well . . . that's *great.* I've, uh, gotta go . . . see you later, Mary-Ellen. Don't smoke cigars, okay? *(Exits)*

MARY-ELLEN *(With a professional comic's timing): Who the hell was that?*

PATTY: He's an old friend of your father's. We went all through school together . . .

MARY-ELLEN: What's his name, so I can tell daddy we saw him?

PATTY: Let's not do that right away, Mary-Ellen. We'll tell daddy later . . .

MARY-ELLEN: When?

PATTY: How's about ten years? *(PATTY laughs. Her laughter is joined by the laughter of three LUMPERS: BOBBY, PORKER and GUS across stage. HAL passes them, nods a greeting. The lights crossfade)*

HAL: Bobby . . . Porker . . . how goes it, Gus?

GUS: Good. How goes it with you?

HAL: Good. *(HAL exits. The LUMPERS exchange an astonished moment)*

GUS: Was that . . . Hal Boley?

BOBBY: Looked like 'im . . .

PORKER: Was. He come into the diner, end a' last week . . .

GUS: You sure?

PORKER: 'Course I'm sure. He was the only one come in all mornin' . . . quarter-pa'hst-six, ordered two eggs over easy and home fries.

GUS: Couldn't've finished 'em, huh?

PORKER: What's that s'pose'ta mean, asshole? Some kind of smartassed diner putdown?

GUS: I just meant 'cause the man's wicked skinny. He couldn't'a ate nothin' . . .

PORKER: Oh, yuh. I see what ya meant.

GUS: Ivy League bullshit, probably. All them top colleges make ya promise ta stay skinny or they won't graduate you . . .

BOBBY: Juicy Reed was sayin' Hal moved back home . . .

PORKER: Two weeks now.

GUS: The man's a waste . . .

BOBBY: He musta changed some, if he's gettin' up for breakfast at quarter-pa'hst-six . . .

PORKER: He wasn't gettin' up. Opposite. Just headin' home. He's stayin' over with Fatso, Tubby Silva.

BOBBY: Oh, yuh.

GUS (Laughs): People don't change . . .

PORKER: He was pretty wasted. I hadda call 'im a taxi.

GUS: Imagine takin' taxies in Glossop? My my, isn't that sophisticated? Must be tough bein' the Son of One and the Son of God, both at the same time! *(The three* LUMPERS *laugh. Their laughter is joined by the laughter of two women:* ALBERTA *and* EMILY FUSCO. *Lights crossfade now to opposite side of the stage,* PATTY *and* MARY-ELLEN *are gone and replaced by the women who are in bed with* HAL BOLEY. HAL *and the two women are all extremely drunk.* HAL *kisses one and then the other. They all laugh)*

Scene Four

HAL: Don't go, huh?

EMILY: We gotta go, Hal. We're both workin' the night shift this week. Really, we gotta . . .

HAL: You don't gotta . . . stay with me, huh? Come onnn . . .

ALBERTA: What for?

HAL: What for? For *me,* that's what for. For me, for your sister Alberta . . .

ALBERTA: I'm Alberta. She's Emily . . .

HAL: Of course you're Alberta. You think I didn't know that? I *knew* that . . .

EMILY: You already slept with us. What's left?

ALBERTA *(Giggles):* Emmmileeee!

HAL *(Loudly):* I have NOT slept with you! I have been awake with you. Fornicating!

ALBERTA *(To the neighborhood, in a good-natured way):* Excuse me, neighbors! Could everybody hear that? *(They all laugh)*

EMILY: What did Tubby Silva tell you about us anyhow? Did he tell you we did doubles? *(The sisters giggle, but* HAL *is oblivious to what they're saying. He is staring up at the sky)*

HAL: Shhh! *(The girls look at him, puzzled)* How come it's dark?

EMILY: Uhhh, lemme guess. 'Cause it's *night?* . . .

HAL: Night! I gotta go!

EMILY: Why? Heavy date? *(Music is heard, electronic, mysterious. The lights crossfade to spotlight on* JACK SILVA, *30, enormously fat)*

HAL: *Heavy* date? *(Laughs)* That's funny . . . *(Whoops with laughter, drunkenly)* that's hilarious! (SILVA *is directing three cohorts,* BARRY, BARDOLPH *and* GADSHILL, *in the stealing of computers and computer parts, stacked in clean carton boxes under a canvas. They carry the cartons offstage quickly and return for others.* SILVA *is not doing any actual labor)*

SILVA: Careful, careful . . .

BARDOLPH: Grab an end . . .

SILVA: I don't grab ends . . .

BARRY: Aren't you gonna *help?*

SILVA: Absolutely not. *(To* GADSHILL*)* Careful with that, Gadshill! That's not your wife, you know, that crate is *worth* something!

GADSHILL: Fuck you, Silva, okay? (LAZZARO, *a stump of a man, enters)*

LAZZARO: What's this I hear, Silva? Six hundred a crate?

SILVA: I know. I'm too generous . . .

LAZZARO: Wiseass! I wouldn't give my *mother* six hundred a crate . . .

SILVA: I don't know your mother . . . but, if you say she's not worth six hundred, your word's good enough for me. But, six hundred's *our* price, Lazzaro.

LAZZARO: Four hundred's my limit . . . *(The lighting shifts to* HAL *leaving the* FUSCO *sisters.* PETEY *calls out to him)*

PETEY: Hey, Hallie! Let's go!

HAL: This is my pal, Petey. This is either Emily Fusco or Alberta Fusco. And this is either Alberta Fusco or Emily Fusco.

PETEY *(Kisses their hands; speaks French):* Enchanté, mesdemoiselles . . .

ALBERTA: What's with the French? You Canadian or something?

PETEY: I'm something. I'm not Canadian.

HAL: Petey's my good friend. He's not my best friend. We're about to rob my best friend.

EMILY: Tubby Silva? You're gonna rob Tubby Silva? He's your best friend, right?

HAL: Well, it's not exactly robbing. It's more like whale-watching, only with guns. *(*PETEY *and* HAL *laugh)*

ALBERTA: Whatcha gonna do to Silva?

HAL: It's Tubby's birthday . . .

PETEY: We're giving him the surprise party of his life! *(*PETEY *and* HAL *laugh again. The lights shift back to* SILVA. *Two other* LUMPERS *stand behind* LAZZARO: *his helpers)*

LUMPER: How many more cartons are goin'? *(From the opposite side of the stage, suddenly, two men call out from the shadows. It is* DAN *and*

HAL, *voices gruffly disguised. They wear comic masks. They appear to have handguns, one in each hand)*

DAN: Everybody lay face down on the ground!

HAL: You heard him! DOWN!

BARDOLPH: Aww, shit.

GADSHILL: Goddam it . . .

THIRD MAN (PETEY) *(Offstage): You heard him!!! All a' you's!!! LAY DOWN!!! (Blinding white quartz light is switched on; shines on to audience, obscuring the stage)*

BARRY: What the fuck gives???

SILVA: Oh. My God. Oh my God . . .

HAL *(Offstage): Lay down and shut up! (Everybody lies down on the ground.* PETEY, *voice disguised, calls out)*

PETEY: We want the keys to both trucks, now! *NOW!!* (LAZZARO *stands, throws car keys, which* DAN *catches.* BARDOLPH *throws another set of car keys which* HAL *catches. A blinding light also shines on* LAZZARO *and* BARDOLPH, *preventing their seeing the "robbers." The light shines from a lamp attached to a video camera in the hands of a fattish man,* FITZIE, *who is videotaping the entire proceedings.* HAL *screams in a disguised voice)*

HAL: Listen! All of ya's: *take off!* Sta'ht runnin'! I said *sta'ht running!* On yo'r marks . . . get set . . . and don't a one of ya's look back, neither! *GOOO! (The men behind the voices begin to laugh. The three* LUMPERS *stand, look at one another quizzically and, one by one, run off.* SILVA *now stands and he begins to run.* BARRY *stands and follows* SILVA. *Now* BARDOLPH *does the same. Now* GADSHILL *follows, as well. All exit. The lights on audience are switched off.* HAL, PETEY *and* DAN *laugh uncontrollably. They turn and face* FITZIE *and his video camera, "filming" the event. They each hold bananas, one in each hand. They laugh uproariously, waving their bananas)*

HAL: Get our bananas! Get our bananas!

FITZIE: Got it . . . (HAL, PETEY, FITZIE *and* DAN *are crippled with laughter and self congratulations*)

PETEY: Oh Goddd . . . did you hear himmm?

HAL *(Laughing; to* DAN): We'd better get a move on. You and Fitzie head over to the Rigger and set up. Petey and I'll put this stuff back . . . (DAN *and* FITZIE *exit and* HAL *and* PETEY *quickly restack the cartons. As they work,* MARK LISSA *enters and stands watching their labor*)

PETEY: That's it . . .

HAL: Great . . . (HAL *turns; sees* LISSA; *jumps*) Jesus! You scared us, Markie . . .

LISSA: What the hell are you doing here, Hal?

HAL: You know Petey Parnell? Petey's Maxie Parnell's boy. (*To* PETEY) You know Markie Lissa? Markie's my father's oldest and closest friend, aren't 'cha, Markie?

LISSA (*To* HAL): You're a fuckin' disgrace, you know that?

HAL (*Smiles):* Okay, well, listen, great seein' you again, Markie. Hell of a night, huh?

LISSA: I'm gonna get your ass for this, Hal. I'm tellin' ya, face-ta-face. (*Lights crossfade to* SILVA, *opposite side of stage, telling his version of what happened that night: he was robbed*)

SILVA: They were humongous but, the leader was off the charts. Six-eleven . . . the one they called "The Little Guy" was maybe six-two, six-three . . . maybe even bigger. (*Lights widen to include* HAL, DAN, FITZIE, *and* PETEY, *facing* BARDOLPH, SILVA, BARRY *and* GADSHILL. *A TV/video monitor is in evidence. All men are holding back laughter*)

HAL (*False amazement; overly innocent):* Jeepers, Tubby, what was it? A basketball team that held you up?

SILVA: I'm tellin' ya's: they hadda average six-six, with the leader six-eleven. On my mother's grave . . . I swear!

HAL: This happened on your mother's grave?

GADSHILL (*Embarrassed*): He wasn't six-eleven . . .

SILVA (*Angry*): He was! He was pointing a stun-gun in my face! We are talking "Miami Vice" here!

HAL: "Miami Vice"? (PETEY *and* HAL *roar.* GADSHILL *laughs, as well.* SILVA *yells at* GADSHILL *first, then at* HAL)

SILVA: What's so funny? What are *you* laughing at? What's so funny? What's so funny? What is so goddam funny?

HAL: Let's watch a little TV, Tubby, huhhh? I think "Miami Vice" might be on nowww! (DAN *and* FITZIE *start the "playback" of the tape on the TV monitor.* SILVA *and others stand watching the tape play back. Everyone other than* SILVA *is hysterical with laughter*)

BARRY: You look great on TV, Tubby!

HAL: So?

PETEY: So?

BARDOLPH and BARRY: So?

GADSHILL, DAN and FITZIE: So?

SILVA (*After a pause*): Nice, really nice . . .

GADSHILL and PETEY (*Sing*): "I'm Chiquita Banana and I'm here to say . . ."

HAL: Happy Birthday, Jack . . .

BARDOLPH: Happy Birthday, Tubby . . .

FITZIE (*Appears with creamy-frosted birthday cake, which all get behind as they march toward* SILVA): Happy Birthday, Jack . . . (*They all sing "HAPPY BIRTHDAY TO YOU." Some sing "Dear Jackieee" and others sing "Dear Tubbyyy"*)

HAL: I wanna make a small speech here. I wanna thank Jackie Silva, a man who's been my best friend since first grade . . . a man who took me back into his life when I came back from the big city . . . destitute, friendless, drunk outta my gourd! I wanna now do for Jack Silva what I have done for no other man . . . (*As they near* SILVA, *he realizes that they are about to hit him in the face with the birthday cake. He backs away*)

SILVA: You wouldn't dare! (*They dare. The birthday cake is added to his face. Blackout*)

Scene Five

Bright, white morning light up, opposite side of stage, on three men in line: GUS *and* PASTA *and* PORKER. *They are joined by a fourth man,* BOBBY.

GUS, PASTA and PORKER: Hey, Bobby . . . Bob . . . etc.

BOBBY: Hey, Pasta, How goes it? Gus . . . hey, Porker. Sorry about the diner.

PORKER: Oh, yuh, well, thanks . . .

GUS: What's with the diner, Porker?

PASTA: Big fuckin' piece in the fuckin' paper last night . . .

PORKER: We're closin' down . . .

GUS: No kidding? (HAL *enters, opposite side, at the same time another burly lumper,* SALVIE REED, *enters. Both* HAL *and* SALVIE *are signing in for work.* SALVIE *and* HAL *suffer from hangovers and from not getting to bed as of yet. They will chat and then join the line together*)

SALVIE: Hey, Hal. Big head?

HAL: Oh, yuh, both of them. I gotta sign in and get myself home ta bed . . .

SALVIE: Must be nice. (HAL *and* SALVIE *join the line behind* PASTA, PORKER, BOBBY, *and* GUS *who do not notice* HAL, *who is the sole "feather-bedder" among them all)*

PORKER: . . . What with my Pa and me workin' long hours and takin' nothing outta the place. Makes no sense to keep it open . . .

PASTA: The fuckin' Lillies are packin' 'em in up ta their fuckin' place . . .

PORKER: They don't hav'ta pay their help like Americans do . . .

GUS: Look'it this: quarter pa'hst nine and none of us workin'. Shit!

PORKER: The cancer's rotting Boley's brain, if you ask me! Harry Percy's got the right idea: dump Boley and the Lillies into the harbor and start out fresh!

PASTA *(Sees* HAL *first):* Yo, Porker, chill! (PORKER *turns to look, bumps into* HAL. *Eye contact. There is a silence. The men all look from one to the other, realizing that* HAL *has overheard everything)*

PORKER: How goes it, Hal?

HAL: Hey, Porker.

GUS: How do you like bein' home?

HAL: It's okay, Gus, it's okay.

GUS: Ain't much like Princeton, huh?

HAL: Well, gosh, I dunno, Gus . . . I haven't been in Princeton since college. About twelve years now.

PASTA: You been livin' down fuckin' New York City, right? That's what the fuckin' paper said . . .

HAL: Yuh, I was livin' in New York, yuh, this is true. *(Smiles)* But, I'm home now. (ANGELO *enters, holding clipboard. He calls out to the men who are waiting in line for assignments)*

ANGELO: That's all the work we got for today. You guys still out here can get your unemployment cards stamped and head down to Salem to collect . . . *(The men respond, grumbling, taking out their proper forms and crowding forward)*

PORKER: This union's a joke!

PASTA: I ain't had fuckin' work in three weeks.

GUS: We oughta try inta Charlestown. I hear they're lumpin' Russian boats . . .

PASTA: I'll lump anybody's fuckin' boat. I don't give a fuck! (HAL *seems confused. He moves forward to* ANGELO)

HAL: You never called me, Angelo. I never signed.

ANGELO: Yuh, that's right.

HAL: I gotta sign.

ANGELO: No go, Hal.

HAL: Hmm?

ANGELO: You ain't signin' . . .

HAL: How so?

ANGELO: Your father's orders. You gotta see him if you wanna straighten it out. *(Lights crossfade to opposite side of stage to* HANK BOLEY)

BOLEY: I don't own the goddam union, ya know. (HAL *turns around and moves to his father, cautiously*)

HAL: Yes, sir, I know that you don't . . . (HAL *is blurry-eyed: hungover. He squints and grins falsely, trying to seem alert.* BOLEY *pauses from time to time, noticing* HAL*'s condition with disgust. Beyond them, through the glass window overlooking the harbor, we see the morning's boat traffic: the flurry of activity, pulsations of labor, of men earning their keep . . . all in contrast to* HAL*'s sleepy-eyed concentration and* BOLEY*'s steely-eyed disgust*)

BOLEY: So, what do you expect?

HAL: Well, it's just that since I came back here, I've been signin' in every morning . . . you know . . . for work and all . . . (BOLEY *stares at* HAL, *who looks down, ashamed, as he continues*) . . . and, well, this morning, I . . .

BOLEY *(Interrupting):* For *"work"?*

HAL: Hm?

BOLEY: You said you "signed in for work" . . .

HAL: Yuh, well, I went to sign in . . .

BOLEY: Are you drunk?

HAL: Drunk? No, it's morning . . .

BOLEY: You don't drink in the morning?

HAL: No. *(There is a pause between them)*

BOLEY *(Pauses):* I'm a sick man, Hal. People know this and it makes them nervous . . .

HAL: I can understand that, yes.

BOLEY: When people heard you were divorced and all and movin' back home, they figured something different . . . *(Pauses)* Princeton man . . . educated . . . comin' home . . . me bein' sick and all . . . *(There is a pause)* Nobody figured you were just a drunk and a whoremaster, comin' home to wait it out . . .

HAL: To wait *what* out? *(There is another pause, longer.* BOLEY *stares at his son)* To wait *what* out, Pa? *(There is a knock on the door.* BOLEY *and* HAL *turn and watch door open.* MARK LISSA *pokes head inside)*

LISSA: Sorry to interrupt, Hank, but, Dr. Nagoa and some others are waitin' already. *(*BOLEY *nods to* LISSA, *who in turn nods to* HAL*)* Hal . . . *(*LISSA *exits.* BOLEY *looks at his son and gets to the question)*

BOLEY: Were you involved in the robbery over at State Wharf?

HAL: What robbery? *(*BOLEY *stares silently)* Nobody stole anything!

BOLEY: But, you were in on it, yes?

BOLEY: It was a joke, that's all, for somebody's birthday. Nothing was stolen.

BOLEY: A *joke?*

HAL: I was the one who put the stuff back. . . . *(Pauses)* I guess you know that already, huh?

BOLEY: I get reports, yuh. *(Pauses, stares at* HAL*)* I'm putting you on three months' suspension. No work, no signin' in for pay, no nothin'.

HAL: For puttin' stuff *back?*

BOLEY: For knowing about the robbery in advance and doing nothing to stop it! *(Pauses)* For thinking that jeopardizing union-protected property is some kind of *joke* . . . something funny . . . *(Pauses)* I got people waiting. Get out of here. *(The lights crossfade to* DR. NAGOA, *a Korean. In the shadow behind* DR. NAGOA *sit other Korean businessmen, silently, straight-backed, in a row, as might birds sit on a telephone wire.* DR. NAGOA *speaks in flawless English)*

DR. NAGOA: We haven't gone to the police and we don't want to . . .

BOLEY: We appreciate that.

DR. NAGOA: Our people mistrust the police . . . our presence in the community causes misunderstanding.

BOLEY: Yes, there's been a great deal of misunderstanding . . . *(Pauses)* I'm sure you know some of the fears people have about your being in town . . .

DR. NAGOA: They think we're going to steal their children.

BOLEY: That's a big one, yuh . . .

DR. NAGOA: The Church of the New Way has been in Glossop for three years. Are there any children missing?

BOLEY: I know that . . .

DR. NAGOA: Glossop is our home . . .

BOLEY: Dr. Nagoa, Glossop was never a rich man's town, but a fisherman or a lumper could count on makin' a buck here . . . feedin' his family. . . . *(Pauses)* The Canadians have been comin' in here with fish prices about fifty per cent lower than ours. . . . *(Pauses)* Now you guys are here, with tuna prices that are gonna put our dealers outta business, . . . *(Pauses)* you really think people are gonna welcome you with open arms? It's just economic. You challenge a man's pocketbook, he fights . . .

DR. NAGOA: Forgive me, Mr. Boley, but it's not "just economic." Nobody ever sank a Canadian boat. There are very few yellow-skinned Canadians. And whoever heard of white people going to jail for a tax discrepancy? We've come to you, Mr. Boley, in trust. We think that we have an understanding with you . . . with *you.* Either you stop whoever's sinking our boats, or we do.

BOLEY: Leave this to me. You can trust me. (NAGOA *bows and exits. A light fades up on* HARRY PERCY, *opposite side of stage*)

HARRY: You guys have questions for me, yes? Tell Boley I haven't got all day. Some of us hav'ta actually *work* for a livin' . . . (BOLEY *turns and faces front. He is enraged. He changes his tone of voice totally from the tone used with* DR. NAGOA. *The lighting on* BOLEY *changes color: new scene)*

BOLEY *(Authoritative; enraged):* We've been too easy-goin' with this kid for way too long! I don't give a fuck whose son he is! I intend to make a stand on this and I don't want anybody thinkin' they can buck me here! *(Lights widen to include full Executive Board of WWFBA.* HARRY PERCY *stands facing the men of the Executive Board and* BOLEY. HARRY'*s father,* TOM, *and* HARRY'*s uncle,* FRANK, *stand just behind* HARRY *and now move forward into the inner circle to join the others at the conference table. The men sit around the table in the following order:* MARK LISSA *sits next to* WALTER BLUNT *and* ANGELO CATALANO, *alongside* BOLEY, *as lieutenants, of sorts. Around the table are four other men:* MORT *and* ARTIE SHIMMA, EDDIE BELL *and* TIMMY JOHNSON. *These four men are young and tough: blue-collar workers.* LISSA, ANGELO *and* BLUNT *are closer to* BOLEY'*s age. All of the men wear sturdy clothing. Flannel shirts are worn under tweed sport coats, by the older men. The younger men wear workclothes: flannel shirts, chinos, boots.* TOM PERCY, HARRY'*s father, like* HANK BOLEY, *has grown older in appearance than his actual years. Unlike* BOLEY, PERCY *is now slightly puffy and slightly soft. He is a pleasant fellow, well-dressed and clean. He and* BOLEY *exchange a knowing glance and a smile.* TOM PERCY *seats himself opposite* HANK BOLEY)*

PERCY: How goes it, Hank?

BOLEY: Fine. Give us half a minute. *(Exits with* LISSA)

PERCY: Eddie, hi. *(Motions to* FRANK *and* HARRY) Sit here. Over there, Harry. (FRANK *sits.* HARRY *doesn't move.* TOM *nods to others)* Mort, Artie, how's your dad?

MORT: Pretty rough still, Tom, thanks.

PERCY: Sorry to hear that. How is the family, Timmy?

JOHNSON: Not so bad, Tom. How's yourself?

PERCY *(Smiles):* We'll tell you in about ten minutes, huh, Harry? (PERCY *smiles at his son.* HARRY *remains silent and stern: unmoving. There is an embarrassed silence and then chatter)* You younger guys all know my brother Frank, or no?

MORT: I don't. I'm Morty Shimma. This here's my brother, Artie . . . that's Walter Blunt . . . (FRANK *smiles.* BLUNT *nods)*

FRANK: Pleasure . . . Frank Percy . . .

ARTIE: You live local?

FRANK: Used ta . . .

PERCY: Frank's down from Worcester . . .

ANGELO: You guys want a coffee and cruller? (PERCY *and* FRANK *shake their heads no.* BOLEY *re-enters with* LISSA)

BOLEY: Let's go!

LISSA: You wanna know this: you're not being charged here formally. Not yet, anyway. We wanna just hear your side of it, then the Executive Board can make its decision . . .

PERCY: We're confident that the Board will see that this has all been a misunderstanding . . .

LISSA: We hope so, Tom . . . for everybody's sake. In the meantime, the WWFBA's got government contracts to protect and we mean to protect 'em at all costs . . . we can't have people scared to pull into Glossop harbor . . .

FRANK: So, you're gonna set up another Percy as a sacrificial lamb. Is that it?

BOLEY: Frank?

FRANK: Just seems to me every time you need a patsy to stick this or that on, one of us gets it in the neck.

BOLEY *(Interrupts):* Get out of here, Frank.

FRANK: Hmmm?

BOLEY: You heard me: out.

FRANK: What gives?

BOLEY *(Pauses):* You weren't invited to this hearing, Frank, so, go: out.

HARRY *(Loudly):* I asked my uncle here!

BOLEY *(Louder):* Hardly your place to, fella! (HARRY *is enraged.* PERCY *puts his hand on his son's arm to quiet him.* FRANK *stands, looks each man in the eye, turns wordlessly and exits the meeting)* What the Lillies claim is that you rammed their boat deliberately . . .

HARRY *(Interrupting):* You takin' their word over mine?

BOLEY *(Continuing angrily, not allowing* PERCY's *interruption):* . . . that you rammed their boat and told 'em your name . . . and warned 'em that you'd be sinkin' more boats . . .

HARRY *(Interrupting again):* I asked you if you were takin' the Lillies' word over the word of one of your own . . .

BOLEY *(Again not allowing interruption, not recognizing that a question has been asked):* . . . and told the Lillie kids to tell their leaders they hadda get off Cape Ann.

HARRY *(Angrily, loudly):* I asked you a question!

BOLEY *(Yells angrily):* You didn't ask a question! You *interrupted* a question: *my* question . . . *(There is an embarrassed silence.* PERCY *flashes a worried look at his son)*

HARRY: What's your question?

BOLEY: Did you sink the Lillie boat, Percy? (HARRY *smiles, takes envelope from his pocket and tosses it on table)*

HARRY: I heard you'd be tryin' to hang this on me, so I saved ya's all some trouble . . . *(Pauses)* Inside is a sworn statement that I was nowhere near the Lillie boat sinkin', *(Shoves statement closer to* BOLEY) Here . . . the statement tells you where I was and it's signed by more'n fifty witnesses . . . all paid up WWFBA members. *(Smiles, pretends to reach for envelope)* Want me to read it out loud or you guys wanna read it to yo'rselves later on . . . ? You got a choice!

BOLEY: No need for you ta ham it up, Percy. We'll read what's in there and make our decision. You done? Anything else we should know?

HARRY: Yuh, there is. I wanna add that I love Glossop and while I ain't myself personally be'n sinkin' no Lillie boats, I'm glad somebody has. The Lillies are out ta destroy fishin' on Cape Ann and I'm glad that somebody's takin' a decisive and manly action against the bastids. That's what I want to add. (BOLEY *stares steely-eyed at* HARRY PERCY)

BOLEY: It's my feeling that you're hopping on to this so-called "Lillie issue" for other purposes, Percy . . .

HARRY: That's yo'r feeling, huh? Well, that is just fuckin' *fascinating* . . .

BOLEY: You keep that mouth of yours shut and do some listening! *(Pauses)* We've got waterfront to protect here and the livelihoods of a hell of a lot of men to protect, too! *(Pauses)* I hope what you say is true. The Executive Board will meet and vote and decide. You'll get a fair shake. *(Pauses)* Now, you have a moment's think, Harold, and you decide if there's anything else you want to say here . . .

HARRY: I said it all.

BOLEY: Okay. . . . *(Pauses)* In the meantime, if you've got any possible influence in this, you see to it that no more of Dr. Lill's boats are bothered. Do you understand? *(No reply.* BOLEY *yells, pounds table) Do . . . you . . . understand???* (HARRY *nods yes wordlessly, through clenched jaw. He is furiously silent.* BOLEY *raps the gavel, three raps)* This meeting is over. *(A light comes up on* FRANK PERCY)

FRANK: You just smile at the bastid and keep your mouth shut, Harry! You hear me? (HARRY PERCY *moves to* FRANK, *as lights fade out on all others*)

HARRY: It just fuckin' galls me!

FRANK: Just cool down, Harry. You're hot . . .

HARRY: Goddam right I'm hot! I got the likes of Hank Boley screaming at me and his pussy-son Hal Boley back in town, blowin' in my ear . . . these things get me hot . . . *wicked* hot.

FRANK (*Snaps at* HARRY *angrily*): You keep a lid on your temper! When it's time to fight, we'll fight fine. It didn't hurt me to leave the meeting then, did it? Didn't I keep my dignity? Didn't I keep a lid on my goddam temper? You think I wasn't burning up?

HARRY: Yuh, okay . . .

FRANK: Trust me . . .

HARRY: I trust *you*. If it were just you I had to trust, there'd be no trouble here . . . (*Lights fade out*)

Scene Six

Lights fade up in BOLEY's *office.* BOLEY *sits atop his desk, feet on floor, facing* TOM PERCY.

BOLEY: You're gonna hav'ta control your son, Tom.

PERCY: How's about you controllin' *your* son?

BOLEY: *My* son ain't out sinkin' boats. Nor is he threatening to take over . . .

PERCY: That ain't what I hear.

BOLEY: What's that?

PERCY: Nothin' . . . *(There is a pause)*

BOLEY: Why's Frank here?

PERCY: I asked him to. *(Pauses)* To help out with the boy. Harry has a great respect for Frank.

BOLEY *(Shrugs):* Frank's not the right influence on Harry.

PERCY: Lay off, Hank. The kid's justifiably very upset by what's goin' on here. You know it and I know it.

BOLEY: How so?

PERCY: You know.

BOLEY: How come you say I know? I *don't* know. I really don't know. Why don't you tell me, Tom? *Then* I'll know. *(There is a long pause.* TOM PERCY *speaks)*

PERCY: I never had any interest in bein' Number One . . . you did, not me . . .

BOLEY: Yuh? And?

PERCY: What we did, we did because it was . . . right. We did what we had to do. For the good of the town . . .

BOLEY: We had reasons, yuh . . . Tom, does your son know anything? (BOLEY *and* PERCY *hold a moment of eye contact)*

PERCY: Absolutely not. Yours?

BOLEY: 'Course not. A sacred promise was made.

PERCY: Henry. Listen to me. This is the honest-ta–God truth I'm speakin' here. I was happy to let you take over the gavel for yourself.

BOLEY: You made out okay.

PERCY: Am I complaining?

BOLEY *(Yells suddenly):* Tom! You got a kid out there sinkin' other people's boats like some kind of *war's* been declared!

PERCY *(Angrily):* And *you've* got a kid who's drinkin' and fuckin' around with women and signin' in for pay without a *lick of work* and my boy, like the rest of the waterfront, is *very pissed off.*

BOLEY: Why? Why's Hal *anybody's business???*

PERCY: 'Cause everybody knows you got cancer, Henry. Nobody wants the gavel to pass from you to your son. (BOLEY *turns and faces* PERCY *silently. They are both old men, proud and worried. The lights crossfade to* HARRY PERCY, *addressing a group of* LUMPERS *and* FISHERMEN *and* FRANK PERCY, *who stands to* HARRY's *right. Among the group is* GUS, PASTA, PORKER, BOBBY, *who all stand listening, paying rapt attention)*

HARRY: Boley was never given leadership of the WWFBA on his own. My father, Tom Percy and Henry Boley were given an equal share. Boley wasn't *born to it* any more than you or me. He grabbed it for himself . . . *(Pauses)* okay, fine. We all know it's survival of the fittest and the meek get shit . . . okay, fine, but just 'cause my father's willing to give in his rights doesn't mean I, his son, am willing to, too. I'm tellin' ya's that I'm not. . . . *(Pauses)* If Hal Boley's a Son of One by some kind of *birthright,* then so's Harry Percy . . . Tom Percy's son . . . *me. (To* FRANK) My uncle Frank here was on the scene when Boley and my father took over. Am I right in saying they were equals?

FRANK: Absolutely.

HARRY: Am I right in saying that I've got as much claim to being the next Number One as Hal Boley does?

FRANK: No question.

BOBBY: This has got nothin' ta do with sinkin' Lillie boats, Harry . . .

HARRY: You wanna try to make your livin' inland, *away* from the water, Bobby, huh?

PASTA: You can't tell me the fuckin' Lillies set up fuckin' George's Bank, can you? That's fuckin' *ludicrous,* Harry!

HARRY: I'm only telling ya's we could make a *living* if the Lillies were outta Glossop!

PASTA: I don't know, Harry . . . seems to me, fuckin' Glossop's fucked! Fishin' and lumpin' are fucked, fuckin' Lillies or no fuckin' Lillies!

BOBBY: Cookie Evangelista pulled the plug on *Bessie II* yesterday, ya know . . .

FRANK *(Interrupting suddenly. False voice):* Okay, boys, let's get back to work! *(All turn to face* MARKIE LISSA *and* ANGELO, *side by side, eavesdropping on everything that's been said)*

HARRY: Markie, Angelo. You guys some kinda Commie KGB here now, or what?

LISSA: You're diggin' your own grave, Harry . . . *(To all)* If you guys are his friends, you'll stop him. *(Nods to* FRANK PERCY*)* Frank. Good to see you on the docks again. Guess you can't keep a good lumper off the docks, no matter how old he gets or how far away he lives . . . he comes back, huh? *(The men break up and move away, not wanting to be associated with* PERCY *as* PERCY's *"gang."* LISSA *and* FRANK PERCY *stare at one another.* FRANK *nods.* HARRY PERCY *laughs aloud, out of context.* LISSA *stares at him. Lights shift slightly to come up on opposite side of stage. Light remains on* LISSA *throughout lighting shift.* LISSA *turns and faces* BOLEY *as* FRANK *and* HARRY PERCY *exit slowly in darkness)* What the hell has Frank Percy got such a hard-on for you for, anyhow, huh?

BOLEY: What? Are you kidding me? Frank Percy was Allie Richards' messenger boy! Frank hates my guts for takin' over Number One. Tom Percy and Frank Percy are like night and day. Always were. *(He pauses)* Tom's boy, Harry, and my Hal, same thing. Night and day. They were born five minutes apart, you know that?

LISSA: I knew they were close in age and all . . .

BOLEY: Within five minutes of each other, up Addison-Gilbert . . . *(Pauses)* Tommy and I used ta stand side by side every night, up the hospital . . . starin' in the nursery windows at our boys . . . *(Smiles)* Ruthie and Ellen used ta link arms and walk up and down the corridor while Tom and I would be standin', starin', makin' big plans for our sons. . . . *(Pauses)* Funny, the way it turns out . . . Ruthie and Ellen both gone . . . (BOLEY *pauses, lost in memory*) I used ta wonder if maybe they switched 'em . . . the babies . . . up Addison-Gilbert.

LISSA: He's still young. He'll come around . . .

BOLEY: I guess. *(Smiles at* LISSA. *Lights crossfade to* HARRY PERCY *on opposite side of stage, on telephone. He is enraged)*

HARRY: What are you givin' me, Matza? Either you're in or you're out. Which is it? (PATTY PERCY *stands upstage of* HARRY, *in shadows, eavesdropping discreetly on her husband's telephone conversation*) Listen to me . . . *LISTEN TO ME!!!* . . . If you don't wanna, don't. That's cool. Just keep your trap shut about it, okay? Yuh, well, you better mean it, Matza. . . . (HARRY *slams down the telephone*) Fuckin' stooge! (PATTY *calls to him, surprising him*)

PATTY: Something wrong, Harry?

HARRY: What were you? Listening in?

PATTY: I just heard you yelling.

HARRY: That was private stuff.

PATTY: I wasn't listening. I didn't hear . . .

HARRY: You sure?

PATTY: What's with you, anyway?

HARRY: I just don't want you listening in on private stuff. That's all . . .
(PATTY *goes to* HARRY)

PATTY: You tired?

HARRY: I gotta go out . . .

PATTY: Now?

HARRY *(Starts to exit):* Yuh, well, I gotta . . .

PATTY *(Without warning):* Did you sink the tuna boat, Harry?

HARRY: What's this?

PATTY: I hear this around town. People say you were the one who sank
the Lillie boat and that you're threatening to sink more. *(There is a
small silence)* You're my husband. I gotta wait up for you. I ought ta
know these things, don't you think? (MARY-ELLEN *enters behind* PATTY,
frightened. HARRY *sees her)*

HARRY: What are you doing up?

MARY-ELLEN: You woke me up, fighting.

HARRY: We're not fighting. We're talking.

MARY-ELLEN: Then how come Mama's crying?

PATTY: I'm not crying. Go back to bed now.

HARRY: Go back to bed. Your mother and I are talking . . .

PATTY: Go on, Mary-Ellen. I'll come right up . . .

MARY-ELLEN: I don't wanna . . .

PATTY: Mary-Ellen . . .

MARY-ELLEN: Okay. Okay . . . (MARY-ELLEN *exits.* PATTY *faces* HARRY, *speaks softly, clearly)*

PATTY: A simple yes or no, Harry. I gotta right to know.

HARRY: What?

PATTY: About the boat. Was that you?

HARRY: Who sunk it? Me? Nope. I didn't.

PATTY: Good.

HARRY: Did *you?*

PATTY: Did I what? Sink the Lillie boat?

HARRY: Mmm.

PATTY *(Laughs):* No.

HARRY: Good. (PATTY *and* HARRY *embrace)* You still in love with me, or what?

PATTY: 'Course I'm still in love with you. Why'd you ask me a question like *that?*

HARRY: No reason.

PATTY: You still in love with *me?*

HARRY: What's with the "still"? When did I ever tell you I was in love with you?

PATTY: That was me, in the church, "till death do us part" . . . remember?

HARRY: That was you? In the white dress?

PATTY: Yup.

HARRY: A promise is a promise, I guess. *(They kiss)* Your old friend Hal Boley's back in town. You know that?

PATTY: Yuh, I know. I, uh, saw him . . .

HARRY: You what?

PATTY: In the car. He was goin' one way, I was goin' the other.

HARRY: He saw you?

PATTY: Huh?

HARRY: That's simple enough: did Hal Boley see you?

PATTY: Me? *(Pauses)* No. *(Lights out on* PATTY *and* HARRY*)*

Scene Seven

BOLEY: How do you know this, Angelo? *How?*

ANGELO: Hank, come onnn. What the hell was Guido Vega doin' out there on a boat that needs a ten-man crew, the minimum, with just his brother? . . . They couldn't'a been fishin'!

BOLEY: Maybe they were pickin' up crew somewhere . . .

ANGELO: Hankie, come onnn . . .

BOLEY: Guido Vega's hard–working, Angelo. He's a boy I've known since he was twelve . . .

ANGELO: Yuh, so? I knew him in the crib and I'm tellin' ya still: Guido pulled the plug.

BOLEY: Bring him in here. Just Guido. I don't want anybody to know I'm talkin' to him . . . round up some of the other captains, too.

ANGELO: The Irish kid from the paper's been snoopin' . . .

BOLEY: Where?

ANGELO: Here. He was out front an hour ago . . .

BOLEY: Tell Guido to come by my house, three o'clock. The others, too.

ANGELO: I dunno if I can find Guido . . .

BOLEY: He's got two dozen cousins workin'. There ain't a one of 'em with decent papers. You find him. (ANGELO *exits. Drumbeat. Light shift.* GUIDO, COOKIE, MORT SHIMMA *and* SALVATORE REED *in semi-circle, facing* BOLEY. *Each wears lumper's clothing and a cap with gold braid signifying ownership of a boat. Each is a captain*)

GUIDO: I haven't made expenses in twenty straight weeks, Hank. I ain't even come close. My insurance premium's due in a month and I ain't got a hope in hell of meeting it. My mortgage on the boat's four thousand a month alone. I grossed $3800 last month and that was my best month outta the last six. . . . *(Pauses)* I used to gross $3800 a week. *(Pauses)* I'm sorry if what I did makes you look bad, Hank. You've been wonderful to me and I don't want anything to make you look bad . . . *(Drumbeat. Light shift.* MORT SHIMMA *speaks)*

SHIMMA: I coulda lied to you. I coulda told you we caught fire, like I told the coast guard . . . but, well, I didn't . . . I'm tellin' you the straight goods. I got eight mouths ta feed. Eight. I love fishin', but well . . . how? They raised my insurance premium from $14,000 a year to $41,000 a year. I tried to find a second company, you know, to change. I couldn't. Nobody else even wanted to insure me . . . I can't pay $41,000 for insurance, Hank. You know that. *(Drumbeat. Light shift.* COOKIE EVANGELISTA *speaks to* BOLEY)

COOKIE: My boat's worth a hell of a lot more to me under the top of the water. I can sell my pier to Phil Duffy for a hundred and sixty thousand, no questions asked, all's I gotta do is pick up the phone. He's developin' condos . . . so what am I gonna bust my balls for, huh?

BOLEY: I don't get it, Cookie. I don't get it. *(Pauses)* I've known you all my life, right? Your father, your grandfather . . .

COOKIE: I've known you as long as I can remember. It's true.

BOLEY: I look at all the problems here on the waterfront: Canadian prices, George's, the Lillies, all of it. Look, I understand when somebody pulls the plug on an old boat to get a new boat. We turn a blind eye to these things. But *forty trawlers?* I do not understand also why half our goddam waterfront's bein' sold to condo developers. Families who've be'n fishing four or five generations are sinking their boats and selling their wharves out from under themselves and WHY??? *I do not understand these things!*

COOKIE: I can't talk to you anymore on this, Hank. Don't make me lie to you. I'm not the right one ta be askin' these questions to . . . I got eight kids. *(Drumbeat. Light shift.* BOLEY *moves to* SALLY REED, *slaps him suddenly)*

BOLEY: Answer me, Salvatore, goddam you!

SALLY: I can't, Hank!

BOLEY: I brought your whole family across, Salvatore. I did that: me! Now, you open your mouth and you speak words, goddam you!

SALLY *(After a long pause):* Cocaine, mostly.

BOLEY: What the fuck are you tellin' me here, Salvatore?

SALLY: It's big, Hank.

BOLEY: How big, Salvatore? Why is this shit startin' up again? And since when, I wanna know! I cleaned this waterfront up with my own hands! I did that! *Talk!*

SALLY: I can't, Hank, I can't . . . *(Drumbeat. Light shift.* BOLEY *returns to* GUIDO, *slaps him)*

BOLEY: Tell me, you little fuck!

GUIDO: I can't hit you back, Hank! I can't raise a hand!

BOLEY *(Threatens a fistfight):* Come on, Guido, raise a hand! Raise one! *Come on!*

GUIDO *(Backing down):* What don't you know?

BOLEY: Let's say I know nothing, huh?

GUIDO: I could wind up dead from this . . .

BOLEY: Fucking "A," Guido. Let me hear some words . . .

GUIDO: I don't know how many boats are runnin' heavy exactly. It's a lot, I know that. Once the coast guard has solid word on a ship, they get their impound orders goin'. You know the rest . . .

BOLEY: You forget? I don't know nothing. Talk . . .

GUIDO: Once the coast guard impounds a boat, it sits at dock for maybe eight or nine months, waiting for trial. The owner can't make a penny fishing while his boat's tied up. The boat's worth maybe a million or two and it's just sittin' there tied up: dead . . . mortgage, insurance, interest keeps clickin' . . . so they pull the plug . . . don't ask me who's runnin' the show, Hank, 'cause I swear to you, I don't know . . .

BOLEY: How many of our boys are wired, Guido?

GUIDO: I dunno . . . *(Pauses)* most everybody's fishin' for a livin'. The boats go down, the insurance goes up, the rest of us get trapped in the middle . . . any goddam shack we own that's close to the water, we can sell like that *(snaps fingers)* for more'n any of us'd clear in two years of fishin' or lumpin' or cuttin'. It's a tough situation here . . .

BOLEY: I must be gettin' stupid! I figured newcomer-yuppies and Boston-Mafioso, yuh, sure! But not *our* people . . . not *Glossop* people. I thought I cleaned this place up, once and for all. I must be gettin' really stupid. Tell me something, Guido. Do you carry drugs?

GUIDO: Never. Not once. I swear on my children. Not even once. All I tried to do was fish. I couldn't make it. *(Pauses)* Maybe if I carried drugs, I could have . . . *(A spotlight, opposite side of stage, fades up on* HARRY *and* FRANK, *as end of Scene Seven overlaps start of Scene Eight)*

HARRY: I ain't sayin' Boley's on Lill's payroll, but, it sure wouldn't change things any if he *were*. Would it?

FRANK: Lumpin's gone sour, too. A lot of boats are avoiding Glossop these days—they're goin' down ta Beverly, into Gloucester, Salem . . . Glossop's finished.

BOLEY: What are you gonna do now, Guido . . . for a living?

GUIDO: I dunno, Hank . . . *(Pauses, smiles ironically)* I was just gonna ask you . . .

Scene Eight

Sunset. PATTY PERCY *stands staring at the sky, lost in a memory.* HAL *calls out from across the stage softly, startles her.*

HAL: You told me to wait here for you and here I am.

PATTY: What? How long have you been standing there?

HAL: About seventeen years.

PATTY: What are you talking about?

HAL: When we were in high school. Right there . . . on that spot. You said, "I'll always meet you here if you need me to. Just wait for me. I'll show up." So here I am.

PATTY: I said that?

HAL: You don't remember saying that?

PATTY: I do. I remember. *(Smiles, embarrassed)* I come here almost every day. I like to watch the sun go down and come up, both of those things. Gives me hope. *(Smiles)* Yuh, 'course I remember. I'm just surprised you did.

HAL: I remember everything you ever said to me, Patty. (HAL *moves to* PATTY, *stares lovingly at her. It seems as though he might kiss her)*

PATTY: I'd better get home. I've got a supper to get in. I've got this family . . . *(She starts off.* HAL *calls to her softly)*

HAL: I'll be here waiting for you tomorrow night. Same time, same place. I need you to meet me . . .

PATTY: I, uh, I better get home and get my supper in . . . (PATTY *runs off. Lights crossfade to* JACK SILVA, *who calls out to* HAL)

SILVA: The word is you're seeing Percy's wife.

HAL: Maybe I am, maybe I'm not.

SILVA: I wrote you a poem on the subject this morning, while I was on the toilet.

HAL: You redefine the word "gross," you know that? Your humor is gross. Your *mind* is gross! Your *ass* is gross! You are gross from top to bottom! You are gross inside and out! You are *gross incarnate!* You are *twelve dozen!*

SILVA *(Takes handwritten poem from pocket):* I don't usually wax poetic, but, écoute, mon frére . . . *(Clears throat)*

HAL: What's this?

SILVA: It's your poem. *(Unfolds paper, clears throat, reads title)* "On My Best Friend's Screwing His Worst Enemy's Wife, A Salacious Sonnet of Sexual Insinuendo, by Jack Silva, A Saint." *(Looks up at* HAL, *smiles)* Wanna hear it?

HAL: What happens if I say no?

SILVA: Read my lips. (HAL *leans in to read* SILVA's *lips.* SILVA *speaks aloud*) I will put beach sand in your condoms. *(Clears throat, prepares to recite poem)* Eat your heart out, T.S. Eliot. *(Clears his throat again, waxes poetic, recites poem)*

> I admit it's your degenerate life to lead,
> But, it's crazy Harry Percy's Wife with whom you breed.
> And, as crazy Harry has a twelve–inch Knife to heed,
> It's Jack's unfathomable mental Strife, indeed!
> As poor Jack Silva simply doesn't want to bleed.
>
> So, for the sake of Jack's Mental Health,
> Put the Questionable Lady-In-Question back up on
>   Percy's Shelf,
> And act with Wisdom! Act with Stealth!
> And get Lady Patty-Cake out from under Yourself!
>
> Think of it as a Favor for your plump, old pal, Jack,
> But, get the fuck offa Percy's Wife's Back!

HAL: Get off of her "back"? Are you calling me a bugger?

SILVA: You know what rhymes with "front"?

HAL *(Shows* SILVA *his fist):* You know what rhymes with "dread"?

SILVA: 'Course I know what rhymes with "dread"! Why do ya think I wrote the poem?

HAL: I'm being totally discreet.

SILVA: "Totally discreet," yuh. About sixteen different people told me they saw you being totally discreet with her under the footbridge at Good Harbor Beach, 6:30, Sunday night.

HAL: One small lapse in otherwise total discretion. Hey, I'm only human. *(The lights crossfade to* HARRY *and* FRANK PERCY, *in a meeting in* HARRY's *house with three* LUMPERS: *"FOGGY" HASTINGS, thirty;* FREDDIE MOWBRAY, *thirty;* HARRY's *cousin,* VERNON KOSKI, *eighteen, all sit around dining table.* HARRY *is the consummate organizer)*

HASTINGS: I don't know if sinkin' Lillie boats is any answer, Harry . . .

HARRY: Definitely not! Not one boat at a time anyhow. But what would you say to sinkin' the entire Lillie fleet? (FRANK *and* VERNON *and others all laugh)*

FRANK: We ain't blamin' the Lillies for all our troubles here. We're blamin' one man and one man alone: Henry Boley. He's the one sellin' Glossop down the river . . .

HASTINGS: So why are you talkin' about sinking Lillie boats? You're running the risk of bringing every cop and every TV camera in the world inta Glossop. I mean, that's kinda gonna make us pretty stupid, right?

FRANK: Exactly right, Hastings! You got it! It's the one thing we can do that's gonna pull Henry Boley off his ass and outta the Number One's seat . . . and put Harry here at the helm where he belongs, so the WWFBA can have proper representative leadership *from the workers themselves* . . . not from the elite rich and not from outsiders! (PATTY PERCY *is now visible in the shadows. She carries a tray with a coffee pot, mugs, coffee cakes. She stops short of entering the room. She stands in the shadows, listens)*

HARRY: You know the tuna contest that Lill sponsors? The entire Lill fleet is gonna be in a straight line, single file headin' past Dogbar, leadin' the contest boats outta Gloucester harbor. It's a beautiful chance to make Boley look like the horse's ass which he is, and run some of his yellow friends right the hell outta Glossop along with him!

MOWBRAY: When?

HARRY: Same day as "Greasy Pole" . . .

FRANK: Right smack in the middle of Fiesta . . . *(The lights fade out on all but* PATTY. *She stands alone in dim light. She pauses, backs up another step, pauses, turns, exits. Blackout)*

Scene Nine

A *light fades up on* JACK SILVA *standing on a stool, reading a listing, an inventory . . . sort of a score card of the "take" for the evening. Enthusiastic applause greets each new item.*

SILVA: . . . Seventeen VCRs, twenty-one CD players and twenty-five stereos . . . thirty-nine TVs . . . twenty-three computers, monitors and printers . . . *and more than thirty-seven hand appliances, such as six gaily-colored blow-dryers and five friendly feminine personal vibrators!!! (We hear applause, as the lights widen to include everyone in* SILVA'*s apartment. There is a party in progress, celebrating a successful night's looting. Among the happy guests are:* EMILY *and* ALBERTA FUSCO; SILVA'*s girlfriend,* DOLLY; BARRY; BARDOLPH; PETEY; GADSHILL; DAN; FITZIE *and a woman named* ALICE QUIGLEY *who is sitting on* HAL'*s lap. The mood is all drunken good cheer. There is a mound of cartons, etc.: the stolen goods.* SILVA *continues)* We had a great, great night tonight . . . a totally successful looting . . . *(Applause),* but while we are all winners for just playing the game, every game has its champion. And champions must be rewarded . . . *(Applause)* I would like to announce tonight's MVP, ladies and gentlemen, the MVP for tonight: our own Kenny *Bardolph! (All applaud enthusiastically.* HAL *seems drunker than usual, peers out from under* ALICE QUIGLEY *who sits on his stomach)*

HAL: What's the noise?

ALICE: Everybody's clappin' . . .

HAL: Who sang?

ALICE: Silllyyy. Tubby just gave Bardolph MVP for stealing more than anybody else tonight. . . . They hit the summah' houses, over Long Beach . . .

HAL: Ohhh.

ALICE: Why didn'tchu go?

HAL: Stealing? Me? Never. I'm not a crook. I'm a bum. Big difference, what's-your-name . . . what's your name?

ALICE: Alice Quigley, sillyyy. Rememberrrr? Afta the Cape race? We snuck upstairs at the O'Malley School . . .

HAL: Of course. *(Pauses)* I don't remember you, actually. Look, could you not sit on me? You're making me sick. I'm sick.

ALICE: You wanna heave?

HAL: I wanna *leave!* You sicken and disgust me . . .

ALICE: Right, well, fuck you very much. (HAL *stands, dumping* ALICE, *starts across room.* SILVA *threatens* DOLLY *with stickpin. They wrestle playfully)*

SILVA: For my dearest Dolly here, I have appropriated this elegant emerald stickpin, for her to stick . . . (HAL *interrupts)*

HAL: You *disgust* me! You *both* disgust me! You *all* disgust me! You are all *disgusting!* (HAL *falls over, dead drunk. Everyone laughs.* HAL *stands, falls again, everyone laughs again.* HAL *feels his way across the room and moves to opposite side of stage, in shadows, to front door. Light shifts to exclude party and include* PATTY, *standing in the shadows at* SILVA's *front door, about to ring the bell.* HAL *rubs his eyes, hugs his knees and looks up at* PATTY) Hiii . . .

PATTY: I've been standing here about ten minutes tryin' ta get up the courage to push it . . .

HAL: To push what, exactly?

PATTY: Your bell.

HAL: Ohhh, of courssse . . . my *bellll* . . . (HAL *tries to be sober, but is incredibly drunk. He smiles out of context)*

PATTY: Can I come up? Are you busy?

HAL: You wanna come upstairs? There? Whatever for? You wanna get debauched? *(Laughs)* Nobody ever wants ta get *bauched*, right? Everybody wants ta get rid of bauch . . . get themselves *de-bauched*, right? (HAL *giggles, tries to kiss* PATTY) Wha's'a matter, Patty-Cake Palumbo? Don'tcha know who I am? *(Stands erect, nearly falls backward)* I am Henry Boley, Jr., the team captain, and you are Patricia Palumbo, head cheerleader, Glossop High . . . I am quarterback, you are "G" . . . wait a minute? are you "G" or are you "L" . . . *(A pronouncement)* I made it with "G," "L," "O," "S" and the other "S," but I drew the line at #2 "O": Rose Mota. She was a *dog* . . . (HAL *tries to kiss* PATTY *again*) Play Patty-Cake, Patty-Cake, will yaaa? Look at meee! I'm handsome Hal . . . I'm gonna *run* this town some day. I was *born to it!*

PATTY: Don't, Hal, please . . . (HAL *gropes* PATTY *sloppily, belching and teetering*)

HAL: A *kiss*, that's all. Maybe a little tongue . . . come onnnn, Pattyyy . . . *(Without warning,* PATTY *hits* HAL. *It is not at all a girlish swat or even a lucky punch.* PATTY *hits* HAL *as if to knock him from the face of the planet Earth. It is a stunning blow.* HAL *flies backwards, out of control. He is betrayed by his very substance which, once rolling backwards, gathers a terrible momentum.* HAL *smashes into the front door pillar and falls in a heap)* Jesus, Patty, that really *hurt!* (PATTY *walks to* HAL *and kicks him cruelly)* Uggghhh . . . (HAL *rolls to one side, feebly trying to protect himself)*

PATTY: I used to have dreams about you! *(Quietly)* I was "L." Agnes Virgilio was "G," Carolyn Russo was "O," and Rosie Mota was #1 "S," not #2 "O." She married Tommy Grilk and they live up Lynnfield and I hear they got four kids and they're wicked happy . . . (PATTY *turns away, stops, looks at* HAL *again. He is down and out)* You shouldn'ta come back. You shoulda died . . . (PATTY *exits, crossing stage. The lights crossfade with* PATTY *standing facing a woman her own age,* MIDGIE, *who holds imagined door open)*

MIDGIE: What gives? It must be ten o'clock . . . .

PATTY: I gotta talk to somebody, Midgie . . .

MIDGIE *(Quietly):* Gus's home.

PATTY: You know what Gus and Harry are planning?

MIDGIE *(Alarmed):* Call me in the morning. Patty, I . . . can't now . . . really.

PATTY: I've got to talk to you, Midgie! When can we talk?

MIDGIE: Gus is home, Patty! For God's sake, I gotta be careful! *(MIDGIE closes imagined door, turns and faces her husband, GUS, who has been eavesdropping, watching MIDGIE and PATTY)*

GUS: What's *she* after? *(The lights crossfade again back to HAL who stays on the ground a moment. Then he sits up slightly. Then he stands and walks back into SILVA's party. The lights widen, on HAL's arrival, to include all party animals. HAL goes as directly to SILVA as he possibly can, given his state of drunkeness and upset. As party animals see HAL weave and bob, they laugh)*

HAL: I need the keys to the van, Jack . . .

SILVA: It's empty. All the stuff's here . . .

HAL *(Yells drunkenly, enraged, totally out of context): I need the fucking keys to the fucking van! (There is a small silence. Then everyone goads HAL with the same line, passed rhythmically from person to person)*

PETEY: Hal needs the keys . . .

BARDOLPH: Hal needs the keys . . .

DOLLY: Hal needs the keys . . .

BARRY: Hal needs the keys . . .

GADSHILL: Hal needs the keys . . .

FITZIE: Hal needs the keys . . .

DAN: Hal needs the keys . . .

ALICE: Hal needs the keys. (SILVA *steps forward, wordlessly hands keys to* HAL. *Everyone laughs.* HAL *staggers slowly to opposite side of stage. The lights shift with him as he goes, feeling his way down imagined stairs to an imagined front door, across an imagined driveway and into an imagined automobile. We hear the sound of a car's engine revving. Ensemble now holds lit flashlights, one in each hand.* HAL *begins to circle the stage, runs faster and faster and faster. Flashlights roam the audience, slowly at first and then madly. We hear the sound of a car out of control: tires squealing, horn blaring, brakes screeching. And then we hear a terrible car crash.* HAL *rolls across the stage madly. He is now drenched in his own blood. The flashlights fly back to the stage, still lit, and come to rest where they will.* HAL *and the flashlights have stopped moving. After a moment's pause,* BARDOLPH *runs center, screams out his message directly to audience)*

BARDOLPH: Hal Boley just totaled the van! They think he killed himself! (PETEY *runs on, opposite side of stage, screams out his message as well. Everyone should repeat message in overlap/cacophony of alarm)*

PETEY AND OTHERS: Hal Boley just missed runnin' down four tourists, over Bass Rocks. He flipped the van over, just missed 'em!

BARDOLPH AND OTHERS: The van flipped over on to the rocks!

PETEY AND OTHERS: Hal jumped out!

BARDOLPH: They got him up to Addison-Gilbert, over Gloucester!

DOLLY: They got him on a machine! They're tryin' ta save him! (*We hear* HAL's *breathing, amplified over speaker in auditorium.* SILVA, BARRY, BARDOLPH *and others now circle* HAL, *looking out at audience)*

SILVA: Did you hear?

DOLLY: Did you hear?

BARDOLPH: Hal.

PETEY: Hal.

GADSHILL: Did you hear?

BARRY: Did you hear?

ALICE: Hal.

EMILY FUSCO: Hal.

ALBERTA FUSCO: Hal.

ALL: HAL!!! *(Drumbeat. All sounds and lights snap off suddenly, but for the still-lit flashlights on the stage next to* HAL *and a single, tight white spotlight up on* LISSA, *center. He talks directly to audience.* HAL *still lies nearby, in pool of blood)*

LISSA: Sometimes, seeing the difference between the force of Life and the force of Death is like seeing the difference between a wave coming in and a wave going out. You've got to pull back and look at the whole beach to know what the tide's accomplished, to figure out which way it's moving. With people, sometimes, you've got to pull back and look at the whole *Life* . . . to see if the person's trying to Live or trying to Die. *(Two white-coated stretcher-bearers walk to* HAL, *place him on a stretcher, carry him off)* Some people dedicate their precious time on Earth to one thing, some to the other. *(Pauses, smiles.*

End of Act One)

ACT II

Scene One

Lights up on HAL, *preparing to leave hospital, with* DOCTOR BERKOWITZ *and* REVEREND SCROOP. PATTY *stands facing* HAL *from across stage.*

PATTY *(Tears streak her face):* I couldn't have beared it . . . if you died . . . and we never talked . . . and you died . . .

HAL *(Touches her teardrop with his fingers):* Oh yuh, that makes two of us! I would've hated that myself, if I died! (DR. BERKOWITZ *enters; talks to* HAL, *sternly)*

DR. BERKOWITZ: It's a miracle you made it through, Hal. I saw the car after they fished it out. It's a miracle. Maybe you can stay away from the bottle now, hmmm? Next time, you won't be so lucky. . . . *(Pauses)* I've signed you out. You can leave anytime this morning. See me in the office next Thursday or so. Call Hazel for an appointment. Okay?

HAL: Okay. Thanks, Dr. Berkowitz . . . (REVEREND SCROOP *enters. He is old; talks to* HAL, *gravely)*

REV. SCROOP: God wanted you to stay alive. He must have some real purpose other than drinking and womanizing.

HAL: I guess, yuh . . .

REV. SCROOP: You're not a child anymore, Hal. (SILVA *calls out from the shadows, opposite side of stage.* SILVA *is shaving, looking in imagined mirror as he shaves)*

SILVA: Look, I'm not saying you're *immature,* but most of us pulled out of the Fuck-Me-Suck-Me-Rubber-Duck-Me Stage when we were about thirteen or fourteen . . .

HAL: It's genetic. I was born very young. (HAL *walks over to* SILVA, *starts to shave, as well)*

131

SILVA: One way or the other, you're lookin' to lose your ass, right?

HAL: How so?

SILVA: Petey said he saw you makin' out with old "L" between "G" and "O-double-S-O-P" over near Salem Willows last night . . .

REV. SCROOP: Pray with me. Hal . . .

HAL: What? *(Looks over his shoulder.* SCROOP's *still there, being reverential)* Oh, yuh, sure, Father. . . . (SCROOP *bows head.* HAL *bows head; looks over to* SILVA, *whispers)* What's the implication here, anyway, Jack-off?

SILVA: You seein' Percy's wife again, or what?

HAL: Why do I feel this question is rhetorical? Is there a rumor around that I'm *not* seeing Percy's wife? *(They laugh. They finish shaving.* HAL *changes his shirt; dresses up)* Did I ever tall you about right after my wife and her money dumped me, down in Noo Yawk City, I was broke. So I took this job, servicing this rich, old, impotent dude's young, fat wife. When I got tired of her, after about four house calls, the old dude comes around to my place, totally pissed off at me, rings my bell, grabs me and goes, "I hear you're not sleeping with my wife!"

REV. SCROOP *(Interjects):* In the Name of the Father, Son, Holy Ghost . . .

SILVA: Take my advice. If you gotta' keep seein' Harry Percy's wife, be smart about it: play it safe and meet her somewhere out of town . . . like maybe Argentina!

HAL: What are you so afraid of, anyway?

SILVA: My blood on these Dhurrie rugs, basically . . . *(Music in. The lights brighten on* HAL *and* PATTY; *fade out on* SILVA. REV. SCROOP *still stands nearby, praying, head bowed.* HAL *and* PATTY *sit cross-legged on stage, facing front, as if sitting on a wall overlooking the sea)*

PATTY: I could sit, starin' at the ocean like this, for all my life . . .

HAL: I dunno, the ocean's always spooked me: it's too big . . .

PATTY: Humbling. That's what my dad used ta say all the time: "The ocean is humbling."

HAL: I totally agree. Many's the time I've looked at the ocean and said, "I never could drink *that* much, I am humbled . . ."

DR. BERKOWITZ: Stay off the bottle and you might stay alive. *(Exits)*

PATTY: What's with you?

HAL: In what sense?

PATTY: How come you are like you are?

HAL: How come I'm *how? How* am I?

PATTY: A drunk. Pissing your life away.

REV. SCROOP *(Punctuates* PATTY's *pronouncement):* Amen . . . *(Exits)*

HAL: Gimme a break, will ya? I *stopped* drinkin', ya know?

PATTY: Oh, yuh? *When?*

HAL *(Looks at watch):* Thirty-one hours, ten minutes, forty-eight seconds . . . forty-nine . . . fifty . . . fifty-one . . . I'm digital! I like it when you worry about me. It's . . . charming.

PATTY: Charming?

HAL: Mmmm.

PATTY: Fuck you.

HAL: That's charming, too. What a mouth! *(Smiles)* I always liked that mouth . . . *(He touches* PATTY's *cheek gently. They kiss)*

PATTY: You got kids? I've been meaning to ask you about your marriage and all . . .

HAL: Me, personally? Nope. The woman I was married to . . . Deborah Coe . . . she had two kids from her first husband. . . . *(Smiles)* She used to introduce me to people as "Harold, my second husband, by marriage." She could make a very dry joke, old Debbie could . . . and a Martini to match! *(Pauses)* I worked for Deborah's father, setting up tax shelters for rich investors. I took a salary from his firm, slept with his daughter, drank his whiskey, babysat his granddaughters, drank more of his whiskey, sailed his boats, drank more of his whiskey, drank *more* of his whiskey . . . eventually, Deborah and her daughters and Deborah's daddy all got really pissed off cause a' my constantly getting pissed . . . I'd constantly get pissed, they'd constantly get pissed off. Fearful symmetry.

PATTY: Is that why you left her?

HAL: I didn't exactly leave *her* . . .

PATTY: You left New York?

HAL: That's it: I left New York . . .

PATTY: And came home . . .

HAL: That was the one thing in life I was trying not to do: come home, come back to Glossop, come back to bein' known most of all as Hank Boley's son, the Son of One, buttt home I came . . . twenty years older . . . my brain pickled . . .

PATTY: . . . Much better-lookin' . . . mmmmmm, s'true . . .

HAL: Boy, you haven't changed at all, have you? One thing on your mind. Always the same. One thing on your mind, all the time . . . two things, actually: *sex* and *lust*.

PATTY: Yuh, right . . . you got it. (HAL *stares at* PATTY, *smiling*) Whatcha lookin' at?

HAL: Somebody.

PATTY *(Simply, clearly):* I've never loved anybody but you in my whole life. I'm ashamed to admit it, but it's the God's-honest-truth . . . *(Smiles, shrugs)*

HAL: Same goes for me, too, Patty. There's only been one woman I've ever really loved and you're it.

PATTY: I've never cheated on Harry before tonight. Not even close. I want you to know that.

HAL: Before tonight? Really? (PATTY *takes* HAL's *face in her hands and kisses him. It is a gentle kiss)*

PATTY: I've got to be careful about Mary-Ellen. She's only little. I've got to be careful . . .

HAL: I promise . . . (HAL *starts to take* PATTY *in his arms, thinks better of it. He is frightened.* PATTY *looks at* HAL, *smiles. She takes* HAL's *face in her hands. They kiss. She is in control. It is a passionate kiss.* GUS *and two* LUMPERS *step out of shadows, watch a moment)*

GUS: Where's Harry?

LUMPER: He should be over Sherm's by now . . .

GUS: Let's head over. This's gonna make his night . . .

Scene Two

Lights crossfade to ANGELO, *carrying clipboard, facing a large group of* LUMPERS.

ANGELO: I got two ships, so there's work for all a'ya's . . . *(The men cheer.* ANGELO *steps to one side, revealing a stack of crates. Some crates are smallish, others are enormous)* This first load's frozen goods, but there's a ten percent pay over-ride. Who wants it? *(One by one, men step forward to start carrying crates.* HAL *is among the men. They all face* ANGELO) Packy, you're on. Tommy D., you got it. Gussie, go for it. *(Sees* HAL) What do you want?

HAL: My suspension time's up . . .

ANGELO: Yuh?

HAL: Today's the day.

ANGELO: Okay, sign in . . .

HAL: Uh uh. I'm workin' . . .

ALL *(Mocking):* OOoooOOOOOooooOOOOOOO! Hal's working!

ANGELO: Yuh?

HAL: Yup.

ANGELO *(To older man):* Okay, Gussie, you're boss lumper. Hal Boley says he's working . . .

GUS *(Smiles):* Okay, Hal. Let's see what ya got . . . grab that top crate. It goes on the stack . . . *there. (The top crate is enormous.* HAL *steps forward and "lumps" the crate, carrying it from one side of the stage to the other.* HAL's *knees nearly buckle under the strain of his load)* Oh, God, Hal, I screwed up. It doesn't go on that stack. It goes on this stack. *(Points to stack near the one from which* HAL *took the crate in the first place.* HAL *moves crate again. He is exhausted, but won't quit. Music in. Lights now full of color, stylized. All jeer. As soon as* HAL *succeeds in getting the crate moved,* GUS *breaks new and worse news)* Oh, my God, Hal, I am definitely Shit–for–brains himself, huh? I was right the first time. That crate goes there! *(Points to stack from which* HAL *just moved crate)*

HAL: You're the boss, Gus . . . (HAL *cannot budge the crate at first. And then he does. He lifts the crate on to his shoulder. His legs start to buckle under him. A young lumper,* BOBBY, *steps forward before* HAL *can fall, grabs an end)*

Jason Robards (right) as Jacob Brackish with Judith Ivey as Kathleen Hogan in the 1992 Broadway production of PARK YOUR CAR IN HARVARD YARD at the Music Box Theatre. *Photo by Joan Marcus*

Jason Robards and Judith Ivey

Jason Robards

Photos of the 1992 Broadway production of PARK YOUR CAR IN HARVARD YARD *at the Music Box Theatre by Joan Marcus*

Members of the original Gloucester Stage Company cast of HENRY LUMPER. *Photo by Clark Linehan*

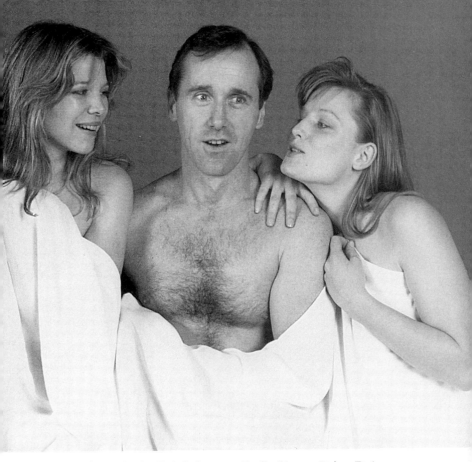

From left to right, Cathy Reinheimer as Emily Fusco, Brian Delate as Hal Boley and Beverly Dretzel as Alberta Fusco in The Working Theatre's 1989 off-Broadway production of HENRY LUMPER.
Photo by Martha Swope Associates/Carol Rosegg

Teade Gormley, Karen Crawford, Michelle Faith, Judith McIntyre, Mary Klug and Geraldine Librandi in the original Gloucester Stage Company production of NORTH SHORE FISH. *Photo by David Benoit*

Laura San Giacomo as Marlena (left) with John Pankow as Porker (center)
and Christine Estabrook as Florence in the 1987 off-Broadway production
of NORTH SHORE FISH at the WPA Theatre. *Photo by Martha Swope*

From left to right, Christine Estabrook, John Pankow, Laura San Giacomo,
Thomas G. Waites, Elizabeth Kemp and Michelle Faith in the 1987 off-
Broadway production of NORTH SHORE FISH at the WPA Theatre.
Photo by Martha Swope

BOBBY: Gimme an end . . . *(To all, in disgust)* we got a boat to unload here, yes? (HAL *and* BOBBY *carry the crate to its stack. The other* LUMPERS *resume their work.* HAL *has, in a small way, begun to gain their respect)*

HAL: Thanks, Bobby.

BOBBY: Hey, no sweat, huh? *(The lights now crossfade to* PERCY, *sitting, watching TV.* PATTY *enters, crossing quietly along back edge of stage, behind* PERCY, *who speaks to her without turning, without actually facing her.* HARRY *speaks with obvious hostility)*.

HARRY: So? You decided to come home? How come?

PATTY: I had to go over to Liberty Tree Mall to exchange something . . .

HARRY: *Really?*

PATTY: Yuh, really.

HARRY: I heard you were over there . . .

PATTY: Over where?

HARRY: Liberty Tree Mall.

PATTY: What else did you hear?

HARRY: All of it.

PATTY: All of *what?*

HARRY: You planning to go out again tonight? *(The lights widen—to* SILVA'S *apartment.* SILVA *and* DOLLY *sit together, watching TV.* HAL *crosses through the room wearing a terrycloth robe, towel on his head, just showered)*

SILVA: I asked you if you were goin' out . . . you gettin' deaf, or what?

HAL: Yes, to your question. I couldn't hear the second part.

PATTY: I gotta, yuh. I promised . . . Midgie.

HARRY: Okay. *(Nods)* Okay. *(The lights fade out on* PATTY *and* HARRY; *brighten on* SILVA*)*

SILVA: Mrs. you-know, *again?*

HAL: Yup.

SILVA: Yup?

HAL: Yup.

SILVA: You're lookin' ta get your balls shot off!

DOLLY: Nice talk . . . *(Doorbell rings)*

HAL: Get that, will ya? I'm late . . .

SILVA: I'm s'pose'ta walk downstairs? For *you???*

HAL *(To* DOLLY*)*: Do you *like* Jack?

DOLLY: I *admire* Jack. *(Doorbell rings again.* HAL *exits into bedroom)* She's nervous . . .

SILVA: She should be nervous. She's married to a certifiable lunatic . . .

DOLLY: What does that make *me?*

SILVA: I don't quite make the connection.

DOLLY: Keep eating Ring Dings and Devil Dogs and you won't even come *close* to making the connection.

SILVA: You have such a remarkably joyous way with words. *(Doorbell rings again.* HAL *yells from bedroom)*

HAL *(Offstage):* Come on, will you? Somebody let her in!

DOLLY: I'll get it . . .

SILVA: Nooo, sit. I'll go . . . *(Turns to* HAL*)* You owe me for this!

HAL *(Yells from offstage):* Tell her I'll be right down! *(The doorbell rings again.* SILVA *stands, yells)*

SILVA: Keep your knickers on, you horny old trollop! (SILVA *crosses the stage. The lights crossfade with him. He descends an imagined staircase, opens an imagined door. He looks around in the darkness. No one there. Suddenly, a hand pulls him out farther into the shadows.* GUS *and* HARRY PERCY *stand in front of* SILVA*)* Hey!

GUS: Who's this?

HARRY: The fat friend . . . (HARRY *and* GUS *each hold knives against* SILVA. GUS *holds a knife against* SILVA*'s throat,* HARRY *against* SILVA*'s stomach)* Tell your pally-pal, Hal, my wife ain't able ta visit tonight, okay? And tell yourself something: if you ever see her come to visit and you let her into your house, I'm going to go even *deeper* . . . okay? *(And with that,* HARRY *allows his knife to pierce* SILVA*'s shirt . . . and the skin on his stomach)*

SILVA: Oww!

HARRY: You follow? You get my point?

SILVA: Yuh yes yesss.

HARRY: Good deal. *(Lights crossfade back to* DOLLY *watching TV.* SILVA *staggers back into room, holding his stomach, which is covered with blood.* DOLLY *sees blood, covers her mouth in terror)*

SILVA: I'm gonna be sick. (HAL *walks out of his room smiling, sees* SILVA *and* DOLLY *and his smile vanishes. Lights fade)*

Scene Three

The lights fade up on a statue or photograph of St. Peter, carried by fishermen. Alongside them, LUMPERS, older men and St. Peter's Club Members, walking in place. BOLEY, LISSA, ANGELO and others parade behind the statue. BOLEY, LISSA and ANGELO wave to imagined crowd. We hear the sound of cheers in auditorium, as well as cheers from all actors.

CHEERLEADER *(In bastardized Portuguese):* "Usseee mussee tutti muttay??? [Translation: "Is everybody deaf?"]

OTHER VOICES *(In response; three repetitions):* Viva San Pietro! (BOLEY *and* LISSA *and others are smiling, shaking imagined hands. All sing "God Bless America." Suddenly, BOLEY weakens, sickens, collapses to ground. ANGELO and LISSA don't notice him at first)*

BOLEY: Markie! *(A woman screams. LISSA turns and sees BOLEY on ground)*

LISSA: Angelo! *Angelo! (All sounds fade under, lightly. Lights crossfade quickly to HARRY PERCY, in front of map of Gloucester Harbor. FRANK PERCY stands beside him. They look out front, using the theatre audience as their own assembled audience)*

HARRY: I hope ya's all can see the map okay . . . on Sunday, Greasy Pole will start at five . . . *(Points to map)* here. And the Lillies'll gather their boats and all the contest boats just inside Dogbar . . . here. They should be in full force at about 1:30, as they're all getting briefed at ha'pahst noon over East Glossop, then comin' across to nest . . . *(VERNON, HARRY's cousin, screams up at HARRY from the rear of the auditorium)*

VERNON: Hank Boley just collapsed in the middle of the parade. They rushed him up to Addison-Gilbert! *(HARRY PERCY looks up, amazed. Sirens suddenly blare out. The lights crossfade to BOLEY, lying in hospital bed, in soft spotlight. PERCY exits in dark. ANGELO, LISSA and others stand in line, in imagined corridor outside BOLEY's room. The amplified sounds of a life-support system are heard in the auditorium. HAL enters on the run, sees the men, stops)*

HAL: There you are . . . where is he?

ANGELO: They got him on a machine. It spread to both his lungs!

ARTIE: He's sleeping . . .

HAL *(Quietly)*: He's alive?

LISSA: No thanks to you . . . (LISSA *walks to* HAL *and spits on him. All are amazed*)

ANGELO: Hey, Markie! What are you doin', huh? (LISSA *turns and exits. All look at* HAL, *who lifts his face, head up. All men but for* HAL *back up, one step.* HAL *speaks to his father*)

HAL: Pa? It's me: Hal . . . (BOLEY *lifts his head, looks at* HAL)

BOLEY: I feel awful.

HAL: It's gonna be different, Pa. I swear to you. (HAL *turns, exits. The lights brighten. All men step forward, two steps. They surround* BOLEY'S *bed.* MORT SHIMMA *is first to speak. Once he does, others join in, speaking rapidly*)

MORT: He's got more than twenty boats . . .

ANGELO: He's got a lot of support, Hank . . .

BOLEY: When?

ANGELO *(After a pause)*: Sunday.

BOLEY: I don't know when that is.

ANGELO: Sunday . . . during Greasy Pole . . . it sounds like he's gone totally nuts! He's makin' his move right in the middle of Greasy Pole . . .

BOLEY: What's today? I've been asleep.

LISSA: Tuesday night. We've only got two and a half days . . .

BOLEY: Ask Tom's kid to come in and talk to me . . . ask him to come in.

MORT: He won't come in, Hank.

ANGELO: We tried already.

BOLEY: Get Tom in here. (*Drumbeat. There is a lighting change. All turn their backs to* BOLEY. TOM PERCY *enters, slowly, looks at his old friend*)

PERCY: I'm sorry, Hank.

BOLEY: It's not your doing. I know that . . .

PERCY: I tried to talk to him, but he won't come near me . . .

BOLEY: He knows you're against him. That's why.

PERCY (*Quietly*): He's my son.

BOLEY: Who can get to him, Tom?

PERCY: Nobody. (*Drumbeat. Lighting change.* HAL *speaks softly from opposite side of stage.* TOM PERCY *turns*)

HAL: Angelo came and got me . . .

BOLEY: I may have to ask you to share something you may not be prepared to share . . .

HAL: Okay . . .

BOLEY: This involves Harry Percy . . .

HAL (*After a pause*): Tell me what you want me to do, Pa, and I'll do it.

BOLEY: Tom? (*Drumbeat, lighting change,* TOM *turns to* BOLEY, HAL *turns away*)

PERCY: What, Henry?

BOLEY: Jesus, I feel awful. I don't have much time, Tom . . .

PERCY: What can I do for you, Hank?

BOLEY: Where's your brother? (TOM PERCY *turns his back. A drumbeat.* FRANK PERCY *and* VERNON KOSKI *enter, move to* BOLEY's *bedside*)

FRANK: I'm sorry you're feelin' punk, Hank.

BOLEY: Thanks, Frankie. Me, too . . .

FRANK: You know my nephew, Vernon Koski? This is my sister's boy, Vernon. He's visiting from Australia.

VERNON: Good to see you, Mr. Boley . . .

FRANK: Vernon's been driving me here and there. My eyes are no good. We get old, huh?

BOLEY: You got to stop him, Frank . . .

FRANK: Stop who?

BOLEY: Frank, it's ridiculous to play games, with me in this condition. I know that Tom's son is going to hit the Lillie boats on Sunday. I know where, when, who's with him. I know it all. . . . *(Pause)* It's a small town, Frank. People know things.

FRANK: What do you want from me?

BOLEY: Stop him, Frank. *(Pauses)* I talked it through with my son, Hal . . . and he's willing to share the gavel with Harry . . . co-Number Ones.

VERNON: Really? (BOLEY *looks at* VERNON: *smiles*)

FRANK: I'll tell him.

BOLEY: Good. *(Drumbeat. There is a lighting change.* FRANK PERCY *and* VERNON *stop downstage two steps.* FRANK *grabs* VERNON *roughly)*

FRANK: He's lying. (VERNON *looks at his uncle)*

VERNON: You *think* so?

FRANK: I *know* so. I go back years and years with Henry Boley. It's the same as it was with your Uncle Tom. Is *he* co-Number One? (VERNON *looks down)* Boley's in like this . . . *(Knots fingers)* with the coast guard. Every last one of us will end up in Federal Court . . .

VERNON: Jesus, Uncle Frank! What do we do?

FRANK: We just shut up about what Boley said to us. We don't say nothing to Harry. We let Harry go ahead and take over . . . *his* way. *(Drumbeat. Lighting change. All men turn and step forward to* BOLEY's *bedside again.* HAL *is among them.* FRANK PERCY *and* VERNON *exit in darkness)*

LISSA: This meeting is official. We have a quorum . . . (LISSA *carries a small wooden box, which he opens and from which he removes the small, solid gold gavel. He hands same to* BOLEY, *placing box on bed)* Hank. (BOLEY *taps the gavel down on the wooden box, producing a fairly meek thud)*

BOLEY: I asked for this meeting and I'm glad you all could come . . .

ANGELO: Excuse me, Hank, but, do you think Hal should be in here now?

BOLEY: Hal's the Son of One.

HAL: I know how you all feel and I, uh, hope I can change your opinion of me . . .

MORT: This is very touchy . . .

BOLEY: I'm dying, Mort. I got no time for what's touchy and what isn't . . . Hal stays in the meeting. *(Pauses)* Anybody hear from Frank Percy, yet?

ANGELO: The word's very bad, Hank . . .

LISSA: Frank double–crossed you . . .

ANGELO: Whatever Frank said to Harry changed nothing. The word is that Percy's got more than a hundred men with him tomorrow . . . (BOLEY *stares, disappointed*)

MORT: The thing is snowballing . . .

ANGELO: The word's very bad, Hank . . .

HAL: I've got an idea . . . if I were to go one-on-one with Percy, early . . . tonight . . . tomorrow morning . . . I could bring this thing to a conclusion . . .

BOLEY: What kind of conclusion?

HAL: I happen to think I can handle Percy. I happen to think I can take him out . . .

LISSA: Takin' out his wife ain't like takin' out the man himself, Hal. You want to be careful.

HAL: *You* want to be careful, Markie. I know you like to think of me as wet behind the ears, as you just spit there, but I gotta warn you: I play to win . . . and I have an excellent memory as to who played on my team and who played against my team. You follow?

ANGELO: That ain't necessary, Hal. Mark Lissa's put his name on the line, many's the time, for your father . . .

BOLEY: None of this is necessary. I won't have you goin' against Harry Percy, Hal. I forbid it. Okay? This matter will be resolved peacefully . . . we wait to see if Harry takes up the offer to share control . . .

MORT: We've got no time, Hank . . . as soon as the tuna-contest boats start out of the harbor, Percy's gonna move against them . . .

BOLEY: Do the Lillies know what's comin'?

HAL: Don't you think if *we* know, *they* know?

BOLEY: Markie, go see Dr. Nagoa. Find out what he's planning.

MORT: Aren't they pacifists?

BOLEY: Oh, yuh, sure. Go see, Markie. . . . *(To all)* Let's reconvene after lunch, after Markie's got an answer. *(Pauses)* Hal, I want you to find out what Frank told Harry. Find out if Harry even knows my offer . . . (VERNON *enters, dribbling basketball)*

HAL: You think that Frank will be straight with me?

BOLEY: No, no, don't waste your time talking to Frank. *(Light shift to* VERNON KOSKI, *opposite side of stage.* VERNON *turns, sees* HAL, *starts to run.* HAL *tackles* VERNON. *They wrestle and roll about, but the boy is no match for* HAL *who is older, larger, stronger and far more determined)*

VERNON: Get off me!

HAL: What did your uncle tell Harry?

VERNON: I don't know nothin'!

HAL: You answer me, Koski!

VERNON: I don't know nothin'! (HAL *whacks* VERNON, *roughly)*

HAL: Talk!

VERNON: I got nothin' to *say!* (VERNON *starts to exit, as* GUIDO VEGA *enters)*

HAL: Did Harry get our offer?

VERNON: I don't know nothin'! Ask Harry yourself! (GUIDO VEGA *walks slowly across the back of the stage, head down, trying not to be seen by* HAL. HAL *spots* GUIDO *and runs after him. Lights shift with* HAL. VERNON *exits in darkness.* HAL *catches up to* GUIDO *who throws a punch at* HAL, *hitting him)*

HAL: Don't, Guido! Talk to me!

GUIDO: Pound sand, Hal!

HAL: My father's dying, Guido!

GUIDO: I can't do nothin' about that Hal, . . . I'm sorry. Leave me be!

HAL: My father's been lookin' after you how long, Guido? How long? *HOW LONG? (There is a long pause)*

GUIDO: It's big, Hal. We could both get killed over this. It's big.

HAL: Tell me, Guido.

GUIDO: I can't, Hal. I'd like to. I would. Your father's like my own to me. Honest to God . . .

HAL: I'll play the fuckin' violin, Guido. My father's layin' in a bed near death and he's countin' on you. Don't tell me what you'd *"like"* to do! Open your mouth and talk, Guido!

GUIDO: I can't, Hal.

HAL: My father's from the old times, Guido. He's naive. He thinks Glossop people are all clean-living, all family. He reads the paper and he doesn't believe it. He doesn't know what goes on here with drugs and money. Don't forget: I've been on the inside here, Guido. *I* know. *(Pauses)* Frank Percy's running cocaine through Glossop, isn't he? *(Pauses) Isn't he? (Pauses) Isn't he, Guido??? (Pauses)* If my father dies knowing you lied to him, Guido, it'll be on your head forever . . .

GUIDO: Come onn, Halll. I was one of maybe a hundred boats. I only carried goods for Frank three times total . . .

HAL: Is Harry Percy in on it?

GUIDO: I don't think so . . .

HAL: So, what the fuck gives? Harry Percy's about to turn Glossop into
the worst place on the map of Massachusetts and that includes
Woburn, Lawrence and East Boston. Why's he doing this?

GUIDO: I dunno, honest ta Christ, I . . .

HAL (*A sudden explosion*): Who are you protecting, Guido? What are
you? On Frank's payroll?

GUIDO: 'Course not! I did maybe three jobs for Frank, total. I made some
pin money—chump change—that's all. I got no other connection.

HAL: Why'd you pull the plug?

GUIDO (*After a pause*): Frank told me to. He's got somebody on the
inside, with the coast guard. They were on to me, that I carried
packages for Frank. (*Pauses, sadly*) So, I got a few bucks now . . . no
boat . . .

HAL: Nobody'll ever insure another boat for you, right?

GUIDO: Yuh, right: nobody . . .

HAL: You help me, Guido, I'll help you. I swear on my mother's grave
. . . (*There is a long pause*)

GUIDO: Frank's using Harry to pull the coast guard's attention off him.
Between the Fiesta and what Harry's plannin', nobody'll be lookin' in
Frank's direction . . .

HAL: Shit! 'Course, he is! Perfect!

GUIDO: Frank's bringin' in enough to retire on. He's buying and sellin'
the protein plant for condos. We're talkin' millions here! He's got a
good bunch of us in on it. We're talkin' very big, very major bucks,
Hal. A lot of guys are makin' big. That's why you gotta promise to

never let anybody know I talked. You gotta, Hal . . . I gotta hold you to that or I'm gonna float up somewhere some day. I'm scared, Hal.

HAL: Trust me, Guido. (HAL, *like his father before him, touches* GUIDO's *shoulder.* GUIDO, *so touched, smiles, as he has before.* HAL *turns from* GUIDO *and moves across stage. Lights shift with* HAL, *at* SILVA *who now faces* PATTY PERCY)

SILVA: You can't come in!

HAL: Let her in, Jackie.

SILVA: Mother of Christ! I've still got a scab on my stomach from her maniac husband! (HAL, *from behind* SILVA)

HAL: I said let her in, Jackie!

SILVA: You promised me, shit-for-brains! You gave your sacred word!

HAL: I did nothing of the kind. *(To* PATTY) Does he know you're here?

PATTY: He knows I'm somewhere.

SILVA: Oh God . . . he knows she's somewhere! You hear that? We are talking Death, here. D.E.A.T.H.! (SILVA *exits, backing away slowly, terrified.* HAL *moves to* PATTY)

HAL: Frank Percy never gave Harry our offer to split head of the union with me. Harry never heard this. I think it's best if it comes from you now . . . maybe he'll still listen, if it comes from you.

PATTY: I'll try. *(Pauses)* We all thought it was complicated when we were sixteen, didn't we? *(Pauses)* Right now, I don't feel like I'm living inside my own *life!* (PATTY *moves across stage slowly. The lights crossfade with her.* HAL *backs off into the shadows. She joins* GUS *and together they move to* HARRY PERCY. *Two other men are with* PERCY)

GUS: It's your wife. (PERCY *turns and faces* PATTY. *He nods to men, who exit the office, leaving* HARRY *and* PATTY *alone)*

HARRY: Why don't you leave me the fuck alone?

PATTY: Please, Harry, listen to me.

HARRY: Yuh, so, what? What do ya want from me?

PATTY: Hank Boley offered you co-Head with Hal. Hal agreed. Your uncle never told you the offer.

HARRY: What are you givin' me here?

PATTY: While you're out there attacking the Lillie boats, your Uncle Frank is bringing a shipment of drugs in. He's using you as a diversion. It's a big shipment . . .

HARRY: Uncle Frank? That's bullshit!

PATTY *(Pauses):* Your Uncle Frank lied to you. He carried an untrue message from Henry Boley . . .

HARRY: How come you know this?

PATTY: Hal told me.

HARRY: You saw Hal again?

PATTY: Yuh, just now.

HARRY: You in love with him, Patty? (PATTY *looks at her husband, answers quietly)*

PATTY: Yuh, I am, Harry . . . (HARRY *walks to* PATTY *and slaps her)*

HARRY: I'm sorry.

PATTY: Me, too. *(They kiss.* PATTY *turns and exits.* HARRY *turns and punches his hand through an imagined window. We hear the sound of glass shattering.* HARRY *turns and faces audience, blood dripping from hand.* GUS *re-enters on the run)*

GUS: Something break? *(Sees HARRY's hand)* What'd you do?

HARRY: I fucked up my hand . . . *(Wraps bandana around gun in hand)*

GUS: What's with the gun? What the hell are you doing?

HARRY: Where's my uncle?

GUS: I dunno . . .

HARRY: Find out! *(The lights crossfade to opposite side of stage, now including* TOM PERCY *staring across at his son. Lights out on* GUS. HARRY *moves to his father.* FRANK PERCY *sits watching TV. Light of TV flickers, sound of late night television show in progress lightly under the scene.* HARRY *has bloody bandana around hand, runs across to* TOM, *yelling "Pa!" Drumbeat)*

PERCY: What is it?

HARRY: Is he here?

PERCY: Who?

HARRY: Uncle Frank . . .

PERCY: Yuh, he's watching TV. I was just upstairs, doin' . . . *(*HARRY *shoves past his father.* TOM PERCY *follows his son)* What's up, Harry? What's the matter? *(*FRANK PERCY, *watching TV, hears commotion, turns and looks, sees* HARRY *standing in doorway. There is a bloody towel covering* HARRY's *hand)*

FRANK: Hey, Harry, how goes it? I was comin' over right after Letterman. What's the matter? What happened to your hand, Harry?

HARRY: Uncle Frank's been telling me all about the old days . . . *(Pauses)* how you and Boley made plans for me to run the union *(Pauses)* How Boley bought you off . . .

PERCY: Nobody bought me off . . .

HARRY: With this . . . this house, the freezer plant . . . half a million dollars . . .

PERCY: What's this? Hank Boley never bought me off. Whatever I have, I earned . . .

HARRY: Uncle Frank's been tellin' me different, hasn't he?

FRANK: What gives, Harry?

HARRY: Uncle Frank's been tellin' me *every*thing. How my wife's fuckin' Hal Boley . . . how the Lillies are fuckin' Glossop . . . how I'm gettin' fucked outta my just desserts . . . *(Smiles savagely)* Uncle Frankie tells me lots! *(Pauses)* Uncle Frankie's been pushin' me . . . pushin' me . . . really givin' me the kinda support you'd expect from family . . . it's been great . . . Uncle Frankie and I have some enormous plans . . .

FRANK: What's the matter, Harry?

HARRY: Uncle Frank's got a shipment of coke comin' into town tomorrow that would sink a battleship, don't ya, Uncle Frankie? Uncle Frankie's wired like a goddam *pinball machine!*

PERCY: What are you sayin'?

HARRY: Uncle Frankie's buyin' and sellin'. He's found himself quite a parcel. Ain't that what they call it when you put the pieces together, Uncle Frankie: a parcel? Quite a parcel Uncle Frankie's got: you're in it, Pa, I'm in it, halfa fuckin' Glossop is in it!

PERCY: What the hell is he talkin' about, Frank?

HARRY: What? That wasn't clear?

FRANK: That was clear . . . (FRANK *takes a gun from his pocket, suddenly, which he trains on* HARRY) wicked clear!

PERCY: Jesus, Frank, don't . . .

FRANK: Back off, Harry . . .

HARRY: Uncle Frank's been plannin' ta use me like some kind of *stooge* . . . some kind of dumb *decoy,* right? *Right?*

FRANK: Yuh, Harry, that's right.

PERCY: Jesus, Frank . . .

HARRY: He's got me out there raising hell with the Lillies, while Uncle Frank's runnin' himself a double-reverse play, right under our noses . . . look at me, Uncle Frank . . . *(Points at* FRANK *with bandaged hand)* I said *look at me!*

FRANK: I'm looking at you, Harry. (HARRY *has a pistol hidden in the bandage wrapped around his bloody hand. He now fires the gun, four consecutive shots, killing* FRANK PERCY)

PERCY: Frank . . . Jesus, Harry . . . Frank's dead . . .

HARRY: Uncle Frank . . . all bloody . . .

PERCY: This is my fault. Get out of here, Harry. I'll take care of this . . . this is my fault. You leave me the gun. Get out of here!

HARRY: I'm not stopping, Pa. I want Number One! It's *mine!*

PERCY: Let it go, Harry . . .

HARRY: *No!*

PERCY: Let Hal Boley have it, Harry. You take your wife and your daughter and you live your life!

HARRY: I got no life to live! *(Waves pistol)* This here's my life! *(Motions to* FRANK) He's your brother. Bury him . . . (HARRY *turns and exits, running past* BOLEY. *The lights crossfade with him)*

Scene Four

In the darkness, we hear the amplified sounds of a life-support system, along with the amplified sounds of BOLEY's *labored breathing. The lights fade up on* BOLEY, *asleep, alone, in the throes of a murderous memory: a nightmare.*

TOWNSPEOPLE (*A low whisper; many voices, in unison*): Murder. (BOLEY *stirs, groans, his labored breathing continues along with his haunting nightmare. The townspeople whisper again*) Murder. (BOLEY *groans again.* ANGELO *enters, suddenly, waking* BOLEY)

ANGELO: Hank? Sorry . . .

BOLEY (*Wakes; startled*): What? What is it?

ANGELO: Frank Percy's dead.

BOLEY: When?

ANGELO: An hour ago . . . gunned down.

BOLEY: Who?

ANGELO: Tom's boy, four bullets, cold blood, he's started.

BOLEY: You sure of this?

ANGELO: Dead sure.

BOLEY: Who's the source?

ANGELO: Usual: our man inside.

BOLEY: Where is he now: Tom's kid?

ANGELO: Back at the wharf, his place, gearin' up . . .

BOLEY: Oh, Jesus!

ANGELO: What do you want me to do, Henry?

BOLEY: Get my son, Angelo. Bring him here . . .

ANGELO: Why, Hank? There's no time . . .

BOLEY: *Angelo, bring Hal here!*

ANGELO: Sure thing. (ANGELO *exits. Drumbeat. Lights shift to* HAL, *at* BOLEY's *bedside*)

HAL: Angelo told me about Frank Percy. Tell me what to do, Pa. I want to help . . .

BOLEY: There's something terrible . . . something you have to know. Listen to me . . . we can't have the police in on this. We have to handle it ourselves . . . (HAL *looks at* BOLEY, *surprised.* BOLEY *speaks with great difficulty*) Years back, when I was your age, lumpin', Allie Richards was wired, runnin' drugs in through Glossop at a time when most of us didn't have a clue what the hell drugs *were*, even . . . it took us no time to figure out what heroin was, what it was doin' to people. . . . *(Pauses)* Tommy and I made a vow to stop him, no matter what. Allie had no wife, no kids, nobody to hand the gavel over to . . . so . . . *(Pauses, groans out his confession)* we killed him, Tommy and me, we killed Allie Richards . . . it was my idea . . . Tommy and I were co-heads . . . co-Number-Ones, just for a while, just for appearance sake, but Tommy never wanted any part of it. He stepped down, I stepped up and that's how I got Number One.

TOWNSPEOPLE *(In a low whisper, in unison):* Murder.

HAL: Pa, I . . . never put the pieces together. Your being Number One always seemed so . . . natural . . .

BOLEY: I've changed my mind. I need to stop Harry Percy . . .

TOWNSPEOPLE: Murder . . .

BOLEY: I can't handle it myself . . .

TOWNSPEOPLE: Murder . . .

BOLEY: Just you and him, like you offered, nobody else. We can't have the police in on this. . . . *(Groans)* It's a lousy goddam time for me to be dying. I'm leaving things in a mess!

HAL: You're not dying, Pa, you're just weak, that's all . . .

BOLEY: I don't need that! Don't, Hal, please! What is *is!* Listen to me, Henry. When the Italians first came to Glossop, everybody said they were gonna ruin the fish business. The same with the Irish, the Finns, too. The same with the Portuguese, when they came. The Lillies are no different from any of us. They're just people come to fish. *(Inhales from pain)* Nature is supply and demand. When a mother stops nursing her baby, the milk dries up in her breast. As long as she keeps nursing, the milk keeps flowing. That's what life is, Hal . . . somebody's got to fish, Hal. If there are no fishermen, the fish themselves will die.

HAL: I'll try, Pa. I'm scared shitless, but I'll try.

BOLEY: Good. Get Markie and Angelo and the others . . . (LISSA, ANGELO, SHIMMA, *others, all turn to face* BOLEY *and* HAL) I don't want to wait. I want the gavel to pass along to Hal, my son, *now* . . .

LISSA: That's not the rule . . .

BOLEY: It's what I *want*, Markie! We got certain things that need to be done right away. We've got no time . . . *(Pauses)* we've got a quorum here. This is what I want. This is probably the last thing I'll ever ask from any of ya's. *(There is a small silence.* ANGELO *speaks softly)*

ANGELO: I move that Hal Boley take over duties as Number One as of now, acting for his father, Hank Boley, who is Number One so long as he lives . . .

MORT: Second.

BOLEY: All in favor? *(All hands go up. As each man raises his hand, he says "aye" and there is a drumbeat. Finally,* LISSA *raises his hand and the vote is unanimous.* BOLEY *hands gavel to* HAL. *The power has passed to* HAL. *Lights fade)*

Scene Five

Lights fade up on HARRY *and* GUS. HARRY, *slightly drunk, is drinking beer.*

GUS: Easy with the brew, huh? We got some work ahead of us, huh, Harry . . .

HARRY: Fuck off, Gus, will ya . . . (HARRY *laughs, drinks from a bottle of beer.* VERNON *enters)*

VERNON: Can I talk to you, Harry?

HARRY: Who's that?

GUS: It's your cousin . . .

HARRY: I got no cousin . . . (VERNON *looks furtively at* GUS, *who is also alarmed)*

VERNON: Harry, I've talked to Boley. (HARRY *turns and faces* VERNON)

HARRY: And?

VERNON: Boley wants to go one-on-one with you . . .

HARRY: What are you? Shitting me? Hank Boley's s'pose'ta be layin' in a sickbed up Addison-Gilbert!

VERNON: *Hal* Boley. *(Pauses)* He took over as Number One last night. Hank Boley's nearly dead. They got him on some kind of machine. Hal's Number One . . . (HARRY *inhales, sharply. He turns away, laughs. He faces* VERNON)

HARRY: What'da'ya mean "one-on-one"? S'that a joke? *Number*-One-on-Number-One?

VERNON: Just the two of you, nobody else. Someplace private. To figure out who's got control . . . (PERCY *goes to* VERNON *and puts a hammerlock on the boy, twisting his arm painfully*)

HARRY: I put four bullets into your uncle. You can only get the chair *once*. Killin' a little pisser like you's *nothin'* ta me. *Nothin'!* (*Twists*) Is it true? Is this a true offer?

VERNON: Ten Pound Island, two o'clock. It's a true offer . . .

HARRY: Are you working for Boley?

VERNON: I ain't working for nobody but myself, Harry. I swear to God.

HARRY (*Lets the boy go*): Me neither, Vernon. (*Smiles*) That's the first smart thing I ever heard you say . . .

GUS: What about our *plan*, Harry? We're gonna get damn close to a hundred men out there!

HARRY: Let 'em surround Ten Pound Island. If Boley's got some kind of funny shit goin', he'll have a *war* on his hands . . . (*Smiles*) if he don't, he'll have a battle, just what he's askin' for: one-on-one . . . we go back all the way to the crib together . . . (*Smiles*) I should'a done the bast'd back then. . . . (*Laughs*) You spread the word, Gussie: circle Ten Pound Island and wait for me. *Then* we go for the Lillies. (*We hear the sound of an amplified Announcer's Voice off in the distance and the sounds of an excited crowd*)

ANNOUNCER: Salvy Benson, ladies and gentlemen . . . the undisputed champion of the Greasy Pole . . . making his second attempt. Salvy Benson . . . (*The lights crossfade to* HAL, SILVA, PETEY, BARDOLPH)

HAL: I'd better be alone in my boat going out there . . . (*The sounds of the Greasy Pole Contest and of the boats' engines should be played under the scene, just barely audible, but* present)

PETEY: You sure?

HAL: If Percy thinks I'm not alone, he'll use his men, too. He's got one hundred piratical lumpers backing him up and all I got is you, Bardolph and tubby Jack Silva, so what's the point? If I show up alone, maybe he'll show up alone. One-on-one's my best shot. I know you're devastated by the news . . .

SILVA: What news?

HAL: You won't be able to go hand-to-hand with Percy and Gus . . .

SILVA: I *won't?* *(False disappointment, badly playacted)* Damn. *(Shrugs)* I'm going back to bed . . .

PETEY: What do you want us to do?

HAL: Just stay back . . . lemme do what I hav'ta . . . *(Pauses)* if it doesn't work out . . . if Percy, well . . . *(Pauses)* you guys come and get me. . . . *(Pauses)* Ten Pound Island's covered with rats. I'd rather have a less ignominious parting . . . *(Pauses)* If it goes wrong, you tell my father, okay, Petey? Get over there fast, so it's you who tells him . . .

SILVA: Why are you doin' this?

HAL: It's a matter of honor.

SILVA: Honor? Honor is just the opposite of "off her." If it were me, I'd be on the shuttle to LaGuardia: now . . .

HAL: I've *been* on the shuttle to LaGuardia. That's the difference between us . . . that and about one hundred eighty-seven pounds . . .

SILVA: You wouldn't want what you just mouthed to be your last words, would you?

HAL: Maybe I would. *(Change of attitude)* Jack?

SILVA: What?

HAL: If I do have the last word . . . if I come back from this . . . things have got to change.

SILVA: In what sense?

HAL: In every sense. (HAL *starts boat's engine—sound of same increases. The lights crossfade to* PATTY. PATTY *moves into shadowy light, calling out to* TOM PERCY)

PATTY: Dad? (PATTY *stops, looks about worried. She smiles and calls out again*) Dad? (PATTY *takes one more step forward, then looks and screams. All women in cast should echo* PATTY's *scream, so that the sound carries from woman to woman and surrounds the auditorium. If scenically possible, lights fade out dimly. We see shadow of* TOM PERCY, *hanging by the neck, dead.* PATTY *walks to grave and takes note from ground, opens same, reads same aloud. The lights cross to* HARRY, *opposite side of stage.* PATTY *turns and faces her husband, reading*) "I claim full responsibility for the death of Alfred Richards and for the death of my brother, Francis Percy. I killed them both with my own hand and by my own hand I take my own life and end this murderous rampage. Whatever I own, I leave to my son, Harold Percy, who I pray will forgive me. . . ." *(To* HARRY) And he signed it . . . *(Weeps)* oh God, Harry, I'm so sorry . . .

HARRY: At least, he found some courage . . .

PATTY: You've got to stop now, Harry. You've got to . . .

HARRY: Opposite . . . what is *is!* Nobody can change it. Nobody can take it away . . . (HARRY *goes to* PATTY *and kisses her, roughly. He turns from her suddenly, leaving her alone, weeping. He calls to opposite side of stage*) Hal Boley! *(Drumbeat)*

HAL *(Offstage, in shadows):* Right here, Percy . . .*(Drumbeat)*

HARRY: You ready, Boley?

HAL *(Enters):* Ready.

HARRY: What's your poison?

HAL: How's these? (HAL *holds up two curved fish knives, high over his head*)

HARRY: Fine with *me.*

HAL: Ten Pound Island, ten minutes, just us . . .

HARRY: Ten Pound Island, ten minutes, just us . . . (HAL *and* HARRY *walk in opposite circles, full perimeter of stage. Lights dim*)

ANNOUNCER'S VOICE *(Over amplifier):* This Greasy Pole Contest is holding for the pleasure boats out there! Somebody tell them pleasure-boat operators we ain't gonna have another walker 'til they move them pleasure boats away from under the Greasy Pole . . . *(Lighting shifts to extremely dim lighting. All cast members, except* BOLEY *and* TOM PERCY *and* FRANK PERCY, *stand in shadows, not recognizable, making sounds of rats. A slight glow now appears center.* HAL *enters, kicking at the imagined rats. Henceforward, drumbeats will punctuate this entire scene*)

HAL: Not me! (HARRY *enters, kicking at the rats as well*)

HARRY: Not Harry Percy! I got a whole 'nother meal planned for you rats: it's called Hal Boley! *(He flashes knife at the imagined rats. We hear the sound of the rats squealing, increasing with their excitement, as stone is hurled.* HAL *looks across, watches* HARRY, *calls out*)

HAL: Harry Percy . . .

HARRY: Hal Boley . . .

HAL: Long time . . .

HARRY: Long time . . . (HARRY PERCY *and* HAL BOLEY *begin to fight, as might two savages. A lifetime of misunderstanding spurs each of them on. The advantage changes and changes again. First,* HAL *is on top, then,* PERCY. *Their sounds are animal-like, joining with the sound of the rats. The fight carries them in and around the audience, up and down ramps and platforms. Suddenly,* HARRY *loses his footing, falters.* HAL *stabs* HARRY *in the stomach. All sound stops. Loud drumbeat)*

HARRY: Oh Jesus!

ALL OTHERS *(A whisper):* Oh Jesus Christ! *(The two young men fall to the ground together. Blood oozes from* HARRY'S *chest.* HAL *cradles* HARRY'S *head)*

HAL: Oh God, Harry, I'm sorry. I am, I'm really sorry . . . Harry?

HARRY: It hurts wicked, Henry . . . *(Pauses)* am I gonna die from this?

HAL: It looks bad.

HARRY: Take me off a' here. The rats . . .

HAL: I will.

HARRY: I'm goin' ta sleep now, Hal. You win . . .

HAL *(Sobbing):* I do, Harry. I win. . . . *(*HARRY PERCY *dies. We hear the sounds of the rats squealing.* HAL *screams)* Noooo! *(*HAL *kicks at the rats. He tosses stones at them. He turns and sees that rats are close to* HARRY'S *dead body.* HAL *screams again)* Noooooooooooooooo! *(*HAL *picks up* HARRY *as best he can and slowly carries* HARRY *in a circle)* I'll leave you in the water, Harry. You'll be safe . . . *(*HAL *buries* HARRY PERCY *at sea. He kneels and says a prayer)* May the soul of the Faithful departed *(etc)*

ALL: *(They all sing "The Requiem" in Latin.* HAL *stands and moves to the full group of spectators who now stand in a cluster, hands at sides.* HAL *runs in circle, ending center. The lights brighten to hot white light)*

HAL: Did anybody tell my father? . . . .

ANGELO: He's . . . gone, Hal. (HAL *screams a primal scream and then faces* ANGELO *again*)

HAL: When?

ANGELO: Noon. It was . . . peaceful. (ANGELO *embraces* HAL. *Lights fade*)

Scene Six

In the darkness, we hear drunken laughter, followed by SILVA's *boisterous voice.*

SILVA: Come on, party-people! We will *own* this town! (*The lights snap on.* SILVA, DOLLY, BARDOLPH, BARRY, GADSHILL, ALBERTA *and* EMILY FUSCO *and others dance on, in the throes of great celebration.* SILVA *sings as he runs on*) You've got to fight . . . for the right . . . to parrrrrtyyyyy! . . . (*They arrive in a cluster*) I *kid* you not! I will be to Hal Boley what Spiro Agnew was to Richard Nixon . . .

DOLLY: Spiro Agnew was Jackie's main hero . . .

SILVA: Spiro Agnew was a *God!* (*All look up to see* HAL *standing, facing them.* SILVA *grins from ear to ear, calls out to* HAL. *All cheer and call out with* SILVA. HAL *cuts them off*)

SILVA & OTHERS: Halll! Hallieeee! Hallll!

HAL: I don't want any of you living or working in Glossop, or anywhere on Cape Ann . . . (*All laugh, cheer*) You've got two weeks to move out . . . (*Laugh*) I know everything about everybody here . . . (*Everyone laughs. And then they don't. One by one, grins fade into something serious, as* HAL *makes his pronouncement*) Glossop's going to change . . . if anyone of you is still here after two weeks, the police will get a full report from me about whatever I know . . . and I know a lot . . . Glossop's off limits to every one of you. No exceptions, two weeks . . . no exceptions. (*All turn away, but for* SILVA. SILVA *and* HAL *make eye contact.* HAL *makes his final pronouncement quietly, sadly*) I don't know you, fat man. (HAL *backs away from* SILVA *and the others, never breaking eye contact. All turn, exit. The lights crossfade to* PATTY *across stage, inside of her house. She is dressed in black dress, her face tear-stained.* HAL *should scream his lines from offstage, behind the audience, if possible.* PATTY *should be alone on stage, calling off to* HAL *through the scene)* Patty!

PATTY: What?

HAL: Where are you?

PATTY: Here. Inside.

HAL: I'm coming in!

PATTY: No!

HAL: Did you hear?

PATTY: Vernon came by.

HAL: There's no other way, Patty.

PATTY: There's no way I'm gonna make you feel better about this. What you did, you did. . . . *(Pauses)* What *I* did, I did. . . . *(Tragic scream)* It's a shame, that's what. *A wicked awful, terrible fuckin' shame!!!*

HAL: I know. I agree. But what is *is*. I can't change it. *(Pauses)* Do you wish Harry killed me?

PATTY: No.

HAL: I'd like to see you . . . talk to you . . . when you're ready . . . do you want to never see me again?

PATTY *(After a pause):* There's a lot I've gotta get done first, with my daughter . . . maybe in a year. I dunno . . . *(There is a small silence.* HAL *calls out to her, softly)*

HAL: Will you see me then? In a year?

PATTY: Yes. *(Lights crossfade to opposite side of stage, where* MARKIE LISSA *and* ANGELO CATALANO *enter from* BOLEY's *graveside. All others surround audience singing "The Requiem" in Latin.* ANGELO *and* MARKIE *stand facing each other, as the others continue and complete the Latin prayer)*

ALL: *Ahhhh-mennn . . .*

ANGELO: Hard to believe . . .

LISSA: Yuh.

ANGELO: Guy like Hank shoulda lived to a hundred . . .

LISSA: Yuh, I s'pose . . .

ANGELO: It's gonna be different. At least we've got Hank's boy . . .

LISSA: What are you? Kidding me? The kid hasn't spoken a civil word to me in months! I'm the one who got him suspended . . .

ANGELO: Yuh, that's tough!

LISSA: An hour ago, at the cemetery, I tried to shake his hand, an' he pushed me aside like I was a nobody . . .

ANGELO: He's a kid still . . . hotheaded . . .

LISSA: Yuh, well, he may be a kid, but he's running the show now, Angelo . . .

ANGELO: He is popular, yuh . . .

LISSA: I'm seventy-one, Angelo. I can't start up fresh. I'm too far gone for lumpin' . . . *(*HAL *enters)*

PASTA *(Calls out):* The new boss, everybody! *(Everyone turns, sees* HAL, *applauds and cheers.* HAL *smiles, waves.* LISSA *walks to* HAL *and offers a handshake. It is a courageous act on* LISSA's *part, as the gesture is now totally public)*

LISSA: I tried to shake your hand at the grave, but you didn't see me, Hal. . . . *(Pauses)* I want to offer you my total support . . .

HAL *(Smiles, looks over at* ANGELO*)*: "Total support"? That's quite an offer, Markie.

LISSA: I know you hate me, 'counta my causin' your suspension . . . but what you did slurred your father. It was a slap in the face of this union and all of us and a slap in your father's face, most of all. . . . *(Pauses)* When you have a son, if he breaks the rules in the same way, he'll be treated by me in the same way. It's a promise I made to your father, years and years ago, and I make it to you right now. Even if you hate me for it, Hal. I know right from wrong . . . *(There is a silence in the room as everyone stares, somewhat embarrassed, deeply aware of what is being said)*

HAL: I pray to God that I'll have a kid someday who'll be lucky enough to have a guy like you around with his eyes on things, Markie . . . *(*HAL *hugs* LISSA, *kisses his cheek. There is a delighted silence, all applaud. We now hear a constant drumbeat)*

ALL: Hal Boley! Hal Boley! Hal Boley!

EPILOGUE

LISSA *moves into a pool of light in front of the townspeople.* HAL *moves up on to a small high platform, into a fiercely white light, gold gavel in his hand.*

HAL: My father believed that any man, woman and child who wanted to live in Glossop and work hard for a living should and would have that chance . . . (LISSA *speaks to audience, as he did in the play's prologue, now in counterpoint to* HAL)

LISSA: The worst and the best of men and trees finally fall forward, dead, to fertilize an earth, so that men and trees might rise and have their time . . .

HAL: . . . No matter if they are Portuguese, Irish, Finnish, Italian, Korean, Protestant, Catholic, Jew, hard-working people will have their chance. I promise this. (*All* TOWNSPEOPLE *cheer. The cheer ends unfinished, suddenly clipped*)

LISSA: Glossop is gone, but for the odd scrap, the odd vestige, a blade of an ice skate, a handle from a glazed ceramic coffee mug. Otherwise, Glossop is gone . . .

HAL: There are plenty of fish in the sea, enough for everybody! My father believed that and I believe that. And I am ready to defend that ideal against any*one* and any*thing* . . .

LISSA: Ideal, like honor, is just another word. A holy war is finally nothing but a war. And murder, in the name of goodness, is nonetheless murder. And fishermen who sink their boats or sell their piers in the name of money can never again call themselves fishermen. They are, simply, ordinary men with pockets full of paper money . . .

HAL: I swear upon the memory of my father to run this waterfront in my father's way. Glossop will be great again! (*All cheer. The cheer ends, suddenly clipped*)

LISSA: The only Lillies left on Cape Ann grow on graves. Where Glossop was now stands a thousand towers: condominiums staring out over a filthy, fishless sea . . .

HAL: I am my father's son. Whatever my father began, I will . . . continue . . . , I promise, with my blood, Glossop will be great again . . .

LISSA: For we the living now, there's still time to take down our "For Sale" signs . . . and to live. (*Drumbeat. The* TOWNSPEOPLE *lift newspapers, reading as they did at the start of the play.* LISSA *now covers his face by opening a Glossop newspaper, too, and reading. Five drumbeats, softly. A moment of silence and then the lights switch out.*

The play is over)

FISH OF THE SEA
(Traditional sea chanty)

Now is the time for fishing
If you mean to have a try,
Get your tackling ready
It's no use to keep them dry.

Shoot your nets out on the briny
And haul them in again,
And you'll get a funny shimmer
In the morning.

Then up jumped the herring,
He's the king of the sea,
He said to the skipper:
"Look under your lee."

CHORUS   Windy old weather, boys,
Squally old weather, boys,
When the wind blow,
We'll all go together.

Then up git the garnet
With pricks on his back,
He jumped on the foredeck
To hook on the jibtack, singing

CHORUS

Then up git the codfish
With his great old head,
He said to the deckie,
"Get a cast of lead," singing

CHORUS

Then up git the haddock,
So sharp and so shy.
He said to the deckie,
"Hook on the lee guy."

CHORUS

Then up git the roker,
So sharp and so rough,
He said to the cook,
"You're burning the duff."

2ND CHOR.

So after it, you bugger,
So after it, you bugger,
When the wind blow,
We'll all go together.

Then up jumped the sprat,
The smallest of all,
He said to the skipper:
"Haul, haul the man's trawl."

1ST CHOR.

North
Shore
Fish

NORTH SHORE FISH was given its world premiere on August 24, 1986, at the Gloucester Stage Company (Israel Horovitz, Artistic Director/Producer; Grey Cattell Johnson, Associate Artistic Director). It was directed by Grey Cattell Johnson with sets by David Condino, costumes by Jeanine Phaneuf Burgess and lighting by B.N. Productions. The cast, in order of appearance, was as follows:

ALFRED "PORKER" MARTINO . . . . Mark Rogers
FLORENCE RIZZO . . . . Geraldine Librandi
ARLYNE FLYNN . . . . Mary Klug
RUTHIE. . . . . Judith McIntyre
SALVATORE (SALLY) MORELLA . . . . . . Theodore Reinstein
JOSEPHINE EVANGELISTA . . . . Michelle Faith
MAUREEN VEGA . . . . Karen Crawford
MARLENA . . . . Teade Gormley
CATHERINE SHIMMA . . . . Tara Dolan

It then went on to a New York production at the WPA Theatre (Kyle Renick, Artistic Director; Wendy Bustard, Managing Director), opening on January 12, 1987. Directed by Stephen Zuckerman, it had sets by Edward T. Gianfrancesco, lights by Craig Evans, costumes by Mimi Maxmen, sound by Aural Fixation, the Production Stage Manager was David Lawrence Folender and the cast was as follows:

ALFRED "PORKER" MARTINO . . . . John Pankow
FLORENCE RIZZO . . . . Christine Estabrook
ARLYNE FLYNN . . . . Mary Klug
RUTHIE. . . . . Cordelia Richards
SALVATORE (SALLY) MORELLA . . . . Thomas G. Waites
JOSEPHINE EVANGELISTA . . . . Michelle M. Faith
MAUREEN VEGA . . . . Elizabeth Kemp
MARLENA . . . . Laura San Giacomo
CATHERINE SHIMMA . . . . Wendie Malick

To the memory
of
Gail Randazza

The People of the Play

ALFRED "PORKER" MARTINO: thirties, small, sadly comic.

FLORENCE RIZZO: thirties, once a high-school bombshell.

ARLYNE FLYNN: late fifties, thin, nervous, Ruthie's mother.

RUTHIE FLYNN: thirties, adorable, enormously pregnant.

SALVATORE "SALLY" MORELLA: early thirties, lean, handsome.

JOSIE EVANGELISTA: thirties, strikingly plump.

MAUREEN VEGA: thirties, tall, thin, bespectacled.

MARLENA VEGA: thirties, Maureen's cousin, quite beautiful: the new girl.

CATHERINE SHIMMA: thirties, slightly up–market look.

The Place of the Play

Assembly line and main plant, North Shore Fish, a frozen fish processing company in Gloucester, Massachusetts.

The Time of the Play

A work day in summer, the present.

The Accent of the Play

Massachusetts North Shore accent, as in "Park Your Car in Harvard Yard."

ACT I

Lights up on line of machinery, interior of fish-processing plant. 1940s assembly line fills stage. Aluminum vats, white-rubber conveyor belt, cement floor, vast space all around. A glass-windowed office overlooks the "line" from above, center stage.

PORKER MARTINO, *early 30s, mops floor. As he mops, he sings "Strangers In The Night,"* taking liberties with song's lyrics. He wears chino pants and shirt; Red Sox cap.*

PORKER:
Strangers in the night . . .
Exchanging glances . . .
Strangers in the night . . .
Taking our chances . . .
We made out all right . . .
Because of lovvvve . . .
How would we have guessed? . . . Dum duh dah
Dum dahh *(Forgets lyrics completely)* . . .
I forget the rest . . . *(Improvises)*
Love was just a glance away . . .
A warm romantic chance away . . . *(Heading toward a big finish)*
We made out all right . . .
Taking our chances . . .
Lovers at first sight . . .
Take off your pants-es . . .
She wasn't too bright . . .
But, we were strangers in the *nighhhhhttttttt!*

(FLORENCE *enters, wearing shorts, bright blouse, sunglasses, carrying two largish pocketbooks, cigarette in her lips. She rubs her hands together, warming them. She listens to* PORKER's *big finish before commenting. Her comment startles him)*

FLORENCE: Jesus, Porker, that you *singin'?* I thought they were stranglin' fuckin' *dolphins* in here! I never woulda' guessed you were stranglin' fuckin' "Strangers In The Night."

PORKER: You sound like a *toilet,* you know that?

FLORENCE: You *are* a toilet! What a sketch, Porker! Moppin' and singin' like whatisname . . . Andy Williams . . . *(Pulls her blouse over her head. She wears a lacy bra)* Turn your head around! I'm changin'!

PORKER *(looks away):* Frank Sinatra, dumbbell.

FLORENCE: How old's he? Eighty?

PORKER: Yuh, right, eighty, you got it . . . (FLORENCE *goes to closet and removes freshly ironed pastel green smock, which she pulls over her head. She puts her blouse in closet)*

FLORENCE: I'm takin' my pants off . . .

PORKER: What am I? S'pose'ta get *excited?*

FLORENCE: Just turn your head around! You're s'pose'ta be moppin', that's all, so *mop!*

PORKER: Hard ta get anything much worked up around your pants comin' off, I can tell you that! It's kinda like gettin' excited about a wave hittin' Good Harbor Beach. (FLORENCE *folds her shorts into the closet with her blouse neatly.* PORKER *continues)* First coupla' waves, you yell "Oh wow, lookit! A wave!" But, after fifty or sixty thousand waves, it's kinda hard ta get anything much worked up in the excitement department, if you follow my message . . .

FLORENCE: What the Christ are you talkin' about, Porker?

PORKER: Your *pants,* Florence! After you take your pants on and off fifty or sixty thousand times, it don't make much of no impression on anybody . . .

FLORENCE: Oh right, I get you, Porker. It's a *jokkke* . . . about me takin' my pants off a lot counta I'm in and out of bed . . .

PORKER *(Adds an "s"): zssszzz* . . .

FLORENCE: Bed*ssszzz* . . . Well, I guess you must be jealous, bein' left out and all, counta you got no dick . . .

PORKER: I do okay . . .

FLORENCE: Is that a fact?

PORKER: What's a *dolphin,* anyhow? Like in the circus kinda thing?

FLORENCE: Dolphins are grey mammals. Dolphins are smart. They got brains. They talk to each other. They got their own language. They *frolic!*

PORKER: I frolic . . .

FLORENCE: Bullllshhhittt you frolic, Porker. You're a hundred per cent glum all the time and you know it! You are next ta pathetic! What's with the air conditioning? It's freezing in here.

PORKER: I already turned it down . . .

FLORENCE: What's Markie planning? Ta freeze the help and cut us up inta *fillettes?*

PORKER: I already turned it down! (ARLYNE *enters with* RUTHIE, *who is enormously pregnant. Both women are smoking. Both carry coffee thermoses under their arms, drink from plastic coffee cups as they enter. They walk directly to their lockers)*

FLORENCE *(Sudden sweetness, to* ARLYNE): Mornin', Arlyne. How's the hip?

ARLYNE: Rough, still, thanks, Floey. How's yo'r mum?

FLORENCE: Doin' better, thanks . . .

ARLYNE: Mornin', Porker. Freezin' in here . . .

PORKER: I already turned it down . . .

FLORENCE: He already turned it down. Mornin', Ruthie.

PORKER: Mornin', Ruthie . . .

RUTHIE: Mornin', Floey . . . Mornin', Porker . . .

FLORENCE: No change, huh?

RUTHIE: Nothin'. I'm ten months, as of this mornin'. Dr. Benoit's
definitely got my due date wrong. I'm thinkin' of changin' doctors, to
tell you the truth . . . (RUTHIE *stops talking suddenly, as* SALLY
MORELLA *enters. He is thin, handsome, thirty. He wears a white shirt,
tie, long white coat, open; hard hat. Without noticing or acknowledging
anyone, he runs up the staircase into kitchen in glass-windowed office
above the "line." He tidies up the place, fussing about, nervously
readying kitchen for new inspector. He Windexes the kitchen window.
He plumps pillow on desk chair. He arranges pens on desk)* What's
with Sal?

PORKER: New government inspector starts today.

RUTHIE: Oh yuh, right. So, how're the kids, Flo?

FLORENCE: Ungrateful, late for school, usual stuff . . . Bradley said he
had a headache, so I said "You're seven, Bradley, you can't have a
headache 'til you're ten. . . ." He says, "Who says?" and I says "It's a
fact, everybody knows it, boys don't get headaches 'til then and girls
don't get 'em til twelve, 'cause they're smarter. . . ." Then, Emily
screams, "You hear that, Breadloaf? Girls are smarter!" And Bradley
throws his goddam egg at her!

ARLYNE: Nooo!

FLORENCE: Yesss!

ARLYNE: Little boys can be very mean to little girls.

PORKER: Raw?

FLORENCE: What's this?

PORKER: The egg: raw?

FLORENCE: Scrambled, shit–for–brains! What? You think I feed my kids raw eggs?

ARLYNE: This mornin'?

FLORENCE: Less than an hour ago . . .

RUTHIE: What'd Emily do? She muckle him, or what?

FLORENCE: No, not much. Bradley's got her scared. I think he hits on her when I'm not home yet. . . . *(Pauses)* She cried. . . . *(There is a pause)* Either of you see the dolphins on TV, last night?

RUTHIE: With the guy speakin' French or something?

FLORENCE: Jock-something, yuh. You see it?

RUTHIE: I switched over. I couldn't stand the foreign words . . .

FLORENCE: There was a simultaneous translation . . . in English . . . a guy was translating over the French . . . at the same time.

RUTHIE: Yuh, but I didn't like it . . . And Earl gets really pissed off when they talk foreign on the TV.

FLORENCE: The dolphins were so wicked smart . . .

ARLYNE: I remember, years back, there was a TV show every week. What was it called?

RUTHIE: I don't know why they don't just put American shows on the TV? I don't know who they think they're tryin' ta please by puttin' all this French crap on. I'll bet we don't have more'n two Frenchmen livin' on Cape Ann, period.

ARLYNE: Uncle Ben?

RUTHIE: That's rice, Ma.

ARLYNE: Something like that . . . there was a show with a "Ben" . . .

PORKER: "Gentle Ben"?

ARLYNE: That's it! That was great!

PORKER (To FLORENCE, confidentially): Stupid fuckin' show.

FLORENCE (Sees that ARLYNE is embarrassed): Will you watch your tongue, cesspool?

PORKER: If that ain't the teapot callin' the fryin' pan black . . . (The three women giggle. PORKER is perplexed) What's funny? What's so goddam funny? (SALLY pokes head out of upstairs office. He calls down to the women)

SALLY: Mornin', girls.

ARLYNE & RUTHIE: Mornin', Sally . . . Hey, Sal . . .

SALLY: Hey, Florence, you got a minute?

FLORENCE: In front of everybody? (Giggles from all)

SALLY: Very comical.

PORKER: Big day, huh, Sally? You ready for this, or what?

SALLY: What's this?

PORKER: You kiddin' me?

SALLY: That? No big deal there ta *me!*

PORKER: You seen her yet?

SALLY: Makes no nevermind to me, whatsoever! (*To* FLORENCE) Can I just see you, please? (SAL *exits into inspector's office again, closing door behind him.* FLORENCE *laughs, goes up the stairs to* SALLY. *She enters office, closes door behind her.* SALLY *and* FLORENCE *are now visible to audience through office window.* MAUREEN *and* MARLENA *enter, all in late 30s.* MAUREEN *and* MARLENA *cross and exit offstage to changing room, smiling to* PORKER *as they go*)

MAUREEN: Mornin', Porker . . . how's the weekend?

PORKER: Not bad, not bad. Yourself?

MAUREEN: Good. It's freezing in here.

PORKER: I turned it down already. (*Sees* MARLENA) This her?

MAUREEN: Yup.

PORKER: How's it goin'?

MARLENA: How's yourself?

MAUREEN: Where's Floey? She sick again? (ARLYNE *and* RUTHIE *point straight above their heads, as if pointing to heaven*)

PORKER: Company business. (MAUREEN *looks up at window.* NOTE: *We now see* FLORENCE *and* SAL *are in a passionate embrace*)

MARLENA: Wow! Who's that?

MAUREEN: I'll tell ya later. Come on . . . (MAUREEN *and* MARLENA *exit.* JOSIE *enters. She is strikingly plump*)

ARLYNE: Morning, Josephine . . .

RUTHIE: Morning, Josie . . . how goes it?

JOSIE: Morning, Arlyne. Morning, Ruthie. It's cold in here . . . Where's Florence? Sick again? *(Everybody points straight up.* JOSIE *looks up and shakes her head in mock disgust)* They were doin' that when I left here, yesterday. They been there all *night?* (JOSIE *crosses to her locker, touching* PORKER's *shoulder as she passes him)* Mornin', Porker . . .

PORKER: Yo, Josie, what's up? . . . I turned the air conditioner down already. New shirt, huh, Jose? *(Rhymes with "hose")*

JOSIE: It's not a shirt, Porker, it's a blouse. Boys wear shirts, girls wear blouses . . . (FLORENCE *re-enters, goes to line sets up for work)*

FLORENCE: Mornin' . . .

JOSIE: I hope you kept your mouth closed when you kissed him!

FLORENCE: You got it: mouth closed, legs open.

RUTHIE: Nice talk! (SALLY *re-enters, whisk broom in hand, sweeps steps to kitchen, vigorously brushing his dirt findings into dustpan. He checks his work, satisfied that steps are spandy clean, goes down steps to handtruck, exits in freezer. Everyone pauses to watch him come, work, go)*

JOSIE: What's *with* him?

FLORENCE: New government inspector starts today . . .

JOSIE: What happened to Haddie?

FLORENCE: She was just a fill–in temp . . .

JOSIE: No kidding?

PORKER: Absolutely. She was just fillin' in 'til the Feds found a full-time replacement for Dorothy . . .

ARLYNE: Poor Dorothy. Hard to believe . . .

JOSIE: Hard to believe . . .

PORKER: Unbelievable . . .

RUTHIE: I still can't believe it myself . . . (JOSIE *and* FLORENCE *exchange a private glance.* FLORENCE *breaks the eye contact; moves upstage.* SALLY *re-enters with handtruck. He sets down pallet with crates of frozen product at head of "line," ready for processing*)

MAUREEN: Mornin', Sal . . .

SALLY: Mornin', Reenie . . .

JOSIE *(Pulling sweater off over head):* Boys, close your eyes!

SALLY: You're supposed to be usin' the big room!

JOSIE *(Wears lacy bra, "flashes" the men):* Cheap thrills!

SALLY: Very comical! *(To all)* I'm tellin' her and I'm tellin' ya's all: you made me set up the big room downstairs with changin' booths and a cot and a Mr. Coffee and bullshit, and if ya's ain't gonna use all that, I'm gonna return the merchandise and use the space for something profitable!

JOSIE: Ain't nothin' profitable goin' on around North Shore Fish . . .

SALLY: I can use it for storage . . .

JOSIE: Keep runnin' the front office the way it's bein' run, you'll be able ta use the whole plant for *storage!*

SALLY: You wanna watch that mouth of yours, sistah, huh? Jobs are gettin' scarce.

JOSIE: I wonder who we get ta blame for that particular turn of events, huh?

SALLY: What's this I'm hearin'?

JOSIE: What's yo'r problem, Sally? Waxey ears? You can't hear clear what I'm sayin'? *(Closer; loudly)* I'm sayin' North Shore Fish is goin' *down the tubes!* (SALLY *blanches white, raises the back of his hand as though he might hit* JOSIE. FLORENCE *steps between them)*

FLORENCE *(Stares him down, eyeball-to-eyeball):* Stay back from her.

SALLY *(puts his hand to his side):* I'm gonna tell ya's all somethin' straight: This is not the day!

JOSIE: What's your plan for the new inspector, Sal? You gonna grab her in the freezer for a cold quickie or are you gonna go for a long and meaningful relationship? Hmmm?

SALLY: Just watch your ass.

JOSIE *(She looks down to her derrière):* Okay, now there are *three* of us watching my ass: me, you and Hotlips Martino. (SALLY *walks to end of "line," moves blocks of frozen fish into position for processing. He then exits into refrigerator)*

PORKER: I got that, you know.

JOSIE: Why shouldn't you have got that? Was anybody speakin' in complex sentences you mightn't comprehend? *(To all)* I'm goin' to the big room to change. I wouldn't wanna be the cause of Sal bringin' our Mr. Coffee back ta Zayre's! (JOSIE *exits.* PORKER *goes to* FLORENCE)

PORKER: What was the implication s'pose'ta be there? That I'm *stupid* or something?

FLORENCE: That was no implication, Porker. That was a *fact of life!*

PORKER: Me: stupid? I ain't the one callin' no TV-dolphin "Gentle Ben." Gentle Ben was a goddam grizzly bear, you dodo! The TV dolphin for about a hundred years, as everybody knows, was "Flipper"! *(To all)* Right? Is this not right? Is this not a perfectly right fact?

FLORENCE: That wasn't me, ya nincompoop! I was just goin' along 'counta I didn't wanna hurt Arlyne's feelin's. If your memory ain't eaten away by the drugs, you might recall it was Arlyne who come up with Gentle goddam Ben and hardly myself! I said nothin' . . . I just went along . . .

ARLYNE *(Eavesdrops; interjects):* Yuh, I think I did and you're definitely right, Porker. Gentle Ben was a bear. Flipper was the porpoise . . .

FLORENCE: Dolphin . . .

RUTHIE: Same thing, if you ask me. They look like big hairy slugs . . .

PORKER: What do you mean "slugs"?

RUTHIE: Slugs. Slugs are slugs . . .

PORKER: Like in a gun in a gangster movie "slugs"?

FLORENCE: Jesus, what a dork!

PORKER: I'm just askin'! I'm just checkin'!

FLORENCE: She don't mean "slugs" like in a gangster movie. She don't mean "slugs" like after you make a bad smell, neither, dork!

PORKER: Will you get off my goddam case!

RUTHIE: What I mean is slugs like you get when you grow your own lettuce . . . in the vegetable garden . . . black fleshy hairy slimey disgusting slugs!

FLORENCE: See?

PORKER: I know that!

RUTHIE: Porpoises are like big bloated-up slugs! Used ta make me sick when we used ta go into North Station to Barnum & Bailey's Circus, when I was little . . .

PORKER: Porpoises?

FLORENCE *(Confidentially, to* PORKER): Don't you correct her, you!

PORKER: Did I say nothin'? *(He shows his palms to* FLORENCE)

RUTHIE *(Continuing; quite disgusted):* These porpoises would come out (big, hairy, slimey, fleshy things with whiskers) and they'd kinda *flop around* . . . all fleshy and slug-like! The trainers would feed 'em live fish, which they'd kinda *suck up,* then they'd bark some kinda weird kinda dog-like soundin' bark, and then they toot out something on car horns or somesuch. I usually had my eyes closed at that point and had my legs clamped together tight, in case they got loose and came at me, and, you know, tried to get under my skirt or anything . . . *(There is a small astonished silence)*

ARLYNE: Jeffrey once put five or six slugs in Ruthie's underpants to scare her, when she was little. She was about ten, maybe eleven . . .

RUTHIE: Gawd, Mama, Jesus!

ARLYNE: . . . I'm never suppose'ta mention it out loud . . .

RUTHIE: Gawd!

ARLYNE: Little boys can be very mean to little girls . . . *(There is another small silence.* SALLY *re-enters with a handtruck with several fresh blocks of frozen fish-product stacked neatly on a pallette, ready for processing)*

SALLY: What is the *matter* with you people? Do you see the clock? We're just about to have a bell! S'posin' Markie comes in early? No saws on, no batter mixed and ready! A new inspector startin' today and nobody set up ta work! This is brilliant, people, huh, with what's goin' down here, huh? Huh? Am I talkin' for my own good here, or am I talkin' for the good of alla' ya's, huh? *(*PORKER *walks wordlessly to the band saw and flips the switch "on."* ARLYNE *walks to the wrapping-sealer and flips the switch "on."* FLORENCE *walks to the batter-tank and flips the switch "on."* RUTHIE *moves along the "line" to the hot-plastic-wrap station; hits the "on" switch.* JOSIE *re-enters with* MAUREEN *and* MARLENA. *They re-join the "line" at their various workstations)* Where *were* you people? You're not even set up!

JOSIE: We were just givin' the new girl the lay of the land.

PORKER *(Guffaws): You oughta know! Haggghhh!*

JOSIE: What's that noise just come outta Porker? Sounded like a trained
seal! Somebody throw Porker a fish! *(Guffaws)*

SALLY: Get set up, okay? (MAUREEN *and* JOSIE *exchange a private glance)*

JOSIE: Sorry I razzed ya', Sal. I know you're feelin' pressured. (MAUREEN
and JOSIE *exchange another private glance.* MAUREEN *smiles
approvingly)*

SALLY: I accept. (SALLY *pats* JOSIE*'s bottom)* Don't sweat it.

JOSIE *(Smiles):* So, how's Carmella and the kids doin'? Okay?

SALLY: Great, great, terrific. *(To* MAUREEN) Get your cousin set up, too,
okay? This is her . . . she . . . right? *(Smiles flirtatiously at*
MARLENA) We ain't been officially introduced yet. I'm Sal.

MAUREEN: Sorry, Sal. This is Marlena, Sal. Marlena, this is Sal. Sal's
foreman.

SALLY: Very pleased ta meetcha . . .

MARLENA: Likewise . . .

SALLY: Maybe we can meet up later and I can show you some tricks . . .
how ta handle product kind of thing . . . (MARLENA *and* SALLY
exchange a flirtatious glance. FLORENCE *flashes an angry stare at* SALLY.
To MAUREEN) Get her set up . . . *(He exits into office. They all set up
to work: get ready for the bell)*

FLORENCE: What gives here?

MAUREEN: I'm just breakin' Marlena in, so's she can cover for me next
month, when Anthony and I are travelin'. She's my cousin. . . . That
there's Florence Rizzo: she batters . . .

MARLENA: Hi.

FLORENCE: Hi.

MAUREEN: These two here are Ruthie and her mother, Mrs. Flynn . . .

ARLYNE: Arlyne . . .

MARLENA: Hi . . .

ARLYNE: Hi . . .

RUTHIE: Hi . . .

MAUREEN *(To* MARLENA*)*: Get boxes off the stack . . . about so many. *(Indicates amount with her hands)*

MARLENA *(En route to box supply, to* RUTHIE*)*: How far along are you?

ARLYNE: She's overdue.

RUTHIE *(Pats her stomach)*: I'm ten months. *(Munches her donut, laughs)* I'm eating for two.

JOSIE *(Pats her own stomach)*: I've been eating for two all my *life!* Anybody got any extra food?

ARLYNE: I've got a ricotta pie from Mike's. You hungry already? Didn't you eat breakfast?

JOSIE: A' course I ate breakfast! That's my point. I was just checking for later. If I eat my lunch early, around ten/ten thirty, which is my plan, I'll get hungry again around eleven/eleven-thirty . . .

ARLYNE: I'll save you half . . .

JOSIE: You're the best, Arlyne! Honest ta God.

RUTHIE: My doctor got my due date wrong, on account of I'm never regular. I think I probably wasn't even pregnant when I first went in

for the checkup, but we all figured it was a definite, 'counta I missed
two months straight 'n all . . . so Earl and I relaxed our system and
next thing I know . . .

ARLYNE *(Completes the sentence):* Pregnant!

JOSIE: Earl and Ruthie use the Basic Cape Ann Catholic System.

RUTHIE: Oh yuh, what's that?

JOSIE *(Shrugs; explains simply):* Getting Pregnant.

RUTHIE: That's about the size of it . . .

JOSIE: *What's* about the size of it? *(Reasonably raunchy laugh from all)*
Gloucester men have it down to a science: they drink 'til about 3 AM
and then they come in making enough noise to wake all the kids up.
Then they roll you over and come, faster than you can say, "I ain't got
my diaphragm in!" Then they drop dead asleep. You miss your period.
They get pissed off. They meet young out-of-town girls who take
aerobics and they move out of the house. *(There is a long embarrassed
pause)*

MAUREEN: Josie's goin' through a bad time.

MARLENA *(Smiles at* RUTHIE*):* You'll probably deliver soon. You're carrying
low.

RUTHIE: I dunno . . .

ARLYNE: She always carries low. I used to carry down around my knees
somewhere.

RUTHIE: I got a lot bigger the last two times. I hope you're right. I'd hate
to stay pregnant for thirteen or fourteen *months!* Jesus, that'd be
awful!

PORKER *(Looks at* MARLENA *admiringly):* So this is the cousin, huh?

MARLENA: Yuh. Hi. I'm Marlena . . . Reenie's cousin.

MAUREEN: That's Porker. He's on the bandsaw. I wouldn't walk too close. It could kill you . . .

MARLENA: His saw?

FLORENCE: His *breath!* *(The women laugh.* PORKER *is disgusted)*

MAUREEN: I hope you don't mind Marlena coverin' for me while I'm gone. Keeps the money in the family . . .

FLORENCE: I don't mind . . .

RUTHIE: It's fine, great, no problem . . .

MAUREEN: I checked it out with Markie . . .

FLORENCE: Sure, no problem . . .

JOSIE: Maureen worried you might be p.o.ed about it, 'counta yo'r mum . . .

FLORENCE: Naw, what the hell, huh? If Markie okayed it, huh? 'Sides, my mum's got a million things ta do. She doesn't miss any of this, I can tell you that . . .

JOSIE: Florence's mum worked here nearly thirty straight years.

MARLENA: Ohhh . . .

FLORENCE: Laid her off a couple of months ago. Bloodless fuckin' people run this place . . . *(The work bell rings. Full sound of machines on tape. All work feverishly. Sounds fade under, work continues)*

RUTHIE: Whose side of the family you on?

MARLENA: How's that?

RUTHIE: Maureen's Da's side or the mum's?

MARLENA: Oh, neither. I'm Anthony's cousin . . .

RUTHIE: Oh, yuh, right . . . (SAL *re-enters from office*)

SALLY: Anybody gonna pack fish here, or what? *(To* FLORENCE) Could I see you private. *Now!* (SAL *exits into upstage kitchen,* FLORENCE *follows*)

MARLENA: Boy, he works ya, huh!

MAUREEN: Yuh, well, business is a little off.

JOSIE: Right! Business is a "little off" and Ruthie is a "little pregnant"!

PORKER: Yuh, well, we can turn it around if we hustle! *(While nobody actually answers* PORKER *in words, they have all now begun their day's labor and seriously)*

MAUREEN: You'll be settin' up boxes, like so . . . tight corners, like so . . . (MAUREEN *demonstrates setting up a box.* MARLENA *watches, imitates)*

ARLYNE: They've gotta be tight and trim.

MAUREEN *(Smiles, imitates* ARLYNE): Tight and trim.

RUTHIE: Earl says he heard some Boston Mafioso's interested in buyin' Markie out . . . *(We now see* SAL *and* FLORENCE, *upstairs in office through window. They are arguing. Work continues full tilt)*

JOSIE: They're fighting again.

RUTHIE: They're either fighting or . . . you know . . . doin' the opposite.

JOSIE *(Laughs at* RUTHIE's *euphemism):* How come Earl's gettin' this secret information about Markie and all? (JOSIE *smiles at* MAUREEN *knowingly)*

RUTHIE: When Earl was pickin' up here yesterday, he saw some big muscleman bodyguard Mafioso-type hangin' around Markie's office—fifth day in a row . . .

MAUREEN *(Filling* MARLENA *in):* Earl's Ruthie's husbin. He picks up our garbage every night . . .

RUTHIE *(Interjects, corrects instantly):* Refuse!

MAUREEN *(Smiles, allows herself to be corrected):* Refuse.

RUTHIE: He seen this humongous bodyguard type hangin' around five days straight . . .

PORKER: I seen him myself.

JOSIE: What's this?

PORKER: There's been this muscleman type—like Ruthie says Earl says —a Mafioso bodyguard kind of person . . . hangin' out with Markie . . .

MAUREEN *(To* MARLENA*):* Markie owns the plant . . .

JOSIE: Markie Santuro's got a bodyguard?

PORKER: Nobody said that! I just said this big jamoca's be'n hangin' out in the front office . . .

JOSIE: What the hell does Markie Santuro need a bodyguard for? This place is gettin' weird! *(Through office window, we see* FLORENCE *and* SAL *are again in a passionate embrace)* They stopped fighting. Now they're back to *(imitates* RUTHIE *here)* ". . . you know . . . doin' the opposite", again.

PORKER *(Eyeing the workload):* We'd better keep it movin', huh?

MAUREEN: C'mon, Porker! We musta' already packed more this week than we did last whole month! *(To* MARLENA*)* Everybody's feelin' the pressure . . . under-the-gun kind of thing, about the plant bein' in trouble'n all . . .

ARLYNE: North Shore Fish was a wonderful place to work, years back . . .

MAUREEN *(To* MARLENA*):* Arlyne's worked here years and years . . .

ARLYNE: Used ta be if you got on a line at North Shore Fish, your worries were over . . . *(At this point in the conversation among the workers, labor should be at a fairly brisk pace. It should be obvious that the workers have sped up the normal pace of their normal labor: that there is concern about the possibility of the plant's closing: that all conversation is simultaneous to labor, but at no time does labor ever stop for conversation.* FLORENCE *re-enters, goes down the stairs to her machine)*

FLORENCE: I'm runnin' outta bricks, Martino!

PORKER: What are you givin' me here . . .

FLORENCE: If this place goes under, it ain't gonna be *my* fault, I can tell you that! *(She re-stocks the "line")*

JOSIE: I'm outta cartons, Porker.

PORKER: Sure thing, Jose. *(To* FLORENCE*)* I'm givin' Josie a hand.

ARLYNE: When my mother first started workin' a line here, it was a very respectful occupation . . . kinda like equal almost to a job a school-educated woman might get. Right up there.

FLORENCE: Hurry it up, Martino! If those blocks melt, the fish'll come back ta life and they are very pissed off about what we've be'n doin' to 'em, I can tell ya that!

PORKER: Hold yo'r hosses!

JOSIE: He's helpin' me! *(*SALLY *exits office, hops down stairs, passes through all, inspecting work-progress en route to freezer. He stops at* MARLENA, *checks her box-making)*

SALLY: Excellent! *(He touches* MARLENA's *cheek, affectionately, setting up a jealousy, a competitiveness. Everybody looks at them)* Good looking and smart, too! *(*FLORENCE *looks over, annoyed and hurt.* SALLY *exits into* *freezer; off.* JOSIE *and* PORKER *are working together, downstage. The lights shift to them slightly)*

JOSIE: So how's Rose and your fatha'?

PORKER: Rose is fine. My fatha's fine.

JOSIE: Good weekend?

PORKER: Yuh, we did stuff. How's about yourself, Jose? Good weekend, too?

JOSIE: Well, you know, it ain't the same . . .

PORKER: Cookie's a good guy, really. I'd call this temporary insanity, more'n anything else . . .

JOSIE: Yuh, well, I guess . . .

PORKER: I guess it's toughest on the kids, huh?

JOSIE: Yuh, well, they know he ain't around, that's for sure. They're fightin' all the time . . .

PORKER: Temporary insanity. He'll be back . . .

JOSIE: Why? You hear anything?

PORKER: Me? No.

JOSIE: You seen them?

PORKER: Together?

JOSIE: Yuh, well, yuh . . .

PORKER: Down the Rigger, just the once, last week. And down the Blackburn, a little more recent . . .

JOSIE: Saturday night?

PORKER: Yuh, well, yuh . . .

JOSIE: Everybody's been tellin' me that. If my fatha' hears, I can't be responsible for what he'll do . . .

PORKER: To Cookie?

JOSIE: A' course to Cookie! *(Leans in; confidentially)* You tell him something for me, Porker. You tell him if my fatha' hears, he's gonna cut his balls off and feed 'em to the seagulls . . . *(Pauses; nods)* You tell him that.

PORKER: Anything else?

JOSIE: Yuh. Tell 'im the kids are fine, not to worry. Tell him I'm startin' ta look around myself, ta see, you know, who's available and who's unavailable sort of thing . . .

PORKER: You want me to *say* that?

JOSIE: Are you my friend or what?

PORKER: Come on, Josie, you know I am, since how many years?

JOSIE: So, you'll tell him?

PORKER: Cookie's my friend, too . . .

JOSIE: Who's closer?

PORKER: Well, you know . . . we were a thing, you and me. Me and Cookie were never a thing . . . (JOSIE *is aware of everyone eavesdropping, she makes a "public" private statement)*

JOSIE: When I start doin' it again with other men, you'll be among the first . . .

PORKER: I know that . . . *(Leans in to steal a kiss.* JOSIE *sees everybody is watching; pulls back)*

JOSIE: What are you? Crazy? . . . (FLORENCE *and* RUTHIE *and* MAUREEN *exchange a smile.* MAUREEN *resumes explaining the labor to* MARLENA. *The lights re-widen to include all*)

MAUREEN: It's pretty much like cuttin', only different. *(To* ARLYNE*)* Marlena used ta cut, up Essex.

ARLYNE: I used ta work live fish, myself.

MAUREEN: Smells better workin' live fish.

FLORENCE: Oh, yuh, the batter's a killer . . . I think they put formaldehyde in it, to keep the fish lookin' tasty! (SALLY *re-enters with pallet truck; he arrives at the end of the "line" with crates of already packaged frozen fish, in individual boxes*)

SALLY: Porker! Gimme a hand here, Pork . . . (PORKER *goes to* SALLY. *Together, they stack the individual boxes on the end table*)

PORKER: Where are these goin'?

SALLY: I dunno', back to Japan. Label's all Japanese. Some Chicago broker called it in . . .

PORKER: Crazy goddam thing, huh?

SALLY: What? Sendin' it back ta Japan? Yuh, well, it's business . . . who cares?

MAUREEN: See how Porker cuts those big blocks down into bricks? The machine is shaping them fish-like and Floey breads them . . . you and me set up the boxes, then Ruth and Arlyne box 'em . . . and Josie wraps and that's it . . .

MARLENA: How come they gotta shape 'em so they're fishlike?

MAUREEN: So they look like fish. You wouldn't wanna eat a fish that looked like a brick, would ya?

MARLENA: Yuh, but if they're already fish, how come they're not already *shaped* like fish?

MAUREEN: 'Cause they're really about a million fish all smashed together . . .

FLORENCE: It's more like a family of fish than just a fish. *(Holds up slab of fish)* See, look close. Piece of a middle, piece of a neck, another piece of middle, little tail . . .

MARLENA: Wow, is that ever *gross!*

FLORENCE: It's nothin' compared to the breading . . .

MARLENA: Is the fish local?

FLORENCE: God, no. The fish is from Boston, mostly . . .

MARLENA: That's where they catch it?

FLORENCE: That's where they buy it. They buy it in auctions, like . . . already frozen. Some of it's Canadian, some of it's Japanese. It comes from all over.

MAUREEN: All the *live* fish is local . . .

MARLENA: Oh, yuh, I know that . . .

PORKER: See these blocks we're cutting up. They're from Japan, 6,000 miles away. All we're doing is cutting them up, spraying a little batter on them and sending them right back to Japan: 12,000 miles round trip. Don't ask me. I only work here.

MARLENA: No kidding? That is *weird* . . .

FLORENCE: Your cousin puts notes in the far-away stuff . . .

MAUREEN: . . . Yuh, well, I do. So what? *(The women laugh at* MAUREEN *affectionately.* MAUREEN *checks to see if* SALLY *is listening)* Sometimes, if stuff is goin' to, you know, Japan or Australia, someplace really *far,* I like to toss in a couple of words. Nothin' too much . . . maybe "Hi, I'm Maureen Vega from Gloucester, Mass., U.S. of A. I'm thirty-one and I like Sylvia Plath and summers." That kind of thing. *(The women continue their labor as they chat. The fish-bricks are moved along to the various stations and the fish is shaped, breaded, wrapped, packed and labeled. Unnoticed at first, at the farthest end of the room,* CATHERINE SHIMMA *enters. She wears a coat, collar up, high-heeled shoes. She is extremely attractive, far more worldly-looking than the other women. She moves to center, pauses; watches)*

ARLYNE: I can remember workin' here some years back when we were still cuttin' live fish, we used ta have two three four Japs standin' lookin' right over our shoulders, makin' bids right then and there, you know, against each other and all . . .

MAUREEN: They are great fish-eaters, the Japanese.

ARLYNE: Oh, you don't have to tell me! I've seen Japs with my own eyes: they have a true respect for fish . . . I wish they didn't bomb Pearl Harbor, but, they must have had their reasons. That's all I'm going to tell ya's . . .

SALLY *(Re-enters with hand-truck; sees* SHIMMA*)*: Can I help you?

SHIMMA: I'm looking for Salvatore Morella.

FLORENCE *(In childish schoolgirl sing-song chant)*: Salll-vaaah-torrr . . . Close-the-doorrrr!

SALLY *(To* FLORENCE*)*: What are you? Demented? *(To* SHIMMA*)* I'm him . . . he . . . this is me: Sal Morella . . . Plant Manager . . .

FLORENCE *(Injects)*: Sal Mo*nilla* . . . the disease!

SALLY: . . . Who are you?

SHIMMA: Catherine Shimma . . .

SALLY: Oh, well, *good.* (SALLY *flashes look of anger at* FLORENCE. *Everyone has stopped work and is staring at* SALLY *and* FLORENCE *and* SHIMMA, *openly.* SALLY *flashes angry looks to all. He then turns again to* SHIMMA, *smiling boyishly)* Let's go up the front office, and meet Markie. He's the owner. Then I'll show you your kitchen . . . (SHIMMA *walks directly to the breading vat, allows breading to flow on to her finger. She tastes the breading. Then she picks up a wedge of frozen fish and breaks it into its component pieces: a few sections of fish-necks, etc. She tosses pieces into tray. Then she looks at* SALLY; *nods.* SALLY *leads her off; she follows)* This way . . .

SHIMMA: After you . . .

SALLY: No, this way . . . After you . . .

SHIMMA: No. You first. *(There is a moment of silence)* Go. (SALLY *obeys; leads the way off. They exit. Everyone stares after them; astonished)*

FLORENCE: She look like anybody?

PORKER: Everybody looks like somebody . . .

FLORENCE: I know she looks like *some*body, wiseass. I mean, does she look like anybody we know?

PORKER: Not ta me . . . *(Shrugs)* She looks kinda', I dunno', so-phisticated.

FLORENCE: I dunno' . . . She's got somethin' familiar goin'.

JOSIE: She looks like me, before I discovered the blueberry muffins down the Glass Sailboat. Thinnish, small knockers. *(She stacks a supply of empty boxes in front of her; continues talking as she continues wrapping frozen breaded fish)* I dunno' why I bother to put the muffins in my mouth. I oughta just apply them directly to my hips . . .

ARLYNE *(As she labors):* You have a nice shape, Josie . . .

JOSIE: Yuh, right, so did last year's Dodge Vans. They had a nice shape, too!

MAUREEN: You read that book about the guy who ran Dodge? What's'name . . . funny name . . . "Coke-head," somethin' odd like that . . .

JOSIE: Sounds great.

MAUREEN: No, it was. Different. Interestin', really. All about how they spied on him and all. Made you think.

JOSIE: I'll have to pick it up and read it. *(They labor a while. Suddenly,* MAUREEN *calls out)*

MAUREEN: Iacocca!

PORKER: What's with her?

MAUREEN: Name of a book.

PORKER: What kind of book?

JOSIE: Squarish, paper pages, with printing all over 'em . . .

PORKER: I love a good joke. I wish somebody would tell me one.

FLORENCE: You *are* one! C'mon, Martino, I'm outta batter!

MAUREEN: Fantastic thing, big business, really . . . (PORKER *brings new supply of batter to* FLORENCE)

PORKER: What are you doin'? Throwing it on the floor?

FLORENCE: When I work, I work . . . when I party, I party . . . 'cause, that's the kinda guy I am . . . *(She playacts being a man: she scratches her crotch and pretends to spit on the floor)*

MAUREEN: Iacocca took Dodge and turned it around . . .

FLORENCE: Whose Dodge?

MAUREEN: The whole company. It was goin' outta business. He put it back into profits, almost by himself . . .

FLORENCE: He know anything about the fish-business? Maybe we can set him up here, huh? *(Laughs.* PORKER *brings her new supply of batter)*

PORKER: We got no problems here so long as we get the product out. *(Everyone labors more enthusiastically, somehow inspired by Lee Iacocca)*

ARLYNE: North Shore Fish has seen good times and bad times. We survive 'em both.

RUTHIE: Where were you born?

MARLENA: Me? (RUTHIE *nods)* Up Newburyport . . . *(Pauses)* We moved down Burlington, when I was nine, but soon as I was old enough to do it on my own, I moved back on the water.

ARLYNE: Oh, I agree! When you're born on the water, you never can live anyplace else!

RUTHIE: My mother and fatha' broke up over water.

ARLYNE: That wasn't the only reason, but, it was *one* of 'em.

RUTHIE: That's the way you always told it to *me!*

ARLYNE: Well, her father was livin' with, you know, another woman and all . . .

RUTHIE: He was workin' up Needham . . .

ARLYNE: He took a place up near his plant and wanted me to move up with him. I couldn't do it . . . I was six months pregnant with Ruthie . . .

RUTHIE: My grandmother and grandfather and aunts and all were in town . . .

ARLYNE: . . . My mother and fatha' were here in Gloucester . . . my sisters, too. I couldn't just pick up and leave all that! Kids, too . . .

(JOSIE, FLORENCE *and* RUTHIE *recite* ARLYNE's *oft-spoken thoughts with her, in unison, lovingly.* ARLYNE *never notices*)

RUTHIE: His job wasn't permanent.

ARLYNE: His job wasn't permanent . . .

FLORENCE: She commuted up weekends.

ARLYNE: I commuted up weekends . . .

JOSIE: Weekends!

ARLYNE: He wanted me there full-time . . .

FLORENCE: He wanted her there full-time.

ARLYNE: He took another woman . . .

RUTHIE: Weekends . . .

JOSIE: Mondays through Fridays . . .

ARLYNE: Two-timer! They're all alike!

FLORENCE: They're all alike!

JOSIE: At least, I'm still in Gloucester, on the water.

ARLYNE: At least I'm still in Gloucester, on the water . . . *(There is a short silence)*

RUTHIE: We live out on the Fort . . .

MAUREEN: Ruthie and Earl live upstairs, over Arlyne.

MARLENA: Can you see the water?

RUTHIE: Oh, God, no! We face in, over the freezer plant. But, we can drive over to Good Harbor Beach in—what?—ten minutes. A' course, you gotta go at *night!*

MAUREEN: Traffic's wicked, summah'time . . . during beach hours . . .

FLORENCE: I tried to get there, day before yesterday, on our lunch break . . .

MAUREEN *(Smiles):* I remember.

FLORENCE: I never fuckin' made it . . . *(Politely)* Sorry, Arlyne . . .

ARLYNE: I don't mind. I know you're angry.

FLORENCE: Two million summah people, one to a car. I dunno why the hell they don't just *team up?* I mean, *none* of us got there! We just sat on Bass Avenue maybe thirty-five minutes I turned around. Took shit from Markie for bein' late comin' back, too . . .

MAUREEN: We all ask, "How's the beach?" 'cause we all figure Floey's beet-red from laying out in the sun. A' course she's beet-red with a fever and all from sittin' in her car in traffic on Bass Ave! (SALLY *and* SHIMMA *exit front office and enter kitchen, closing door behind them.* SALLY *makes "Keep it down" signal to all before closing door.* PORKER *slides upstage, plants himself under window to kitchen in order to spy on* SALLY *and* SHIMMA *inside)*

FLORENCE: This new one ain't gonna buy his greaseball charm, I can tell ya's all *that!*

MAUREEN: If our product's good, what's the diff? She's not inspectin' Sal, she's inspectin' product, right?

FLORENCE: Yuh, so, if that's true, what's he tryin' ta get into her pants for? Answer me that?

RUTHIE: Nice talk, huh?

FLORENCE: Yuh, well, I'm just not up for bein' outta work all next year, that's all . . .

PORKER: Come on, Florence. Sal can handle this. I'm gonna watch closer. (PORKER *moves upstage, spies on* SALLY)

MARLENA: What's she sayin', Maureen?

MAUREEN: Florence is a little negative, on accounta this and that.

MARLENA: Which and what?

FLORENCE: I heard that, Reenie. I ain't a "little negative." I am *very fucking negative!* Look around you! You see how empty it is here? This place looks like a fortune cookie, after somebody took the message! There's nobody here, Reenie! This is a dead place. The fish business has had it! *Absolutely definitely had it!*

ARLYNE: Florence Marie Rizzo, you close that mouth!

FLORENCE (*Sincerely, childlike*): Sorry, Arlyne . . .

ARLYNE: What if your mother heard you . . . ?

FLORENCE: I know . . .

ARLYNE: Businesses have ups and downs.

FLORENCE: It's true.

ARLYNE: The fish business just has fewer ups and more downs, that's all . . .

FLORENCE: I suppose . . .

ARLYNE: We are fish people. We are doing what we were born to do . . .

FLORENCE: I don't think that . . . (*thinks better of it*) I guess . . . (FLORENCE *and* RUTHIE *and* ARLYNE, *in unison, complete* ARLYNE's *oft-spoken thoughts*)

ARLYNE & OTHERS: "Negative criticism will only bring the very thing you dread right down onto your head . . ." (FLORENCE *smiles at* RUTHIE *gratefully*)

ARLYNE: That's what my mother used ta say ta me, and she was right. That's all I'm gonna tell ya's . . . (RUTHIE *and* FLORENCE *exchange another conspiratorial glance and smile)* She was a smart woman, my mother. We worked together . . .

ARLYNE: . . . elbow to elbow, side by . . .

ALL OTHERS: . . . elbow to elbow, side by side . . .

ARLYNE *(Alone):* It's a wonderful thing when you can earn your livin' workin' side-by-side with people who care about you . . .

FLORENCE: I know . . . (FLORENCE *moves upstage with empty stock-tray, which she will replace with full stock-tray)*

ARLYNE: And it's a wonderful thing to live your life overlookin' the water.

MARLENA: Oh, I agree. There's something so special about livin' on the water . . .

RUTHIE: Definitely! The water gets in yo'r blood . . .

MARLENA: . . . takin' walks on the shore . . .

FLORENCE: My fatha' used ta be able ta name all the flowers over Braces' Cove . . . dropwort shoots and so forth . . . angelica and stuff. You'd think you were hearin' some kind of Ha'vid professor, honest ta God! *(We see* SALLY *above in office touch* SHIMMA's *cheek.* FLORENCE *sees as well.* SHIMMA *pulls back, angrily)* Ah shit . . .

RUTHIE: That's the thing: knowing you know everything about the ocean, because you've lived your life on it . . . naming all the fish right. That sorta thing . . .

MAUREEN: I like thinkin' about what's out there . . . across from us . . .

JOSIE: I got enough trouble thinkin' about what's right under my nose . . . *(Eats a Snickers bar)* Oh God, I ate it! I was gonna save that for afta lunch!

MAUREEN: You know, if you go straight out from here across the northern part of England, there isn't a single mountain range between us and the Ural Mountains in Russia . . .

MARLENA: Is that right?   JOSIE: No kidding?

MAUREEN: If you could blow hard enough, you could blow out somebody's birthday candles in Russia, and that is a fact . . . (SHIMMA *is clearly annoyed with* SALLY)

PORKER: I think they're fighting . . .

FLORENCE: You say something?

PORKER: I think Sally's yellin' at the new inspector . . . *(They all turn and look.* SALLY *storms out of the kitchen, slamming the door. He runs down the stairs. Each worker busies herself with her labor.* SALLY *moves directly to the refrigerator, about to exit. He stops, thinks better of it; talks)*

SALLY: I want every fifth fillette weighed. I want no light product. And check the batter. I want no thick breading. If this bull-dyke wants to play it by the rules, I say fine! I say we give her perfect product and let her break her own dyke balls and if anybody here says different, let them bread their own ass too thick and find work elsewhere, 'cause this plant is not goin' under! *(And with that,* SALLY *exits into the freezer. After a pause, he re-enters)* Porker, I want sixty crates of the Howard Johnson's out and ready to rewrap with Stop'n'Shop!

PORKER: That order ain't due for three and a half weeks . . .

SALLY: I give *no shit!* The second that vicious mother of a bitch rejects one miserable underweight or triple-breaded fillette, we go off the fresh-frozen and right the fuck on to re-wraps. *Bang! (Punches crate, violently)* I got Stop'n'Shop re-wraps, I got Jap re-wraps, I got next year's Daitch-*Shopwell* re-wraps. I do not give a shit. Is this okay?

PORKER: It's okay.

RUTHIE: It's okay.

MAUREEN: Okay . . .   JOSIE: Okay . . .

SALLY: I apologize sincerely for my filthy mouth, Arlyne, but as you can see, I am overwrought . . .

ARLYNE: That's no excuse . . .

SALLY: Arlyne!

ARLYNE: "A filthy mouth speaks the thought of a filthy mind!"

SALLY *(Head down, he "mouths" precise sentence with* ARLYNE *in unison):* ". . . of a filthy mind . . ." *(He goes to* ARLYNE*)* Arlyne, we have trouble here! I think I have to warn nobody. I think you can see from the three closed-down lines and the many laid-off close friends and loved ones, this plant is on no solid ground and should she fuck us over, we could go down if not under. *(He spots* SHIMMA *walking down staircase from her office)* Here she comes! *(He runs into freezer.* SHIMMA *walks to "line", carrying a tray, wordlessly. She smiles at everyone officiously. She places six samples of breaded fish on her tray.* SHIMMA *purposefully exits the "line" area, and re-enters her kitchen.* SALLY *peeks out from behind the freezer door)* What I smell here is not good . . . Porker, come here . . . *(To* PORKER*)* I'm goin' in to Markie. Any kind of move at all: report. You follow me?

PORKER: Yuh, sure . . .

SALLY: What'd I say?

PORKER: I got you . . .

SALLY: *What'd I say?*

PORKER: I'll get you . . .

SALLY: Martino, I am in no fucking *mood!*

PORKER: You're in with Markie. If she makes a move, I'll come get you . . .

SALLY: No, this is exactly what I do not want! *(Moves to* PORKER) You know Markie's position here, which I am laboring to change, yes?

PORKER: I have a good idea, yuh . . .

SALLY: What the fuck do you mean "I have a good idea, yuh"? I *told* you exactly what his position is on this, right?

PORKER *(Looks around; worried):* Yuh, well, shhh, yuh, okay, Sal . . .

SALLY: If she makes a negative move or a rejection-like move involving product, this is what you come get me for . . . but don't . . .

PORKER *(Finishes the sentence):* . . . let on to Markie!

SALLY: *Exact! (He realizes that everyone stands, staring)* Hello? Are you being paid to work, or is this the company clambake, huh, people? Thannnkk youuuuu! *(Everybody starts working again.* SALLY *looks up at* SHIMMA, *through window. He then looks over at* PORKER; *exits. Through the window, we can see* SHIMMA, *in her office/kitchen, cooking the frozen fish in a microwave oven. She opens the oven, takes out a filet of cooked fish, replaces it with a filet of frozen fish, shuts oven, hits "ON" switch. She weighs cooked fish. She tastes cooked fish, chews it awhile, spits what has been in her mouth into a plastic-bag-lined garbage container; begins to write a report)*

MARLENA: Look, Reenie, she's eating our fish!

MAUREEN: That's how they do the test: they cook it up and taste it . . .

MARLENA: Hey! She spit it out!

JOSIE: They always spit it out . . . They taste maybe eighty, ninety pieces of fish a day. Imagine what they'd weigh if they didn't spit it out? I never spit it out. I swallow everything.

PORKER: *Everything?*

JOSIE: You're an embarrassment to the Italian race, you know that? *[If actor playing* PORKER *is fat,* JOSIE's *line changes to "You're an embarrassment to fat people! You know that?"]*

MARLENA: What if she rejects it . . . the fish?

RUTHIE: We have to throw out the batch . . .

ARLYNE: . . . Clean the breader, make new batter . . .

JOSIE: That's what Dotty did . . .

ARLYNE: Poor soul . . .

JOSIE: She was rejecting everything at the end . . .

MARLENA: Who's Dotty?

FLORENCE: Dorothy Fabiano. She was Government inspector here for seven years, nearly eight . . .

MARLENA: She quit?

MAUREEN: She was the one I was tellin' you about . . .

MARLENA: Oh . . .

FLORENCE: She died . . . she was having a serious thing with Sal for the last four years or so . . .

JOSIE: Then, Sal got interested elsewhere . . .

FLORENCE: What's this, you?

JOSIE: Just talkin' . . .

RUTHIE: Sal's married . . . and he got Dot pregnant . . .

MARLENA: Reenie was tellin' me . . .

FLORENCE: The way people around here see it, Sal was the definite cause of Dot's dyin' . . .

ARLYNE *(Shocked):* Florence Marie Rizzo, I am not going to let you incriminate Sal so viciously. We are all Catholics here, mostly, and this sort of incrimination is hardly the way we were taught!

FLORENCE: I'm entitled to my opinions, Arlyne. Even though you're Ruthie's mother, I am . . . (PORKER *and* FLORENCE *exchange a glance.* PORKER *shakes his head in disgust.* FLORENCE *returns to her battering)* I'll stay out of it . . .

JOSIE: For the last couple of months or so, Dotty'd wait 'til we get set up with a fresh batch of batter, then she'd come out, get a fish, cook it, shake her head, come out and put her thumb down. No words, nothin', just her thumb down. Sally used ta fuckin' *burn* . . . *(Laughs)* Sorry, Arlyne . . .

ARLYNE: I know it's something that angers us all . . . *(Pauses)* Dorothy was a lovely, lovely, lovely girl . . . local, too. We all knew her family . . . motha', two brothers, sis'tah. Her sistah's teachin' up at O'Malley School right today. Very lovely family, honest ta God . . .

PORKER: She's comin' out! (SHIMMA *enters; looks about; speaks to* PORKER)

SHIMMA: Where is he?

PORKER: Front office.

SHIMMA: Get him. (PORKER *pauses a moment; then runs to door to* MARKIE'S *office; exits.* SHIMMA *looks at* FLORENCE *and others)* Beautiful day out there. Beach weather. Shame to be trapped inside . . .

JOSIE: Ain't I seen you drivin' around town with the "GOLF" license plate?

SHIMMA: Oh, yuh, that's me, yuh . . .

FLORENCE: What's this? You live local or something?

SHIMMA: Oh, no. I live up Woburn.

FLORENCE: Oh, yuh? Woob'in? *(To all; sarcastically)* Figures.

SHIMMA: Why? You got somethin' against Woburn?

FLORENCE: Me? Naw. So long as I don't hav'ta drink the water . . .

JOSIE: She's got a plate with "GOLF" on it.

SHIMMA: I do, yuh . . .

MAUREEN: There's a blue Duster out in the lot with "GOLF" on it!

JOSIE: That's *her.*

SHIMMA: That's me.

MAUREEN: You play golf?

SHIMMA: Me? Uh uh. It's my husbin's plate. It's mine, now, but, it *was* his . . .

FLORENCE: Don't I know you?

RUTHIE: *What?*

FLORENCE: I'm not talkin' to *you,* Ruthie, I'm talkin' to the new inspector: her. *(Steps toward* SHIMMA*)* You look wicked familiar to me.

SHIMMA: We met. My husbin's got cousins who are yo'r husbin's cousins. He told me ta ask after you when I sta'hted out this mornin' . . .

FLORENCE: Is that a fact?

RUTHIE: She's Floey's cousin! See? You never know . . .

JOSIE: You *always* know! Everybody's related to everybody else around these parts. We're even cousins, distant, right, Arlyne?

ARLYNE: I don't think so . . .

JOSIE: Aren't you related to the Asaroes?

ARLYNE: No, that's Florence.

FLORENCE: That's me, cupie doll.

JOSIE: If there's anything I hate more than bein' fat, it's bein' *wrong!* *(To* SHIMMA*)* So, how come you got "GOLF" on your plate? Yo'r husbin some kinda big golfer?

SHIMMA: My husbin? Uh uh. He's never played any golf . . . *(There is a pause)* I got him a vanity plate for his birthday and it came through with "GOLF" on it . . .

JOSIE: You didn't ask for "GOLF"?

SHIMMA: Not really. There was a buncha spaces for choices . . . I asked for "Billy" first, on accounta that's his name; then "Bill"; then "Willy" . . . his brother used ta call him "Willy" . . . but, then, there was this fourth empty space for a choice. I shoulda thought ta put down "William," but nobody ever calls him that and I guess I forgot that was in the runnin', even. I used ta drive by this golf club every day when I worked over Wakefield . . .

RUTHIE: Bear Hill . . .

SHIMMA: That's the one, yuh. I always thought it would be really—I dunno—sophisticated if he took up golf, so, I just wrote it in the empty space. I guess "Billy," "Bill" and "Willy" were taken and when the plate came through I got fuckin' "GOLF"! *(She laughs embarrassedly)*

MAUREEN: He doesn't *ever* play golf, your husbin?

SHIMMA: Naw, never, no sports at all. He used ta bowl before I met him . . .

JOSIE: Didn't he get pissed off, when you gave 'im the plate?

SHIMMA: Oh, yuh, *wick'id!* That's why *I'm* drivin' the car. He won't *touch* the thing! (SALLY *runs into room, followed by* PORKER. SALLY *doesn't see* SHIMMA *at first, as she is among the workers*)

SALLY: *Where is this dyke?*

PORKER *(Sees):* Oh, my God . . .

SALLY *(Sees. His attitude changes entirely. He smiles seductively):* Alfred came got me. You sent him? *(Motions to* PORKER*)* Him. (SHIMMA *stares wordlessly at* SALLY) So? What's up? (SALLY *smiles his most boyish smile at* SHIMMA)

FLORENCE *(Disgusted):* Jesus! (SHIMMA *walks silently into her kitchen; leaves door open.* SALLY *looks around at the women*)

SALLY: What gives? What were you jawin' about with her? *(He looks them over, one by one)* We got a plant ta protect here, ya know, so's don't any of ya's play it too *sma'ht,* if you're able ta get my point . . .

FLORENCE: A good couple'a us have *had* your point, Salvatore! It don't look like it's gonna work with this one! *(Motions toward* SHIMMA*)* You might hav'ta use yo'r *brain* for change, ladykiller.

(SALLY *walks to* FLORENCE, *slowly, angrily. He stares at her a moment, silently, then turns, moves up staircase to kitchen, tentatively. He then enters kitchen, closing door behind him. We can now see* SHIMMA *and* SALLY *in conversation.* PORKER *moves to* FLORENCE, *subtly; silently. When next to her, he speaks quietly*)

PORKER: What's the matter with you?

FLORENCE *(Choking back anger):* Fuck off . . .

PORKER: You lookin' to get smacked, or what?

FLORENCE *(Angrily):* Leave me alone . . . *(Turns upstage; moves off from others, alone. She paces; angrily; enraged)*

JOSIE: What'd you say to her, Porker?

PORKER: Oh, yuh, sure . . . *me!*

ARLYNE: Just leave her be. Let her collect herself . . . that's the best.

RUTHIE: It's embarrassing when you cry . . .

ARLYNE: It's better to stand off, alone, get a grip . . .

RUTHIE: Collect yo'rself . . . *(Pauses;* FLORENCE *paces like a caged cat upstage)* Get a grip . . . *(Pauses;* FLORENCE *continues to pace)* Stand off, alone . . . it's embarrassing when you cry . . . (MARLENA *looks to* MAUREEN *for an explanation.* MAUREEN *speaks to* MARLENA *quietly, but, certainly not discreetly)*

MAUREEN: Florence and Sally there are on-again/off-again kind of thing . . .

MARLENA: Oh, yuh? Her, too?

JOSIE: Italian men are the worst . . .

MAUREEN: Italians, Portegees, Irish and English: the worst!

RUTHIE: I'd say Jews were the best.

JOSIE: You've never *seen* a Jew!

RUTHIE: I know Mr. Linsky . . .

JOSIE: I mean a young Jew: a Jew under thirty . . .

RUTHIE: Oh, no, I don't know anybody like that.

JOSIE *(Smiles):* Mr. Linsky must be seventy-five . . .

ARLYNE: *Sixty*-five . . .

MAUREEN: Everybody's nice when they hit sixty-five. They get kinda *beaten into it!*

ARLYNE: I wouldn't say Linsky's so nice . . . *(They all look at* ARLYNE*)* I could tell you a couple a' stories about Linsky! *(They all smile, enjoying their game)*

RUTHIE *(The widest smile of all):* She's still mad at him over something.

ARLYNE: It ain't money, neither!

RUTHIE: She went out with him once . . .

ARLYNE: I wouldn't get too close to Jews if I were you!

RUTHIE: I always bring it up ta get her goat . . .

ARLYNE: Jews are loose with their hands! That's all I'm gonna tell ya's . . .

RUTHIE *(Giggles):* Never fails me . . .

ARLYNE: They can sweet-talk you, all right, but when push comes to shove, stay clear of Jews. That's all I'm gonna tell ya's . . .

RUTHIE *(Imitating her mother's voice):* They can break yo'r heart, too . . .

ARLYNE *(Exact same voice, but, tearfully):* They can break yo'r heart, too . . .

RUTHIE *(Giggles):* Never fails me! (SALLY *and* SHIMMA *argue, in kitchen, upstairs.* FLORENCE *paces away, upstage, alone. She is extremely upset. She watches* SALLY *and* SHIMMA, *through kitchen's window-wall, above)*

JOSIE: So that rules out Jews, Italians, Portegees, Irish, English . . . what's left?

MAUREEN: Frenchmen.

MARLENA: Frenchmen?! You soft in the head? Frenchmen'll fuck *lobsters* if you hold their claws open! Frenchmen are the *worst!*

MAUREEN: How about Frenchmen from Montreal or from up Vermont? How do you feel on *them?*

MARLENA: That's what I'm *tellin'* ya's! *(Pauses)* We had a shed built once. Six Frenchmen, all brothers. *(Pauses)* My husband's upstairs, shavin'. One of the Frenchmen asks me if he can use the downstairs toilet. Another one wants a glass of water. He has his own *glass!*—(I shoulda known something funny was comin', right?)—I'm in my housecoat still, 'counta it's maybe 6:30, 6:40 . . .

RUTHIE: In the mornin'?

MARLENA: A' course in the mornin'! My husband only shaves in the mornin'! *(Takes a breath)* The one with his own glass comes up behind me and like presses himself against me. The older one—with the muscle-shirt—he presses himself against me, in front, kisses me. The younger one reaches under and up, around front . . .

MAUREEN *(Interjects):* You are *kidding* with this!

MARLENA: . . . and I, of course, cannot make a *peep* . . .

MAUREEN: . . . 'cause a' Frank . . .

MARLENA: . . . 'cause my husband's upstairs, shavin', not thirty feet away. *(Pauses; then smugly)* So, you wanna tell me about Frenchmen? *(There is a long astonished pause.* PORKER *is first to break the silence)*

PORKER: So what did you do? *(They all look at* PORKER, *as if surprised by his participation)*

MARLENA: I didn't know he was listenin' . . .

JOSIE: Jesus, Porker, you got no *shame?* *(To* MARLENA) Porker's a tell-me-a-story freak.

PORKER: I wasn't listenin' . . . *(To* MARLENA) I wasn't listenin' . . . *(To all)* We need more bricks! (PORKER *goes to saw, saws down blocks into smaller brick shapes. The women continue their labor; wordlessly. After a while,* MAUREEN *talks to* MARLENA)

MAUREEN: You ever tell Frank? *(We become aware again of* FLORENCE *upstage, stopped now watching* SALLY *and* SHIMMA *in kitchen-office through window.* SALLY *touches* SHIMMA'*s cheek again.* SHIMMA *slaps* SALLY'*s hand)*

MARLENA: You kiddin' me? I'd hav'ta have been lookin' to get beat black and blue. *(There is another flurry of wordless work.* JOSIE *breaks through)*

JOSIE: So what did they do? *(*MARLENA *looks at* JOSIE*)* The Frenchmen . . .

ARLYNE: Josephine!

RUTHIE: Jees, Josie . . .

JOSIE: *Why?* Am I the only one interested?

MARLENA: They just kinda groped around for a while and then they left . . .

JOSIE: That's it?   RUTHIE: That's all?

*(*MARLENA *shrugs, shows her palms.* PORKER *cannot resist a question)*

PORKER: Did you pay 'em? *(*MARLENA *and all look at* PORKER*. He explains quickly)* For the shed . . .

JOSIE: What is *with* you, Porker?

PORKER: It's just a question, that's all! I'm just interested! *(*MARLENA *is done with her story, done talking on the subject.* PORKER *shrugs, shows his palms, sets stack of bricks in front of* FLORENCE *at breading machine.* FLORENCE *is back at work, but still not in commune with the others)*

JOSIE: Porker forgets from time to time. He thinks he's one of *us.*

MAUREEN: They say that dogs do that. Somebody dies in a house, the dog gets depressed. Divorce, too, does the same thing. I read that . . .

(SALLY *storms out of the kitchen, swaggers down staircase. He is in a rage*)

SALLY: Burn the crop! Dump it all! I don't want no arguments here, just dump the whole batch! Porker, I want all the HoJo crates . . . all of 'em . . . (*Screams at* PORKER) *MOVE!* (*To* ARLYNE) Get the Stop'n'Shop labels, Arlyne, and I want ya's all ta hear this: the only way this plant's stayin' open is if we can cover our asses for this loss and the losses for the last four months and even then I'm promisin' nobody nothin' . . . except for that leaky douche-bag, who I am promisin' that I will process no fish whatsoever, if that's the way she wants it. I will find orders on re–wraps and re–wraps only. And if she wants ta turn down our re–wraps, she can sue the Federal Inspector who approved 'em in their last wrap, 'cause they are all approved, all registered, and I don't care if we spend the rest of our lives takin' Howard fucking Johnson labels offa fish and puttin' Stop'n'fuckin' Shop labels *onta* fish . . . if that's what she's lookin' for, that's what she's gonna find . . . 'cause I say "Fuck the dyke!" . . . and what I say *goes!* (*Screams at* PORKER) *MOVE!* (*To all*) You all heard me: dump the product, clean the breader. I ain't havin' her fault us on no fuckin' cleanliness . . .

ARLYNE: Is she going to test you on *language,* Salvatore . . .

SALLY: Oh, gimme a fffff . . . a *break,* Arlyne, will ya! You *see* what I'm goin' through here?

ARLYNE: This is not an excuse!

SALLY: Ar*lyyyyyynnnnne!*

ARLYNE: Out of memory for your mother . . .

SALLY (*To* RUTHIE. *He knows he's beaten*): Will you talk to her?

RUTHIE: Just say you're sorry. What's the big deal?

SALLY (*Angrily*): For the love of Christ, Ruthie, I . . . *Okay!* All right! Fine! (*Sweetly, head down; like a four-year-old boy*) Arlyne, I'm sorry I swore so much. Okay?

ARLYNE: I understand there's a terrible problem, but does foul language help anything . . .

SALLY: No, but it helps *me!* It makes me feel a little better.

ARLYNE: Do you work alone?

SALLY *(Still a boy):* No . . . *(Raises his head and attitude, slightly)* Come *onn,* Arlyne, we are in trouble here!

ARLYNE: *Salvatore!*

SALLY *(Head down again):* Okay, okay. I said I was sorry. *(To* RUTHIE*)* Tell her! Didn't you hear me tell her I was sorry? Didn't I?

ARLYNE: I accept. (ARLYNE *offers her cheek for* SAL *to kiss. He does, head still down.* ARLYNE *kisses* SAL's *cheek. All is forgiven)*

SALLY *(Regains the old manly control):* Get set up . . . all a'ya's!

JOSIE: Good for you, Arlyne.

RUTHIE: My motha' is *tough!*

ARLYNE: You have to stand your ground. You have to stand up to them. You can't let them get an edge.

RUTHIE: She's known him since the crib. (SALLY *is humiliated. He storms into locker area, where* FLORENCE *stands, smoking a cigarette)*

SALLY: Get out here and pull your part of the load! What da ya think you are: *special?* I told ya ta lay offa me today, didn't I? I told you I had enough pressure on my head without your bullshit, didn't I? But could you back off? Nooooo! Could you give me a break for even *one* measly day? Noooooooooo. And I'm s'pose'ta take you serious when you ask me ta think about what you're askin' me ta think about? What are you: off yo'r gourd? (SALLY *storms off, to freezer, screaming for* PORKER) Yo, Martino! You partying in there? What's up? (SALLY *enters freezer, slamming door closed behind him. All eyes on* FLORENCE, *who exits locker area and moves to "line." Suddenly,* FLORENCE *starts flinging frozen fish sticks about the room furiously, in a rage. Some of the fish sticks clunk against the kitchen-office window, causing* SHIMMA *to stand and look down, frightened)*

FLORENCE: I've had it! I have fucking *had it!!!*

JOSIE: Hey, Floey . . .

FLORENCE *(Dumps breading onto the floor, making a horrendous, disgusting mess):* Fucking men!

MAUREEN: Hey, Flo, come onnn . . .

ARLYNE: Florence . . .

RUTHIE: Floey, heyyy . . . (FLORENCE *knocks one of the tables over.* PORKER *and* SALLY *enter, pushing handtrucks with crates of already wrapped/labeled frozen fish. They see* FLORENCE *and stop in their tracks)*

SALLY: You'd better do something . . .

PORKER: Me? Shitt . . . (PORKER *runs to* FLORENCE *and she beans him with a breaded frozen fish brick)* Heyy, you tryin' ta kill me, or what?

FLORENCE: LEAVE . . . ME . . . ALONE! (FLORENCE *paces, trapped, caged)*

SALLY: What the hell gives here? Did you do this, Rizzo?

FLORENCE *(To* PORKER, *about* SALLY*):* Just keep him the fuck away from me!

PORKER: Just let her calm down a little, Sal . . . (SALLY *cannot believe his eyes; rages at* FLORENCE*)*

SALLY: What are you? *Warped?* With a new inspector around? You make this mess? What are you? Flipped out? You need a strait jacket, or what? You want me ta call down ta Danvers . . . have 'em bring the nut-wagon over? Or what? (FLORENCE *charges at* SALLY, *slapping him, scratching him, kicking him.* SALLY *does nothing offensively. He ducks*

*her punches, absorbs her slaps, twists out from under her scratches,
dances away from her kicks. For him, it is all accomplished quite
easily. He giggles and guffaws, childishly, cruelly)*

FLORENCE: I'll kill you . . . I'll kill you . . .

SALLY: Look at her! Look at this one! What? You wanna kick me? You
wanna scratch my eyes out? C'mon, c'monnn . . . what's yo'r
trouble, huh? Come onnn, dooo ittt . . .

ALL OTHERS. *(Call to them)*:
—Hey, Floey . . .
—Knock it off, you two . . .
—Grab Florence . . .
—Poor kid . . .
—Do somethin', Porker!
—Grab her, Porker!

FLORENCE *(Screams, suddenly)*: Fuckin' coward . . . hitting women
. . . beatin' women . . . murderer . . . everybody knows . . .
everybody knows . . . murderer! *(During the fight,* SHIMMA *has
quietly exited the kitchen and entered the main work area, standing
upstage, watching.* SALLY *stops his giggling on* FLORENCE's *final
"Murderer!" and grabs the now-hysterical* FLORENCE *by the throat with
his left hand and he raises his right hand, poised to strike* FLORENCE.
PORKER *screams at* SALLY)

PORKER: *Hold it, Sal! HOLD IT!*

SALLY: What, Martino, what? You don't want me ta hit your girlfriend?
You don't think I should make over her face? What?

PORKER: You're bein' observed . . . *(He nods towards* SHIMMA)

SALLY: What? *(Looks, sees* SHIMMA; *snarls at her)* What are *you* starin' at?
This is a private matter. This is company business . . . *(*SHIMMA *stares
at him, silently.* SALLY *releases* FLORENCE, *shoving her away from him)*
You're free, you . . . *(*FLORENCE *circles the plant floor, still in a rage.
Animal-like moans issue from her: deep-throated, primal.* SALLY *goes to*
PORKER *and "sucker-punches" him in the stomach; hurting him,*

humiliating him) That's for your girlfriend, you . . . (PORKER *skids and falls in a crumpled, humiliated heap)* Get back to work! Get set up for re-wraps! *Hustle!* You're all gettin' paid, *yes? (The women restart their labor in near-robot fashion, mechanically, automatically. Their eyes meet, one by one.* SALLY *is deeply ashamed and embarrassed, but unable to apologize. He cleans some of the mess. Suddenly,* SALLY *screams at* SHIMMA) You won't close us down, sister! No matter how much you shove, North Shore Fish is stayin' on its feet . . . *(To the Women)* I'll bring the product out . . . *(To* PORKER) Get up and gimme a hand, you!

(PORKER *stands, silently. He starts toward* SALLY *after flashing a look at* FLORENCE, *who stands facing* SALLY, *her body heaving a silent sob every tenth count, as does a child after a tantrum.* SALLY *yells at* FLORENCE, *through clenched teeth, pointing his finger)* If you ever, *ever,* come at me again, I'll . . . *(He doesn't complete his sentence. He moves to the freezer)* I'm getting the product. Get set up . . . *(To* PORKER) You comin', or what? (PORKER *moves to* SALLY, *wordlessly. He is embarrassed, beaten into humiliation, hangdog.* SALLY *and* PORKER *exit into the freezer. There is silence, but for* FLORENCE's *sharp sobbing intakes of breath: her post-tantrum gasps for oxygen.* SHIMMA *is shaken. She holds back her tears, makes pronouncement to women on the "line"*

SHIMMA: You tell that blow'ah I ain't passin' no fuckin' inferior product for *noooooooobody.* You tell him I got people lookin' over my shoulder . . . and I'm coverin' my own ass, no matter what. Even if I have ta close this plant down. If I hav'ta, I hav'ta! I'm just doin' a job. You get my point here? *(All nod understanding)* You tell that blow'ah what I just spoke . . . (SHIMMA *turns, exits into kitchen, slamming door closed behind her. After the door slams, there is a small silence. We see* SHIMMA, *through the window. She sits in chair, bows her head, extremely upset. The women watch her a moment, then look at one another, gravely concerned.* ARLYNE *cocks her head. She is worried. The lights fade to black)*

ACT II

Scene One

Lights out in the auditorium. In darkness, we hear the sound of a radio playing: a song such as Willie Nelson singing "All Right Woman, All Right Man."

Lights up in plant. Five hours later. The women are squashed together on either side of the end of the processing "line," at the wrapping table. They are all involved in the unwrapping and re–wrapping of frozen fish dinners: boxed. At the moment, they are stripping the boxes of their "A&P" labels and re–wrapping the boxes with "Good Deal Market" labels.

Neither PORKER *nor* SALLY *is on stage.* SHIMMA *is in her kitchen, at the typewriter, writing reports.*

The women sing along with the song. PORKER *and* SALLY *enter, wheeling handtrucks loaded with fish product in crates. The women are all singing full-voiced, wholeheartedly.* PORKER *and* SALLY *stop, astonished, as they head toward a big finish.* SHIMMA *hears* SALLY, *looks up and out, as* SALLY *switches radio off.*

SALLY: What's up? What gives here? We workin' or we partyin', huh? We got a plant fallin' apart here and what are you all doin'? Singin'? This is very bright, very *swift!*

JOSIE: C'mon, Sally, we've been singin' all afternoon and we still wrapped sixty crates of Stop & Shop.

SALLY: I just walked in here and half of you wasn't doing a single stick of work.

RUTHIE: We're almost finished, Sal.

PORKER: Maybe if they just played it and didn't sing along?

SALLY *(Turns on* PORKER *cruelly):* What is this I'm hearin' now?

PORKER *(Shows* SALLY *his palms):* Just an idea . . .

229

SALLY: You wanna come in to Markie with me and maybe take it up with him? *(Pretends to be* PORKER *talking to the boss)* "Markie, I know we're goin' outta business and all, and I know we got a new inspector turnin' down every piece a' product we process and you're probably gonna hav'ta sell the building and the land and all, but couldn't the girls just have some music ta listen to, instead of doin' their last couple'a days of paid work? *Hmmmmmmmmm?*"

PORKER *(Interjected into above speech):* Right, okay . . . okay, Sal . . . okay, we'll drop the playin'-music idea . . .

SALLY: What have you got? Some private income?

PORKER: Okay, okay, you made your point . . .

SALLY: I don't hear an answer to my question, Martino!

PORKER: C'mon, Sal, enough, huh?

SALLY: I would like to hear an answer to my question, Martino!

PORKER: C'mon, Sal, will you?

SALLY: I would like to hear an answer to my question, Martino . . .

PORKER: Come onn, Sal, a joke's a joke, huh!

SALLY: I said that I would like an answer to my question. Did you not hear me?

PORKER: Okay, fine. What's your question? *(The women all stand silently watching)*

SALLY: Do you have a private income?

PORKER: No, Sally, I don't. I don't have a private income. (PORKER *is humiliated; head down.* FLORENCE *walks to radio, switches it back on. James Taylor's "Fire and Rain", blares out.* SALLY *turns and faces* FLORENCE)

SALLY: What's this? *(There is an enormous tension now in the plant.* SALLY *moves to* FLORENCE, *who stands her ground, defiantly, sings along with the music for a few beats. The music continues on, but without* FLORENCE *now, who stands her ground, silently staring at* SALLY. *There is a long "hold."* SALLY *talks to* PORKER, *without ever breaking his stare at* FLORENCE) Turn it off. Martino, turn off the radio.

PORKER: Hey, Sally, will ya' . . .

SALLY: You workin' for North Shore Fish or what?

PORKER: I'm workin' . . .

SALLY: Turn it off. *(After a long, tense pause,* PORKER *heads toward the radio. As he passes* FLORENCE, *they share a moment. He cannot find the strength she wants him to find: He goes to the radio; switchs it off. Whilst looking at his shoes,* PORKER *speaks)*

PORKER: I'll be right back. I gotta go to the bathroom . . . *(*PORKER *exits upstage, out of sight lines. There is another moment's pause.* SALLY *feels he has won;* FLORENCE *absorbs* PORKER's *small defeat)*

SALLY: I called the broker, myself. We can move now on the re-wrap job for A&P . . . eighty thousand units. Everything's in house. I got the labels, I got the product . . . *(*PORKER *speaks up. He hasn't, of course, been to the bathroom. He has simply stepped out of sight)*

PORKER: What product?

SALLY: We're gonna re–wrap everything we got. Tommy Fusco's brought me labels from Mass Coastal. We're in business here, yes?

ARLYNE: *You* did this, Salvatore?

SALLY: I did, yuh, I made the call myself . . . I made the sale.

JOSIE: Does Markie know this?

SALLY: I told Markie I could move the stock, yes . . .

FLORENCE: We're selling off all the stock we've got?

SALLY: I'm making work. I'm covering overhead . . .

ARLYNE: Are we makin' a profit?

SALLY: What is this? I have to make reports to the wrappers? (False laugh. After a pause, SALLY continues; answers ARLYNE) We're breakin' even. We're payin' ourselves. We're makin' our own work . . . (There is another small pause. Then SALLY screams his orders officiously) I want everybody on unwrappin'. I want all the labels pulled and then we'll all go on to wrapping. . . . Could we please start? (Everybody starts unwrapping boxes of frozen fish) Porker, go get the rest of the stock . . . (nods to PORKER) let's go. (PORKER and SALLY exit with handtrucks after leaving crates at end of wrapping table)

ARLYNE: I don't like the sound of this . . .

JOSIE: It doesn't sound great . . .

FLORENCE: Looks like the end of the road.

RUTHIE: How so, Floey?

FLORENCE: You can't sell fish if you got no fish to sell!

MAUREEN: Sally must know what he's doing . . .

FLORENCE: How come you say that, Maureen?

MAUREEN: I dunno.

MARLENA: He's good looking . . .

FLORENCE: Right. You got it. . . . (Smiles, nods to MAUREEN) Your cousin catches on fast.

MARLENA: Something wrong?

FLORENCE: Nope. (PORKER *re-enters with handtruck loaded with cartons of frozen product*)

PORKER: This don't look good . . .

RUTHIE: It's work, like Sally said . . .

PORKER: If we sell off all our stock, under-priced, then we ain't got nothin' ta play with . . . to broker. I mean, where's the future? (FLORENCE *laughs.* SALLY *re-enters, unloads his truckload of frozen product*)

SALLY: If ya's all are smart, you'll work hard now and save yo'rselves a job for tomorrow . . . if you get my message. (SALLY *exits again. The women unwrap product, diligently*)

ARLYNE: No harm in workin' hard . . .

JOSIE: When have we ever done anything but?

MARLENA: Hard work's the best thing in the world, really . . .

MAUREEN: The Japanese give their first loyalty to their work, second to their families. That's why their country's making so much money . . .

FLORENCE: Same thing here, ain't it? Who do you know who's givin' their first loyalty to their family? (FLORENCE *moves upstage to breading machine. After a moment's work,* ARLYNE *sings alone, not conscious of anyone listening, or caring*)

ARLYNE: "If you want a dooo-right-all-night's womannnn . . ." (*Thinks; speaks*) If John Wayne had been a singer, he would have sounded just like Willie Nelson . . .

JOSIE: I think that's true . . .

FLORENCE: After Willie Nelson's dead, he'll sound just like John Wayne.

PORKER: I don't get it.

FLORENCE *(Explains):* John Wayne's dead now. After Willie Nelson's dead, they'll sound alike. Get it?

PORKER *(Disgusted):* What's *with* you?

RUTHIE *(To* MARLENA*):* My mother's hung up on John Wayne . . .

ARLYNE: I'm not "hung up." I *like* John Wayne. I enjoyed his acting. He was excellent!

JOSIE: They say he had a tiny organ. Miniscule.

PORKER: I'm in the room, ya' know.

JOSIE: So what?

PORKER: I hear what you're sayin'.

JOSIE: "Miniscule" isn't dirty, Porker. It means the same as "tiny" . . .

MAUREEN: . . . like your Toyota . . .

RUTHIE: . . . like your Christmas bonus . . .

FLORENCE: . . . like your *mind* . . .

JOSIE: . . . like John Wayne's wee-wee!

PORKER: What is *with* this one?

RUTHIE: John Wayne's real name was Marion Morrison . . .

ARLYNE: She does this to annoy me.

RUTHIE: It was *so!*

FLORENCE: Marion?

RUTHIE: It's in my "What To Name The Baby" book. Marion Something Morrison. They have this whole long list of famous name-changes.

PORKER: John Wayne was a fag?

FLORENCE: What's this?

PORKER: Isn't that what Ruthie just said? John Wayne had a girl's name
. . . (SALLY *re-enters with another handtruck load*)

SALLY: Now, what's the chatter?

PORKER: John Wayne was a fag!

SALLY: What's this?

PORKER: Ruthie found it in a book. He was a fag. He had a girl's name.

SALLY: What are you saying, Martino?

PORKER: John Wayne's real name was a goddam *girl's name* . . . The
Duke, huh? The *Duchess*, that's what!

SALLY: If you ain't the fuckin' limit! (SALLY *dumps the contents of his
handtruck and exits, angrily*)

PORKER: What's with Sally? Everything I say pisses him off.

FLORENCE: Maybe 'cause Sally's a girl's name, huh?

PORKER: What the hell are you *tellin'* me here? You *know* somethin'?
What's with this insinuendo, huh? (*The women roar with laughter.*
SHIMMA *walks down staircase from kitchen above. End of laughter*)

SHIMMA: I called into Boston. I can't allow the re–wraps to go out of
here. I don't care if you've been doin' it before. I can't allow it to go
out of here now. (*Pauses*) It's not my decision . . .

PORKER: What are you saying here?

SHIMMA: Once product is wrapped, it's wrapped and it's gotta be
shipped.

PORKER: But we didn't wrap it! It's bought already wrapped. It's our stock. That which we don't process and pack ourselves we buy already wrapped. It's our stock. That's the business . . . oh shit! (PORKER *runs offstage, to get* SALLY. *There is a pause*)

SHIMMA: It's not my decision . . .

FLORENCE: So if you get this plant closed down, then what?

SHIMMA: I'm not lookin' to get this plant closed down. I'm just doing my job. If I don't, somebody else will come in and do the very same thing. . . . *(Shrugs)* I'm not lookin' to get any plant closed down . . . (SALLY *enters on the run; skids to a stop*)

SALLY: What's this?

SHIMMA: I can't approve the re–wraps. There's no way.

SALLY: There's nothin' you can do about it. There's a government pass on every package . . . it all passed.

SHIMMA: Not after you unwrap the package there isn't . . .

SALLY: The government doesn't pass the label. It's the *product* that's been passed . . .

SHIMMA: You've never heard of shelf life? This stuff's double-dated . . .

SALLY: What shelf life? These are frozen goods! What the hell are you talking about?

SHIMMA: It's not my decision. I called Boston . . . I gotta red-tag.

SALLY: Now wait a minute. Wait a fucking minute here . . . you ain't gonna red-tag none of this product . . . (SALLY *starts to move in toward* SHIMMA)

PORKER: Hey, Sally, come on . . .

SALLY: You ain't closin' us down, sistah!

SHIMMA: I'm only doing my job! (SALLY *arrives at* SHIMMA, *grabs her, backs her against wall. He raises his fist*)

FLORENCE: *Don't, Sal!*

PORKER: *Sal!* (SALLY *is about to hit* SHIMMA *when suddenly* RUTHIE *screams out*)

RUTHIE:
Oh God, Mama, it's coming! The baby! Oh God! (*Everybody turns and looks*) *Oh God, Mama, it's coming NOW! It's coming FAST!* (*There is a moment's pause. Blackout*)

Scene Two

Fade in music: Otis Redding sings on tape: "Oh, she may be weary . . . Young girls do get weary . . . wearing that same shaggy dress . . . but, when she gets weary . . . try a little tenderness . . ." Music fades out.

Lights up in plant, fifteen minutes later. MAUREEN, FLORENCE *and* MARLENA *are sitting center, smoking cigarettes. The first glow from their cigarettes is the cue for the stage lighting.* RUTHIE *and* ARLYNE *are offstage, in the lounge.* RUTHIE *is about to deliver her baby.* JOSIE *and* SALLY *are with them.* SHIMMA *is in her kitchen on the telephone.* PORKER *enters from offstage.*

FLORENCE: How's she doin'?

PORKER: Any second now . . . any word from the doctor?

FLORENCE: She's callin' his office. He shoulda been here by now . . .

PORKER: He can't be here if he doesn't know about it . . .

MARLENA: I was born on my father's boat. . . . (*Pauses*) My mother was overdue, so my father took her out for a ride on the boat, to shake her up . . . it worked. . . . Of course, I was a third baby for my mother. (*Pauses*) I guess I came too fast . . .

PORKER: You *what* too fast?

FLORENCE: Jesus, Porker, you are *disgusting!* *(To* MARLENA) *One* thing on his mind! Honest ta God!

PORKER: What's with you? I was just interested in what she was sayin' . . .

FLORENCE: Oh, yuh, sure . . .

PORKER *(To* MARLENA): I was born on my father's lobster boat. Same thing, kinda. My mother was frightened she'd have me while my father was out on the boat . . . so, she came along. . . . I was her fourth baby. *(Smiles)* They say they figured if she went into labor, they'd have time to get up to Addison-Gilbert, 'counta they weren't too far out, just lobsterin' off of Bass Rocks . . . *(Shrugs)* I guess they figured it wrong . . .

FLORENCE: A long line of great thinkers . . .

MAUREEN: My Uncle Kevin got born in the old Central Grammar School. My grandmother used to clean there. Then he went to school there himself . . .

FLORENCE: Didn't he teach there, too?

MAUREEN: That's my point. After he finished college up to Salem Teachers, he taught there . . . all his life 'til they retired him at sixty-five. . . . Now, it's city-subsidized housing and he's movin' in there. Imagine: born in the same buildin', school in the same buildin' . . . and now he'll be livin' there!

FLORENCE: The Central Grammar School?

MAUREEN: Practically the same room he taught in . . . Same floor. It's amazing, huh?

FLORENCE: I got two aunts livin' up there. Nice place . . .

MAUREEN: A whole life, in one building . . .

FLORENCE: Arlyne's like that with this place. She started here, same as my mum, when she was about fifteen. She must be, what?, sixty, now?

MAUREEN: Close to it . . . she's been shop stewardess here, probably thirty-five years . . .

FLORENCE: That's why my mum was so happy ta get laid off. It was like a ticket *outta* this place . . . *(Pauses; then bitterly)* Bloodless, fuckin' people, layin' her off after so many years, huh?

PORKER: Puts the food on the table . . .

FLORENCE: What the hell are you *sayin'*, Porker?

PORKER: I'm just sayin' that workin' here puts food on the table. That's not too complex an idea, is it? What's with your attitude? *(We hear siren, offstage, to indicate arrival of police car. We might also see the glow of a flashing red light reflected on a wall.* SHIMMA *enters from kitchen, then goes offstage to back room to* RUTHIE. JOSIE *pokes her head in from back room, calls to* FLORENCE *and* PORKER*)*

JOSIE: He's here. *(*JOSIE *disappears back into back room. There is a moment's pause. The sound of the siren stops. The car has arrived.* ARLYNE *appears, poking head into room, then re-exits into back room. There is another moment's pause.* SALLY *appears from back room for a brief statement)*

SALLY: The doctor's here! *(Nervous laugh)* I sent him around back to the loading door. *(*SALLY *re-exits into back room)*

FLORENCE: Gives me the creeps, havin' the police come here like that again . . . so soon . . .

MAUREEN: Me, too . . .

FLORENCE: Seein' the son-of-a-bitch comin' in, same look on his face . . . *(She imitates* SALLY*)* The doctor's here . . . *(Adds in* SALLY*'s nervous laugh.* FLORENCE *punches her fist into her hand)* Gives me total willies, that's what. Saddest thing there is. Saddest goddam thing there is, I swear to God! (FLORENCE *turns away.* MAUREEN *explains to* MARLENA)

MAUREEN: When Dot died—She's the one we was tellin' ya' about—the doctor showed up in the Gloucester police cruiser, same way.

MARLENA: She died *here?*

MAUREEN: We found her in the freezer, when we opened up.

PORKER: *I* found her.

MARLENA: Oh, Jees. That must'a be'n *weird!*

MAUREEN: Same exact sound: police cruiser with the sireen goin' soft-like, then the brakes screechin', stoppin' . . .

FLORENCE: Mist'ah Macho comin' in with that same look on his face: half puppy-dog, half shit-eating grin . . . *(Imitates* SALLY *again, words and laugh)* "The doctor's here . . ." *(Pauses)* Saddest goddam thing there is . . .

PORKER *(Softly):* Floey? Hey, Floey, c'mon, huh . . . (FLORENCE *looks at* PORKER, *half smiles, bravely. The two old friends share a private moment of grief)*

MARLENA *(After a pause):* What . . . happened?

PORKER: I opened up, same as usual . . . hit the daytime generators, mopped up, set out the waste cartons, the usual. Then I went into the freezer to load a pallet with blocks. We were doin' Grade "A" orders for McDonald's then . . . before we lost the account . . . the freezer was full of exhaust fumes. . . . *(Without pause)* Dotty was on her back on top of a stack of #6 blocks. She was wearin' her dress, street shoes, lab coat on top, open . . .

MAUREEN: She killed herself . . .

MARLENA: No kidding?

MAUREEN: Length of garden-hose tapped into the freezer-engine . . .

PORKER: The fumes were wicked. . . . *(Pauses)* To tell you the God's honest truth, I still didn't think she was dead. Her eyes were open and she was starin' straight at me . . .

MARLENA: That musta be'n creepy!

PORKER: She was kinda half-smilin' . . . her eyes all sad . . .

MAUREEN: The doctor caught a ride up in the police cruiser. They were all in Dunkin' Donuts when the call came in . . .

PORKER: Coincidence . . .

MAUREEN: Same exact sound: police cruiser with the sireen goin' soft-like, then the brakes screechin', stoppin' . . .

PORKER: She was in the family way. The G.D. *Times* said she was "despondent" . . .

MAUREEN: She was havin' Sal's baby . . .

FLORENCE: No, she wasn't. She killed it, two days before, over Beverly. She went to Sal and he told her to kill it . . . set it up for her . . .

MAUREEN: Dot's a super devout Catholic, too. Her whole family. Her brother's a priest, down Revere . . .

FLORENCE: It drove her nuts, killin' off the baby . . .

PORKER: Made her despondent . . .

FLORENCE: Sal made her kill it . . . *(*SALLY *enters, looks about, smiles)*

SALLY: Any second now. . . . *(Laughs)* Too much for meee . . . *(smiles)* it's an amazing thing. Absolutely amazing . . .

JOSIE *(Pokes her head into room; excitedly):* It's the baby! The head's come out!

PORKER: Boy or girl?

JOSIE: Just a *head's* out! Jesus, Porker! (JOSIE *exits again into back room.* SALLY *looks up at* FLORENCE, *not smiling*)

FLORENCE: Are you gonna shoot this one with a gun? Or are you gonna let this one live?

SALLY (*Shows his palms to* FLORENCE): Right. Great. Fine.

PORKER: What's this?

FLORENCE: You're quite a fella', Sal . . .

SALLY: That's what they tell me.

FLORENCE: I hope you die.

PORKER: Hey, Floey, what gives here?

SALLY: I probably will . . . fifty-sixty-seventy years after you do, I hope . . .

PORKER: Hey, Sally, what gives? (*We hear the sound of a baby crying softly offstage.* MAUREEN *crosses herself, as do* MARLENA *and* SALLY) Goddd . . . (JOSIE *runs in*)

JOSIE: It's a girl! (*Everyone cheers enthusiastically.* JOSIE *runs off, returning to* RUTHIE *offstage*)

MARLENA: I love girls.

SHIMMA (*Enters, smiling*): It's a girl! (SHIMMA *goes upstairs, to her kitchen, closes door.* ARLYNE *enters, smiling*)

ARLYNE: Girl! (*Everyone cheers, again. They gather around* ARLYNE, *hugging and kissing her: children around a triumphant mother*)

MAUREEN: How's Ruthie?

ARLYNE: Hardly a peep. We deliver easy. *(She looks around at* PORKER *and the others, smiling at them, happily)* Wonderful thing, isn't it, bein' born right here, right in the middle of it . . . *Gawdd! (Sobs)* I wish my mother coulda' been alive ta see it. Gawdd! *(Smiles, instant recomposure)* It's a girl! Ruthie's fine. You wanna come see?

MAUREEN: Great! *(To* MARLENA) Wanna?

MARLENA: Great! (MAUREEN *and* MARLENA *exit into back room.* JOSIE *re-enters, momentarily)*

JOSIE *(To* ARLYNE): She's askin' for ya . . . (JOSIE *and* ARLYNE *exit.* SALLY, PORKER *and* FLORENCE *are alone on stage.* SALLY *nods to* PORKER)

SALLY: Give us two minutes to ourselves here, okay?

PORKER: I'm not listening. *(Showing his palms)* I'm not listening! (SALLY *goes to* FLORENCE)

SALLY: Can I try to explain something here? (FLORENCE *looks at* SAL, *wordlessly; shrugs)* I was seventeen, Carmella was sixteen. Alla' fuckin' *Gloucester* knew what was happening! I mean, come onnn . . . two kids leave high school and get married 'cause they're *so in love?* Seventeen years old, standing up in Our Lady Of The Good Voyage Church, looking out the door to Destino's while Father Gambriana's sayin', "Do you, Salvatore, take this woman . . . ?" And you know what I'm really doin'? I'm lookin' out the door across the street and I'm seein' Porker's girlfriend, Jumbo-jet Josie Evangelista, hoppin' up the steps to Destino's for her second cold-cut sub of that particular morning and I'm thinkin' about what it would be like to be bouncing up and down on her moons-over-Miami! (PORKER *quickly runs to top of stairs to basement/changing room; checks to be certain that* JOSIE *can't hear)*

PORKER: Josie's nothin *like* my girlfriend!

SALLY: Yuh. Sure. And you're not in love with Florence here, neither, right?

PORKER: What's this?

SALLY: I thought you wasn't listening!

PORKER: I'm not!

FLORENCE: Did you?

SALLY: Did I what?

FLORENCE: Bounce on Josie?

SALLY: I did . . . about two weeks after the wedding. *(Pauses, looks away: a private moment)* I'm seventeen and Carmella's *six*teen and nobody's got the sense ta get it taken care of! I mean, come *onnn.* Carmella was probably second or third best grades in the whole junior class . . . already accepted down to Salem Teachers, right? Futures? Forget about it! "The family *pride,*" my father's tellin' me. Her old man . . . you remember looney Yo-Yo Shimmataro, before he fell out of his brother's dragger?

PORKER: I remember Yo-Yo . . . No great brain *there* . . .

SALLY: Yuh, well, Yo-Yo corners me, over back of the old Rockaway. I was drinkin' beers all night with Bootsy McMahon and I'm off havin' myself a piss . . . my thing is out and allsa sudden there's Carmella's old man right beside my doo-dad. I'm thinkin', "Swell! He's gonna cut it off!" and I hear Yo-Yo sayin' in this sincere fuckin' voice, "I knocked her mother up same way and we've been together thirty-something years already and we're *pretty happy,* sometimes. I'm glad Carmella's marrying a *man!*" What'd he think Carmella was marrying: a fucking *toad? (Pause)* Seventeen years old: they fix us up with a two-day honeymoon in some summah cottage Carmella's mother cleans, over Riverdale. She's got the key so we use it for two days . . . the place stinks of mold and mustiness. Then we both start workin' here at North Shore Fish: Carmella stays on the line wrappin' 'til she's big like Ruthie . . . me: I start right out in the office, coverin' Markie Santuro's ass, which I will never stop doin' til I fucking *die!* And Carmella goes home to mind the baby. She closes the door behind her and she never gets to see daylight again! *(Confidentially to* FLORENCE, *trying to exclude* PORKER) Let me ask you a question, Florence, straight and simple: Knowin' how I wrecked Carmella's life as I did . . . not to mention knowin' how I've probably been the worst husbin in the history of the whole North Shore, tell me something: How'mI s'pose'ta walk out on this person, Florence? How?

PORKER: Walk out on who, Sal? Walk out on who? *(To* FLORENCE*)* What's he sayin', huh? What's he talkin' about? Come on, you guys? What gives? (JOSIE *re-enters, she is upset, holding back tears. She makes eye contact with* FLORENCE *and* SALLY, *smiles, bravely)*

JOSIE: Nice little girl . . . *(Then, without warning,* JOSIE *goes directly to* PORKER *and folds herself into his arms, weeping)* Makes me so sad. . . . *(Sobs)* Oh, God, it makes me so sad . . .

PORKER: What does, Jose?

JOSIE: Babies bein' born. . . . *(Sobs)* If I weren't so fat, he'd come home, wouldn't he?

PORKER: You're not fat! *(To* FLORENCE *and* SALLY*)* Is she fat? (FLORENCE *shrugs.* SALLY *shrugs.* PORKER *makes a fist at both of them. He grabs a coffee mug, fills it from* MAUREEN*'s thermos, hands mug to* JOSIE*)* Drink some of my sister Rose's coffee. It'll make your troubles seem miniscule. *(She takes mug, sits on steps. She tries not to cry. She sips the coffee. She makes a face.* PORKER *sits beside* JOSIE *on steps)* I think she adds oregano. (JOSIE *smiles briefly and then she speaks, sadly)*

JOSIE: He used to touch me all the time. I don't just mean high school, I mean years and years afta. . . . *(Sobs)* I don't know why I eat so much, Porker. I get so *frustrated* . . . doin' the same things day in and day out . . . havin' no money . . . seein' the same buncha ya's day in, day out . . . sayin' the same dumb things. . . . *(Sobs)* Don't take this personal. It's not personal. It's not against any of ya's, honest ta God, but, I really hate my life. . . . *(Pauses)* I'm sick of the neglect. Being his wife is like being a dog in a dead man's house. (JOSIE *is now a sobbing jelly-mass in* PORKER*'s arms.* PORKER *looks around helplessly at* FLORENCE. FLORENCE *starts to cry. She holds her stomach and she wails with grief.* SALLY *goes to her, speaks softly)*

SALLY: Floey?

FLORENCE: What?

SALLY: I'm tryin' to say something to you, Florence. Something about *life* I think I'm finally learnin' . . . something that's, I dunno, *appropriate* right now about, well, *us*.

FLORENCE: Yuh, swell, let's hear it.

SALLY: People like us are like pieces of wood floating on the water. We float in—sometimes we touch—sometimes, we even *bang together* . . . but, then we float off. We're not really in control of these things, Florence. There's like some *big tide* moving us here and there . . . we can't really be *blamed*. (FLORENCE *hits* SALLY. *It is a startling backhand blow*)

JOSIE: Hey! Florence!

PORKER: Ah, shit, you guys, c'mon, will ya's . . . (SALLY *holds his hand to his cheek*)

FLORENCE: Tell Carmella to set a couple of extra places at the table for next Christmas dinner. Tell Carmella I'll be comin' over for next Christmas . . . me and the baby.

SALLY: I'm s'pose'ta walk out on her 'cause you and I are *so much in love*, right? What a joke, huh? I oughta send it in to CBS-TV. They can use it on the television! (*He starts away from* FLORENCE, *stops, turns to her again*) You wanna' tell Carmella and Little Sal and Michael and Angela about everything, this is fine with me, you do that! You do that . . . and a' course, then I get to tell Bradley and Emily about their mother bein' the Town Pump, right? (FLORENCE *points her finger at* SALLY *and seems to want to yell something accusatory, but cannot form the words. She sobs instead, pointing her finger inscrutably.* SALLY *moves towards* FLORENCE, *just as* MAUREEN *and* MARLENA *re-enter. They are both smiling brightly*)

MAUREEN: She's beautiful . . .

MARLENA: She's *sooo* nice!

MAUREEN: You should go in and see her, Josie. It'll make you feel good.

MARLENA: She's really such a nice little baby . . . (MAUREEN *and* MARLENA *feel the pain in the air*)

SALLY: I'm gonna go tell Markie. I gotta tell him about the baby and about the red-taggin'. I gotta report in to Markie. (SALLY *turns on his heel and exits into back office*)

JOSIE: It's all big loud thunder and very little rain. You know what I mean? (*Sighs*) Cookie's giving me about half what he used ta . . . and that's with me hounding him day and night. My fatha keeps tellin' me to take nothin' . . . to let him pick up the bills and just throw Cookie out altogether . . . (*Pauses; weeps*) I'm thirty years old. I don't want my fatha payin' my bills. . . . (*Sobs*) My fatha wants to kill him, ya know. My fatha knows that Cookie's be'n beating me. (*Sobs*) Before you beat a dog, you better make sure whose dog it is. That's the way I see it.

FLORENCE: A dog is a dog. That's the way *I* see it.

JOSIE: I don't like that mouth of yours, sistah! You got something shitty between you and Salvatore, this is fine, this is great, but this is between the rotten two of ya's, so don't be draggin' us all inta the middle! Nobody's got the guts ta bring it up, but we all remember the price certain people paid for gettin' caught between the pair of ya's sluggin' it out, okay?

PORKER: Maybe you oughta just leave it be, Josie, huh?

FLORENCE: What are you gettin' at?

PORKER: Me?

FLORENCE: Her!

JOSIE: What I'm sayin' here is maybe if you never started in with Sal, things mighta be'n a little different for Dot, huh? You ever think of that?

PORKER: Hey, Josie, Jesus! Is *that* what you were sayin'?

FLORENCE: Yo'r mouth is as big as your ass, ain't it?

PORKER: Hey, come *on*, will ya's!

FLORENCE (*Circling towards* JOSIE): I seen Cookie down the Rigger, ya know . . .

JOSIE: Yuh, so?

FLORENCE: So, am I sayin' things out loud?

JOSIE: What am I sayin' out loud?

FLORENCE: What are you? *Simple?* Your ears can't hear what your mouth is speakin'?

JOSIE: I didn't say nothin'! Did I say anything bad, Porker? You're right here. You heard! Did I?

PORKER: What do I know? People say things. It's intense around here right now. No big deal . . .

FLORENCE: Not to you, maybe, shit-for-brains, but, if I'm carryin', that's my personal stuff and havin' it talked about in front of everybody is no little deal to *meee!*

JOSIE: Who the hell said you was carrying?

PORKER: Now, you lost me there, Flo . . . I gotta tell you: You lost me there . . .

JOSIE (*To* PORKER): Did you hear me say she was carrying?

PORKER: Carrying what?

JOSIE: A baby, you dodo!

PORKER: A baby? You're having a baby, Florence?

FLORENCE: Come off the shit, Porker! Sal told you. He wouldn't keep something like that to himself . . .

PORKER: Cross my heart!

FLORENCE: *Porker!*

PORKER: Okay, so he said something, but honest ta God, I didn't believe him for a second. Sal's always braggin' about this and that, right? . . . How far along are you?

JOSIE: Jesus, Porker, what's *with* you?

FLORENCE: I'm havin' it taken care of during lunch break, tomorrow. I made the appointment . . . over Beverly. That's where lady-killer sends his ladies, right?

JOSIE: Don't let Arlyne hear . . .

FLORENCE: What do I care? You think the Pope's gonna be any happier if there's one more pathetic kid runnin' around Gloucester, wonderin' where the hell his fatha is . . . wonderin' why the hell he was put on Earth? For *this*? For cutting and packin' TV-fucking-dinners? Taste-O-The-fucking-Sea Fish Fingers??? What are you all? *Crazy???*

JOSIE: You know what Arlyne will say to that: "We're in the fish business. We're fish people. We're doin' what we were born to do . . ."

FLORENCE: Can you believe this one? This is not the fish business, Josephine! This is the non-union, bottom-of-the-barrel, end-of-the-road, frozen, breaded *dung* business! I know what fish is. Fish is alive until you kill it. Fish is something that bleeds when you cut it open. You see this already-wrapped-and-unwrapped-twenty-seven-times frozen *dung*? *(She breaks apart a frozen fish brick into its component parts)* One little fish neck, two little fish backs, piece of a tail, piece of another tail . . . answer me a question: Did you ever in your entire life see anybody actually *eat this shit*? *(*SALLY *walks out of the back office, re-enters, stands facing* PORKER, FLORENCE, MAUREEN *and* MARLENA. *He is ashen, whitefaced)*

PORKER: Sally.

FLORENCE: *What?*

PORKER: Sally's back . . .

FLORENCE: So what?

SALLY: I think one of you should stop me . . .

PORKER: What?

SALLY: Me: I should be stopped.

PORKER: From what, Sal?

SALLY: You'll see from what when I get to her goddam door . . . (SALLY *climbs stairs to kitchen. He screams at* SHIMMA) Get out here, you Commie KGB pig! (SHIMMA *presses her nose against the window, frightened. She locks door. Satisfied that door is locked,* SALLY *goes to door, bangs on same)* GET . . . OUT HERE!!! GET (Bang) OUT (Bang) HERE (Bang, bang, bang) !!! (SHIMMA *stares out from behind the glass, trapped, but safe from* SALLY's *rage.* SALLY *kicks the door, three sharp kicks. He then climbs on structure, screaming in through window at a terrified* SHIMMA)

PORKER: Hey, Sally, what's *with* you?

SALLY: You better stop me, Martino, or else I'm gonna break this door down and murder this one . . .

PORKER: Why now? What's she done now? She couldn't have red-tagged nothin' more 'cause we haven't mastered nothin' more. Nothin's gone into the master pack for more'n an hour and a half.

SALLY: Markie's sold the plant.

PORKER: What?

SALLY: You have waxey ears or what? Markie's sold the goddam plant out from under us . . .

FLORENCE: What are you sayin', you?

SALLY: Am I not speaking the King's fucking English? Markie Santuro has sold the plant. North Shore Fish is sold.

FLORENCE: To who?

JOSIE: To who?

MAUREEN: To whom?

MARLENA: What's happening?

MAUREEN: He's saying the plant's been sold . . .

MARLENA: Will you still get your paid vacation?

MAUREEN: Jesus, Marlena, I'm just hearin' this same as you . . .

MARLENA: I don't wanna be a pain in the ass, but, I've got to schedule out my time . . .

MAUREEN: Shut up! (MAUREEN *moves to* SALLY) Who'd Markie sell the plant to, Sal? (SALLY *doesn't answer*) Sal?

SALLY: It's gonna be a fitness center . . .

FLORENCE: What?

SALLY: Nautilus, aerobics classes, that shit . . .

JOSIE: I'll join up! My prayers are answered!

PORKER: Are you shittin' me, Morella? This plant is *sold?*

SALLY: Sold. The equipment goes on the dump. The new people move in as soon as possible . . .

PORKER: Like when?

SALLY: I dunno . . . Tuesday, Wednesday . . . We hav'ta clear our personal stuff outta here, today . . .

PORKER: Wait a minute, wait a minute. North Shore Fish is sold and it's gonna have weight-lifting and dancing classes startin' *Tuesday* or *Wednesday? (Laughs)* This is a fact of life?

SALLY *(Smiling):* This is a definite fact of life. There is no changing this. Markie's had these fitness people "on hold" for about six weeks, 'til he saw whether or not the business turned around. He's pretty torn up about it himself, I can tell you that. This plant's been in the Santuro family more'n a hundred years . . .

PORKER *(Laughing and snorting):* Wait a minute, wait a minute, wait a minute! This plant is definitely sold and weight-lifting and Nautilus are definitely comin' in here as soon as possible, maybe Tuesday or Wednesday of this coming *week?*

SALLY *(Starts laughing, infected by* PORKER'*s laugh):* Definite, definite, definite . . . (FLORENCE *and the others giggle as well, also infected by* PORKER'*s laugh)*

PORKER: You're not my boss, anymore, Morella? You're not over me? I'm not under you? This here set-up between us is over and done?

SALLY *(Laughing):* Over and done. *(Without warning, with total purpose and precision,* PORKER *goes to* SALLY *and punches him in the stomach)*

PORKER: You miserable prick! You greaseball, fuck-your-own-children, miserable brown-nose prick! (PORKER *pummels* SALLY *with slaps, swats and punches. This is the fight that* PORKER *has stored away for some twenty years: since fifth grade. The fight is, thus, like that: formless; childlike . . . a school-yard brawl)*

MAUREEN, FLORENCE & MARLENA: —Hey, Porker, off him . . .
—Hey, Porker, stop . . .
—Grab his arms . . .
—Porker, knock it off . . .

—He's killin' Sal!

—Stop it, Alfred!

—Stop punching, Porker!

—You split his lip!

—Porker, you'll kill him! *(Instant chaos:* PORKER *and* SALLY *are in a heap. The women pile on and try to pull* PORKER *off of* SALLY)

PORKER *(A tad hysterical):* I'LL KILL HIM! I'LL RIP HIS HEART OUT! I'LL BREAK HIS ARMS OFF! GIMME HIS MISERABLE TONGUE AND LEMME PULL IT OUTTA HIS MISERABLE MOUTH! LEMME KILL HIM! I WAITED MY WHOLE FUCKIN' LIFE FOR THIS! GIVE HIM TO MEEEE!

FLORENCE *(Sees* RUTHIE *coming up stairs, from below):* The baby! Stop! The baby! (RUTHIE *enters, supported by* ARLYNE. RUTHIE'*s hair is matted, stringy. She is sweaty, exhausted, but joyously aglow. She wears* SHIMMA'*s white lab-coat; carries her baby, swaddled in white towels.* PORKER *stops his rant when he sees* RUTHIE. *All others look up as well, amazed. The women pull* PORKER *off of* SALLY, *who rises from the floor slowly. His lip is split, bloodied.* SALLY *holds his jaw;* RUTHIE *holds her baby. A unique class-reunion photo could be shot now)*

RUTHIE: I'm totally fine. Don't any of you worry. They're takin' me up Addison-Gilbert, but it's only for the rules. I could go straight home if I had to. I'm totally fine . . .

ARLYNE: I'm gonna run up to the hospital with Ruthie while they check her and the baby out . . . if that's okay with you, Sal . . .

FLORENCE *(To* SALLY; *sternly):* Don't you tell her!

SALLY: It's fine, Arlyne, fine. No problem. Have a good weekend.

ARLYNE: What happened, Sal?

SALLY: Why? What's the matter?

ARLYNE: Your lip's all bloody.

SALLY: I fell down.

ARLYNE: The doctor's still out in the cruiser, if you hustle out there . . .

FLORENCE: He's okay.

MAUREEN: He's fine, Arlyne. It's superficial.

ARLYNE: It's on your coat, too. It looks like you've been cleaning live fish.

FLORENCE: Dead fish.

ARLYNE: Hmmm?

FLORENCE: He's fine, Arlyne. Go with Ruthie . . .

RUTHIE: I'm naming her Roxanne . . . *(There is a embarrassed pause: un ange qui passe)*

FLORENCE: Don't do that, Ruthie. Roxanne is a shitty name . . .

RUTHIE: You think so?

FLORENCE: It's *horrible.* She'll hate being Roxanne . . .

RUTHIE: You all think so?

MAUREEN: I don't like it . . .   PORKER: I wouldn't . . .

JOSIE: It sounds kinda *cheap,*   SALLY: I wouldn't, Ruthie.
don't'cha think? . . .   Roxanne's not really too great.

RUTHIE *(To* MARLENA): How about you? I know you're temporary, but I'm kinda interested . . .

MARLENA: I dunno . . . Roxanne's okay, I guess . . .

ARLYNE: I thought Roxanne was elegant.

FLORENCE: It's shitty, Ruthie. Trust me.

RUTHIE: How about Florinda?

FLORENCE *(Rolls her eyes to heaven):* Jesus, Ruthie!

RUTHIE: Well, how about Joyce?

FLORENCE: Yuh, well, maybe . . .

JOSIE: Maybe . . .

PORKER: Nothin' wrong with Joyce!

FLORENCE: I would go with Joyce, Ruthie.

RUTHIE: Maybe I'll wait and go through the what-to-name-the-baby book
again tonight. . . . *(To the baby)* You don't mind not havin' a name
one more day, huh? *(To all, with a giggle)* She's cute, isn't she?

FLORENCE: I haven't seen her. . . . *(Walks to baby; looks)* She's
beautiful, Ruthie. She looks just like . . . you and your mother.
Same eyes.

RUTHIE: Yuh . . . (RUTHIE *crosses slowly, painfully, to the door; stops at
threshold. To baby)* Say "bye-bye" . . .

ARLYNE: She'll be back . . .

RUTHIE: No, she *won't*, Ma! *(Embarrassed by the suddenness of her
response; to all)* Just joshin' . . . *(To* ARLYNE*)* I'm feeling just slightly
weak. We'd better go . . . *(To all)* I'm really fine. Don't any of ya's
worry.

MAUREEN: 'Bye, Ruthie. Congratulations . . . congratulations to Earl,
too!

MARLENA: Nice to meetcha.

RUTHIE: I'll probably be back in a week from Monday, Sal, if that's okay?

SALLY: Whatever you want, Ruthie, that's fine.

RUTHIE *(Affectionately; admiringly):* You're the greatest, Sal!

PORKER *(Disgusted)*: Oh, *yuh!*   SALLY *(Touched)*: Nawww!
"You're the greatest, Sal!"   Congratulations, Ruthie, huh?
                                      . . . and say congratulations
                                      for me to Earl, too . . .

RUTHIE: I will. Come visit, everybody . . . *(Giggles)* I guess you've seen
the baby already, but come visit anyhow . . .

FLORENCE: We will,   JOSIE: I'll come by,   PORKER: 'Bye, Ruthie!
Ruthie!   Sunday!

SALLY: 'Bye, Ruthie!   MARLENA: Nice to meet you both!

ARLYNE: Good weekend, everybody. Don't do anything I wouldn't do!
*(*RUTHIE *and* ARLYNE *exit the play. There is a moment's pause. Suddenly,
as though by some force of elision,* PORKER *attacks* SALLY *with precisely
the same schoolboy intensity as before)*

PORKER: Miserable prick! Lemme kill you! Lemme put you outta' yo'r
misery! *(Once again,* PORKER *muckles* SALLY *and once again the women
pile on top, pulling* PORKER *from* SALLY *before he does mortal damage)*

MAUREEN, FLORENCE & MARLENA: —Porker, come onnn . . .
—Grab his arms . . .
—You'll kill him . . .
—He's a lunatic!
—Get off, Porker . . .
—Stop hitting . . . Porker . . .
—Jesus, Porker, STOP!

PORKER: I'LL RIP HIS HEART OUT! I'LL TEAR HIS MISERABLE
TONGUE OUTTA HIS HEAD! *LET ME!!!*

(The two men are once again separated. SALLY's *lip is again cut and bleed-
ing.* PORKER *rages out of control, moaning and ranting. The three women
try to hold him back)*

FLORENCE: You gotta calm down, Porker. You'll bust a blood vessel!

PORKER: Let me go, Florence! Let me at him!

FLORENCE: I can't do that, Pork!

PORKER *(Breaks loose; charges at* SALLY, *swatting him with terrycloth towel):* You blew it, Morella! My grandfather worked in fish, my father worked in fish and I am gonna work in fish. You can sink and submerge this plant, but you can't pull real people like us down with you! I will bury you before I'll sink with you and that is a fucking fact of life, you *faggot!*

SALLY: You split my lip, you *dick!*

PORKER: I'll split your dick, you *derr . . .* you *peckerhead . . .* you *pussy . . .* (SALLY *finds a wet rag and swats back at* PORKER)

SALLY: I didn't put this plant under, you *dink . . .* you *donk . . .* you *diddlyshit.* I kept this plant goin'! I kept this plant alive! I breathed precious life inta' this operation. I put the food on your goddam table, Martino! *(To all)* All of ya's! I kept you workin' . . . kept you earnin' money. I put the food in your babies' mouths, if you wanna know the goddam truth of it! And this is the thanks I get!

FLORENCE: What are you? *Demented?*

SALLY: Yuh, right, I'm demented. Takes one to know one, Florence . . .

PORKER *(Screaming):* Don't dignify the dork, Floey! Honest ta Christ, just treat him like somethin' dead. Just treat him like a bad smell. Just act as though he ain't happenin', 'cause you *ain't,* Morella, you really *ain't!*

MAUREEN *(Out of nowhere):* Is my vacation paid or what, Sal?

SALLY: What's that s'posed'ta mean?

MAUREEN: What's that? Too *complex?* Is my vacation a paid vacation or a vacation that is not a paid vacation? Which?

SALLY: The plant is closin', Maureen. Closing. C-l-o-s . . .

MAUREEN *(Picks up* JOSIE's *half-filled mug of* ROSE's *old, cold coffee):* Don't you fuckin' spell at me, you! (MAUREEN *pours coffee on* SALLY's *head)*

SALLY: Nice, thanks, Maureen, very nice . . .

MAUREEN: You're lucky it wasn't boiling, 'cause that's what you deserve! You're lucky it wasn't a knife in your heart, 'cause that's what you *really* deserve! (MAUREEN *goes to* SALLY *and spits at him*) Scumbag! *(To* MARLENA) He's playin' up ta all of us, all this time. He even comes on ta old Arlyne, this one . . .

SALLY: Come on, Maureen, huh?

MAUREEN: Sweet talkin' shit, keepin' all the girls scared they're gonna get laid off if they don't come across . . .

JOSIE: We all know the opposite to "laid off" workin' a line under you, don't we, Sally-boy?

SALLY: I never touched you once, Josephine, and you know it!

JOSIE: What are you? *Brain-damaged?*

SALLY: When? Name a single touch!

JOSIE: I'm s'pose'ta spiel off when you touched me, in front of Floey and Reenie and Hotlips Martino?

SALLY: One touch: come on . . . let's hear!

JOSIE: Greasy-Pole Contest, Stage Fort Park, under the old bandstand floor!

SALLY: That was years ago!

PORKER: What's this?

JOSIE: How'd you lose your memory? Horse step on your head?

PORKER: Is she makin' this up or *what?*

SALLY: That was years and years ago!

JOSIE: Not so many . . .

SALLY: Eight!

JOSIE: Five!

SALLY *(Shrugs):* Five.

JOSIE: You were married to Carmella, already . . . I was workin' under you, already . . .

FLORENCE: Hard to find anybody who hasn't been workin' under this one . . . if ya catch my drift.

PORKER: What am I hearin' here?

FLORENCE: Kinda' hard ta grasp, ain't it, Pork?

SALLY: I never thought I'd see the day you'd be blurtin' it out in front'a everybody . . .

JOSIE: Every dog has her day, Sal . . .

SALLY: You were goin' with Cookie, already, ya know . . .

JOSIE: "Goin' with" is hardly "married to," you cheatin' bastid!

PORKER: See? That's why I never did it . . .

FLORENCE: You never *did it,* Porker?!

PORKER: Ho, ho, that's rich. That's why I never got *married* . . .

JOSIE: What's why?

PORKER: On accounta there's no point to it if nobody's ever gonna be *faithful.*

FLORENCE: Also, on accounta the fact that every goddam one of us said "no" when you asked us . . .

PORKER *(After a beat):* Now, that was a miserable cruel thing ta say out loud.

MAUREEN: It was, Flo.　JOSIE: It was pretty　SALLY: It was, Flo.
low, Flo . . .

FLORENCE: I guess . . .

MARLENA *(After a pause):* Is it true? Did he ask all'a ya's?

PORKER: Will you come on?

FLORENCE: All of us, all of Rockport, Manchester, Ipswich, Essex, even Woburn! *[Pronounced "woobin"]*

PORKER: Nice.

MARLENA *(To* SALLY*):* Does this mean my workin' here next week is off or what? Hey, I'm askin' you a question!

SALLY: What?

MARLENA: Does it?

SALLY: The plant is closed. Closed. What do you think it means? We clear out our stuff, we go home, we never come back unless we're takin' aerobics. Is that clear enough for you?

MARLENA *(After a pause, to all: screams):* He grabbed me in the freezer, you know . . .

SALLY in unison with PORKER: Come onnn . . .

MARLENA: Both of 'em! First him, then him! The greaseball pretty-boy jumped me and started pawin' all over! The little one snuck up and started in kissin' me. In the freezer!

FLORENCE: Teamed up?

MARLENA: Uh–uh. One at a time. That one asked me to give him a hand with fish fingers, then he jumped me on this huge frozen grey lump of something. I whacked my leg wickid!

PORKER: When was this?

MARLENA: About 11, maybe 11:30, this morning . . .

PORKER *(Disgusted):* Jesus, Sal . . .

SALLY: What's with the "Jesus, Sal"? When did *he* come at you?

MARLENA: At least he said something nice! You just grabbed like I was, I dunno . . . *product!*

SALLY: I got no time for this. Come on, Martino. We got a freezer to inventory . . .

PORKER: Do it yourself.

SALLY: What's this?

PORKER: Fuck you.

SALLY: This is exactly the gratitude I expect . . .

PORKER: Fuck you and fuck your grandmother!

SALLY: This I won't be forgetting . . . (SALLY *makes a sign of the curse [Italian variety] at* PORKER; *exits, swaggering, into the freezer.* PORKER *is smiling)*

FLORENCE: What'd he say?

MARLENA: Hmmm?

FLORENCE: This one: Porker: what "nice thing" did he say?

PORKER: What is the matter with you?

FLORENCE: Just curious, Pork . . . *(She smiles at* MARLENA; *pauses)*

MARLENA: I don't remember. . . . (Pauses) Something about me being "special" . . .

FLORENCE: Special?

MARLENA: I dunno. . . . (Pauses) Something about me bein' "different from the hometown pigs" . . .

JOSIE: Nice, Porker. Tasteful, too . . .

FLORENCE: What? Like your bein' an out-a-town pig kinda thing?

MAUREEN: Come on, you two!

MARLENA: I oughta warn you that once I start swingin', I don't stop. I mean, I gotta be stopped. You follow my point?

FLORENCE: No, I can't follow your point. I got dropped on my head and I'm a stupid fool. . . . (Talks to herself) Show her. How many fingers am I holding up? (Holds up three fingers; answers her own question) Dahh, I dunno, Flo, six? (To MARLENA, menacingly) You wanna' swing, Suzie, you swing! If I ain't afraid of him or him, I certainly got no fuckin' fear of a bimbo like you!

PORKER: Hey, come onnn, will ya's, no rough stuff! (Without warning, both FLORENCE and MARLENA slap PORKER, at precisely the same time. PORKER reels backwards, holding his face. He is totally humiliated. He confronts the women, MARLENA first) I ain't gonna hold you responsible for this, so, don't worry . . . (To FLORENCE) You neither . . . (To MAUREEN) Your bein' her cousin doesn't phase me against you, neither . . . (Nods in direction of freezer, where SALLY exited) It's the asshole in the freezer I'm gonna kill! (PORKER charges off into the freezer, screaming at SALLY) Dukes up, Morella! You're gonna be dead meat! (All pause. We hear: The sound of the freezer door slam shut. MARLENA looks at FLORENCE)

MARLENA: I apologize for losing it. I was a little wiped out to hear the news that I was workin' for no money . . .

FLORENCE: It's no sweat. I'm a little wiped out myself. (SHIMMA *enters from office. She walks to* FLORENCE)

SHIMMA: This wasn't my doing. I asked the owner straight out. He's had this offer on the table for two months, maybe more. This wasn't my doing . . .

FLORENCE: What's the diff?

SHIMMA: I just wanted to say that . . . I mean, this puts me out of work, too, you know . . .

FLORENCE: No problem . . .

SHIMMA: I've been waiting for this job to clear for me for weeks and weeks. I'm out now, too . . .

FLORENCE: Nobody's pointing fingers. Don't sweat it . . . (PORKER *enters on the run, worried*)

PORKER: Sally's knocked out . . .

JOSIE: Hey, good goin', Porker . . .

PORKER: It wasn't my fault. He slipped . . .

JOSIE: Don't be modest, Porker . . .

PORKER: He hit his head and cut it . . .

FLORENCE: What are you sayin'?

MAUREEN: Is he critical?

JOSIE: Is he dead?

PORKER: No, but he's hurt. He knocked himself out. We were rollin' around in the freezer and he whacked his head on this big chunk of tuna Markie keeps in there for personal use . . . Maybe I should get the doctor back . . .

MAUREEN: Is he still out cold?

PORKER: He came to, but he's groggy and his head's hurt bad . . .

FLORENCE: Gushing?

PORKER: No, but cut . . . and banged.

SHIMMA: Put some ice on it.

PORKER: You think so?

SHIMMA: I took First Aid in school . . .

PORKER: Where'll I get ice?

FLORENCE: I thought you said you were in the freezer.

PORKER: Oh, yuh, right . . .

FLORENCE: Jesus, Porker . . . (PORKER *exits off again, on the run. There is a moment's pause. The women begin to pack their belongings, ready to leave*)

SHIMMA: This is the first work I've had in four months . . . at least I've got no stuff to pack up . . .

FLORENCE *(Emptying her locker)*: Makes no difference to me. . . . *(Pauses)* I'm just about breaking even, anyhow. . . . *(Pauses)* Babysitters make just about the same as me, after I pay tax and dues. . . . *(Pauses)* My mother ain't gonna live forever. . . . *(Pauses)* Makes no difference to me . . . anybody got an extra shopping bag?

MAUREEN *(Tosses bag to* FLORENCE*)*: Here . . .

FLORENCE: No sweat. I should chuck all'a this . . .

MAUREEN *(Packing)*: Me, too . . . Anthony and I have been plannin' this trip for about two years now. . . . *(Pauses; smiles)* He'll probably be happy to call it off now. I don't think he ever wanted to go, really . . .

he was just being nice . . . he's got no real interest in seein'
Connecticut . . . just me.

FLORENCE: Connecticut? Is that where you were goin'? Connecticut?

MAUREEN: Connecticut has great natural beauty.

FLORENCE: You've never been to Connecticut?

MAUREEN: Yuh, well, so what?

FLORENCE: Don't miss Bridgeport. *Full* of natural beauty . . .

MAUREEN: I'm not goin' anywhere. Anthony's gonna be scared about
makin' our mortgage payments, with me outta work again . . .

JOSIE: At least you own a house . . .

MAUREEN: Yuh, I guess . . .

JOSIE: You could sell it. Arlyne said her cousin just sold her house over
East Main Street for two-hundred-thousand. . . . They moved to
Vermont—got a gorgeous place.

MAUREEN: I don't wanna move to Vermont.

SHIMMA: We tried to buy something in town here . . . couldn't even
come close . . .

JOSIE: How come you wanted to buy here?

SHIMMA: My husband's from here . . .

FLORENCE: From Gloucester?

SHIMMA: Yuh. Years back . . .

JOSIE: What's his name?

SHIMMA: Billy Shimma . . .

FLORENCE: He about thirty-eight?

SHIMMA: Thirty-seven . . .

FLORENCE: There you go . . .

JOSIE: Where'd he live?

FLORENCE: Lane's Cove, over by the sauna . . .

SHIMMA: That's right.

JOSIE: *That* Billy Shimma? With the pink Buick?

SHIMMA: I never saw the Buick. I only heard about it . . .

JOSIE: Small goddam world, huh? (PORKER *leads* SALLY *on.* SALLY *holds a packette of frozen fish product against his head wound)*

PORKER: I think he needs some stitches . . .

JOSIE: Is he gushing?

PORKER: No, but it's open. . . . Somebody ought to run him up to the hospital . . .

MARLENA: I'll do it. I've got a car. . . . (*Everybody looks at* MARLENA; *surprised)*

FLORENCE: The new girl.

MARLENA: I'm heading home anyhow. No point in paying a sitter for *this*. My kids are home from school already. No point in paying a sitter if the plant's closin' down . . . (*Goes to* SALLY, *looks at his head wound)* I'll take you . . . you know the way?

SALLY: I'm gonna be okay. . . . (*To all)* Don't any of ya's worry. I looked at my reflection in the chrome cover on the freezer pump and I've seen worse, so don't any of ya's worry. . . . (*Pauses)* Listen, I've got feelers out already and I've already gotten nibbles from a couple of places . . . maybe something's gonna open up at Gorton's, for example. There's also something I don't wanna mention, yet, but I want ya's all ta know, definitely, when I'm settled, you're settled and that is a promise . . .

JOSIE: We know, Sal . . .

SALLY: To tell you the God's honest truth, I'm glad Markie sold. He's been threatening for so long now . . .

PORKER: Sally's be'n keepin' it from ya's . . .

SALLY: I didn't want none of ya's ta worry . . . but I've seen this fitness clown hangin' around Markie for a couple'a weeks now . . .

PORKER: The weightlifter type of musclebound Mafioso jamoca Earl kept seein' when he picked up our garbage. I kinda suspected som'pin, myself, personally . . .

SALLY: I kept it under my hat. I saw no point in every one of ya's bein' under the gun too . . .

PORKER: . . . feelin' the pressure kind of thing . . .

SALLY: To tell you the truth, I'm glad it's finally over. This way, I can set up something solid for all of us . . .

JOSIE: We know you will, Sal . . .

SALLY: You guys all . . . mean something to me . . .

JOSIE: You mean something to us, too, Sal . . .

SALLY: I swear this to ya's all: I'll set up something new for all of us inside of three months, four at the very max . . .

MAUREEN: We know you will, Sal. You've got my number, right?

SALLY: 'Course, I do. I got everybody's . . .

FLORENCE: Yuh.

SALLY *(Pauses; touches head):* I'd better head up there . . .

MARLENA: It was nice meeting you all . . .

FLORENCE: Oh, yuh. It's gotta have been one of the absolute high points of my life . . .

SHIMMA: I'm sorry it didn't work out. My husbin'll never believe this one, really . . . *(Goes to* SALLY; *offers hand)* No hard feelin's, I hope . . .

SALLY: Naw. I know you were just doin' a job . . .

SHIMMA: Well . . . *(Looks at all; shrugs)* Good luck, everybody. I loved meeting ya's . . . *(Exits)*

JOSIE: Me, too . . .

MAUREEN: Me, too . . .

MARLENA: We'd better, huh?

SALLY: Yuh, sure . . . (SALLY *moves to* FLORENCE) I'm gonna be sayin' goodbye now . . . (FLORENCE *turns away from* SALLY. *He starts to move to door; stops; turns again to face everyone. Suddenly, without warning,* SALLY *begins to cry. He sobs and moans, openly, like a hurt child)* It ain't fair, it ain't fuckin' fair! It ain't my fault. I did my job. I got out the product . . . I got out the product! *(To all, embarrassed)* It's the loss of blood that's gettin' ta me, probably. *(Pauses, clears his head; makes a pronouncement)* I loved every woman who ever worked for me. I did. I'm not ashamed of it, neither. I'm a natural leader . . . you watch me: before Labor Day. You watch me. I'll have ya's all workin' back under me in some local fish situation, before Easter. *(Exits)*

MARLENA: 'Bye, everybody . . . *(Exits.* MAUREEN *moves from her locker, carrying a huge stack of papers, books, stuff)*

MAUREEN: I need a Sherpa . . .

JOSIE: What's a Sherpa?

MAUREEN: They live in Nepal. They carry stuff up Mount Everest for explorers . . .

FLORENCE: You know everything, don't you, Maureen?

MAUREEN *(Blushes):* I like to read about things. . . . *(Shrugs)* Things interest me. . . . *(Drops some books)* Shit! *(Picks them up)* Lookit all this stuff. I never thought I'd be leavin' here. Got my own little Sawyer Free Library goin'. . . . *(Picks up topmost book; looks at it)* A book on fish. I don't know anything about fish, really . . .

FLORENCE: Who knows anything about fish? I mean, fish don't tell you anything much, do they? You ask 'em a question, they flop around. . . . *(Ruefully, suddenly)* What's the secret of life, Reenie?

MAUREEN: For fish, it goes like this. The female gets pregnant because she drops eggs and the male swims around and shoots his sperm at 'em . . . at the eggs. The eggs pop open and about a million little fish swim around together. The females drop their eggs, the males shoot their sperm on 'em and about ten million more fish pop out, swim around . . .

FLORENCE: I'm sorry I asked . . .

MAUREEN: The schools . . . the fish that swim around together . . . they're all the same age. They never see their fathers again, after the sperm gets shot, never. They just swim around with fish their same age and have their own little fish. . . . *(Smiles)* Wanna borrow the book?

FLORENCE: It sounds too depressing. I'll stick to *Cosmopolitan.*

MAUREEN: If Anthony and I bag Connecticut, maybe you and I can spend a morning down Salem? . . . in the historic houses?

FLORENCE: Again?

MAUREEN: I was just thinkin' . . .

FLORENCE: Sure. I'd like that, Reenie . . . as long as we can skip the House of Seven Gables . . . looks just like what I grew up in . . . hit your head every time you move . . . (MAUREEN *suddenly cries*)

MAUREEN: I never thought we'd actually close up . . .

PORKER: Don't cry, Reenie . . .

MAUREEN: I better go. . . . (*Suddenly*) Do you mind puttin' this stuff in the dumpster, Porker? There's nothin' here I need . . .

PORKER: No problem . . . you sure?

MAUREEN: I'll call you guys. 'Bye, Josie! (JOSIE *moves from locker, carrying plastic bags filled with her belongings, to* MAUREEN. *The women look at each other for a moment, silently, sadly. Suddenly, they hug*)

JOSIE: I'll call you later, Reenie!

MAUREEN (*Sadly*): I'd better go. (*Turns; exits.* JOSIE *moves forward, carrying her belongings, ready to leave*)

JOSIE: What a miserable effin' day, huh? Call me, Porker, huh?

PORKER: Uh, yuh, sure, Jose, sure . . .

JOSIE: See ya', Flo . . . (JOSIE *starts to exit;* FLORENCE *stops her*)

FLORENCE: Who's gonna take Arlyne and Ruthie's stuff to them?

JOSIE: Want me to?

FLORENCE: Uh uh. It's okay. I'll take it. I just didn't want you stickin' me with the errand. Long as you offered no matter . . . I'll take it to them . . .

JOSIE: That reminds me. I left a whole buncha ice cream and stuff in the freezer . . . (JOSIE *exits into freezer.* FLORENCE *looks at* PORKER)

FLORENCE: You and Josie are doin' it, huh?

PORKER: What's with you?

FLORENCE (*Imitates* JOSIE): *Call me, Porker, will ya?*

PORKER: Don't talk stupid. . . . (*Pauses*) It's none of your business . . . (*Smiles*)

FLORENCE: I knew it! (JOSIE *exits refrigerator; crosses to* PORKER, *winks at him, exits, carrying bag of ice cream containers*)

JOSIE: See you guys . . . how's about I call you after supper, Floey? About 6:30?

FLORENCE: 6:30's fine . . . (JOSIE, *by habit, pulls her timecard from the rack and punches out. The clock's bell rings sharply.* FLORENCE *and* PORKER *turns around, startled. They smile.* JOSIE *shrugs, smiles, exits the play. There is a pause.* FLORENCE *turns to* PORKER, *who looks down*) I s'pose with Jose you get more for your money . . .

PORKER: I won't dignify that smart remark . . .

FLORENCE: You wanna go out with me, Porker?

PORKER: Tonight like?

FLORENCE: Tonight, tomorrow night . . .

PORKER: You know I do.

FLORENCE: Okay. We'll go out.

PORKER: That is *great!*

FLORENCE: What's gonna become of us, Porker?

PORKER: In what way?

FLORENCE: Life is so full of shit . . . *(She looks about the room; sadly)*
My motha was thirty years here . . . breading, wrapping. For what,
huh?

PORKER: Come onnn. She *loved* it!

FLORENCE *(Smiles):* She did, yuh. . . . *(Pauses)* She's really lookin' awful
lately, Porker. Thirty years, not once bein' out sick, not once bein'
late, not once leavin' at the bell neither and they lay her off like she
did somethin' wrong. I mean, that's what she's thinkin'. That's what
she's tryin' ta figure out: what wrong thing did she do that she got
punished for? She's got nothin' . . . nobody's got nothin' . . . none
of us. None of the old people . . . I mean the real people, the
Gloucester people . . . I'm gonna end up just like my motha, Porker;
wicked miserable lonely, cookin' too much food when somebody
finally breaks down and visits, chewin' stuff over and over again that
happened years and years ago, makin' out that it was good, makin' out
that somethin' that happened to her mattered . . . goin' over and
over the past. No plans for nothin' . . .

PORKER: Come onn, Floey. Sally'll hook up to something soon. He's
workin' on four–five possibilities. . . . *(Shrugs; smiles)* We can collect
. . . the weather's good . . .

FLORENCE: I guess. . . . What're we s'pose ta do now, Porker?

PORKER: Us? I dunno . . . we'll clean up. We'll put out the lights, we'll
go home, wash ourselves up, you'll cook somethin' up for Bradley and
Emily, I'll eat some of my sistah Rose's horrendous cooking, we'll go
ta sleep, get up in the morning and face the fact we got no jobs, kill
the day, maybe meet up and go down ta the Capri in Beverly, get sick
on pizza, catch a movie, get married . . . I dunno. Why don't you go
home, start pickin' out somethin' to wear? *(There is a noise overhead.*
PORKER *and* FLORENCE *are both startled; look up)* What gives?

FLORENCE: Somebody's breakin' in! *(Two legs drop into sight: gabardine*
slacks, black wing-tip shoes . . . we've seen this costume)

PORKER: Sal! (SALLY *drops down, on to the top of the breading machine,*
eyes wild with determination)

SALLY: I've been up on the roof, watchin' and listenin' to what everybody's been sayin' about me. I know that you and my friend Martino here have always been attracted to each other and that now you're both available for each other and all, so before you go runnin' off with my friend Martino here, I want to tell you something, Florence.

FLORENCE: What's this?

PORKER *(To* FLORENCE*)*: He's always been jealous of us . . . ever since second grade! *(To* SAL*)* Nobody's runnin' off, Sal. We're just talkin'! Honest to Christ!

SALLY: Florence, I . . . I love you, Florence.

PORKER: Your foot's in the breading, Sal. Watch it!

SALLY: I've gotta talk to Florence, Alfred . . . *alone,* okay?

PORKER: Yuh, well, I can see that. I'll wait in the freezer . . . (PORKER *starts off.* FLORENCE *yells out)*

FLORENCE: Stay, Porker! (PORKER *starts to stay)*

SALLY: I have to talk to her, Pork . . .

PORKER: She wants me to stay, Sal . . .

SALLY: Porker, please . . . I'm askin' ya like a friend . . .

PORKER: I . . . *(Exchanges a glance with* FLORENCE*)* I'll stay, but I won't listen. (PORKER *gets mop. He starts to mop, as he did at start of play. He looks around at* SALLY*)* I'm not listening. Honest to God. *(Mops a moment; calls out)* What? I'm not listening. (SALLY *whispers to* FLORENCE, *as confidentially as he can manage to be)*

SALLY: I love you, Florence. I couldn't go off without you hearin' that from my mouth.

FLORENCE: What about your stitches?

SALLY: My stitches can wait, Flo. I'll risk it.

FLORENCE: Just be careful you don't fall off the breader.

SALLY: I'm leaving Carmella, Florence. I decided.

PORKER: What are you *sayin'*, Sal? (FLORENCE *throws a stay-out-of-this look to* PORKER. PORKER *returns to his mopping*)

FLORENCE: What are you sayin', Sal?

SALLY: Jesus, Florence, pay attention! All my life, you've been *it*. When we were in fourth grade, I was already serious in love with you! Of all the girls I've ever loved, you've always been *it*, Florence. I was just now driving up to the hospital for stitches and I'm thinkin' to myself, "Sally, you're screwing it up with Florence in a big way. You're gonna get your stitches, you're gonna go home to Carmella and that will be it for the next forty–fifty years until you get some devastating dread disease and croak!" I'm doin' it, Florence. Even though Carmella will probably drown herself off Bass Rocks and my kids will turn out to be junkies. Also I'm a Catholic, so my soul will no-doubt-about-it burn in hell for forty–fifty thousand years, but I'm doin' it . . . for you, Flo. (SALLY *stares into space, suddenly silent.* PORKER *and* FLORENCE *look at each other. He looks up at* FLORENCE, *eyeball to eyeball. He makes his pronouncement*) I'm moving in with you, Florence. I'm leaving Carmella and the Church. As soon as my divorce comes through, you and I are getting married.

FLORENCE: Are you asking me to marry you, Sal?

SALLY: Isn't what I said clear?

FLORENCE (*After a substantial pause*): No.

SALLY: No, it's not clear or no, you won't marry me?

FLORENCE: No, I won't marry you. (PORKER *laughs, discreetly, turning away from* SALLY *as best he can*) Go home to Carmella, Sal. It's okay. Go home.

SALLY: I don't want you to hate me, Florence.

FLORENCE: I don't hate you, Sal. But, that's no reason to be married to you.

SALLY *(He means what he says):* I'm sorry, Florence.

FLORENCE: Me, too . . . *(Suddenly, the back door opens. To everyone's amazement,* MARLENA *enters, looks around, sees* SAL*)*

MARLENA: I'm *fryin'* out there! It must be a hundred! You said five minutes about a half hour ago! I gotta get home!

PORKER: Jesus, Sal . . .

FLORENCE: Jesus, Sal . . .

SALLY: I told her not to come in, no matter what! *(Yells at* MARLENA*)* Didn't I tell you not to come in, no matter what? *(To* FLORENCE*)* This doesn't mean there's anything between me and her at all, Florence. She's just drivin' me . . .

PORKER: How come you need a ride? Where's your car?

SALLY: *Stay out of this!* *(To* FLORENCE*)* Can I call you later, Florence?

FLORENCE: I . . . for what?

SALLY: For *talking!* To talk to you!

MARLENA: I'm not getting in the middle of *nothin'!* I'm goin'! *(*MARLENA *leaves in a huff, slamming door behind her as she goes.* SALLY *looks worried. He's in a bind.* FLORENCE *sees this and laughs)*

FLORENCE: You'd better go.

SALLY: I'd better.

FLORENCE: You'd better . . .

SALLY *(Wants to stay and wants to go. Makes moves in both directions. Suddenly, he points at* PORKER*)*: This was all private stuff, Martino!

PORKER: Hey, c'mon, huh? Mum's the word, Sal. Trust me. (SAL *starts to speak again to* FLORENCE, *but has nothing further to say. He looks at her and then at* PORKER*)*

SALLY: We've only got each other, right? We came in together, we go out together. That's friends. (SALLY *exits the play.* FLORENCE *stares after him a while, thoughtfully. She turns and sees that* PORKER *has mopped and tidied the work area: it sparkles)*

FLORENCE: What's with you? The plant's closed . . .

PORKER: No reason to leave it filthy . . .

FLORENCE: You're okay, Porker . . . *(She starts to weep, doesn't)*

PORKER: Yuh, well . . .

FLORENCE *(Tries not to weep, turns, starts to exit):* See you around, huh?

PORKER *(Stops her; sings with Sinatra voice):* "Love was just a glance away . . . a warm, romantic chance away . . ." (FLORENCE *stops, laughs, turns and faces* PORKER, *sings)*

FLORENCE: "If you want a dooo riiiight allll niiight's womannn . . ."

PORKER: You wanna get married, Florence?

FLORENCE: What's this?

PORKER: If you're carrying and all, you oughta be married . . .

FLORENCE: What about Carmella and their kids?

PORKER: To *me*, Florence. I mean to me. *(There is a long, long pause)*

FLORENCE: I think your mind's snapped, Porker, 'counta the plant closin' down and all . . .

PORKER: A baby oughta have a fatha . . . (FLORENCE *stares at* PORKER, *suddenly cries*) You don't have to answer right away. We'll be goin' out and all . . . (PORKER *moves to* FLORENCE, *wants to embrace her, thinks better of it*) I'll ask you again, maybe Tuesday night, say . . . *(Pauses.* FLORENCE *is really in trouble: She is sobbing)* Are you cryin' 'cause I asked you to marry me?

FLORENCE: That isn't it . . .

PORKER: I can understand and all . . . getting stuck, just 'cause of yo'r situation and all . . .

FLORENCE *(Looks around at empty plant):* This is all I know how ta do, Porker. Me, my mother, my grandmother, all of us . . . we know the fish business. *(Pauses)* I've got nothing left to teach my children, Porker. They're gonna look at me and that's what I'm gonna think. . . . *(She sobs, chokes back her tears, continues)* I got nothin' left to teach my children . . . (PORKER *looks sadly at* FLORENCE; *tries to cheer her)*

PORKER: Don't cry, Flo, huh? *(Motions to boxes on assembly line)* It's only *work. . . . (Shrugs)* It ain't *life!* (FLORENCE *sobs.* PORKER *goes to her, they embrace. He sobs as well. Music in: repeat of lyric that started scene: Otis Redding, singing "She may be weary . . . young girls do get weary . . . wearing that same shaggy dress . . ." The light begins to fade.* FLORENCE *sobs in* PORKER'*s arms. They stand under one of the industrial lights over assembly line: in their own "natural" spotlight. The stage lights are now out. Otis Redding completes lyric: ". . . try a little tenderness . . ." and the industrial light—their spotlight—fades to black. The play is over)*

ABOUT THE AUTHOR

Israel Horovitz was born in Wakefield, Massachusetts in 1939. His first play, "The Comeback," was written at age seventeen. In the thirty-six years that have followed, nearly fifty Horovitz plays have been translated and performed in as many as twenty languages worldwide. Among the best-known Horovitz plays are "The Indian Wants the Bronx" which introduced Al Pacino and John Cazale; "Line" which introduced Richard Dreyfuss; "It's Called The Sugar Plum" which introduced Marsha Mason and, subsequently, Jill Clayburgh; "Rats" which introduced Scott Glenn to the American stage; "Morning" of the Horovitz-McNally-Melfi Broadway triptych "Morning, Noon and Night"; "The Wakefield Plays", a seven-play cycle; and "The Primary English Class" which starred Diane Keaton in its New York premiere.

For the past several years, Mr. Horovitz has been at work on a cycle of plays set in his adopted hometown, Gloucester, Massachusetts, all of which have had their world premieres at The Gloucester Stage Company, a theatre founded by Horovitz thirteen years ago and which he still serves as its Artistic Director and Producer. Other of Horovitz's Gloucester plays are "The Widow's Blind Date," "Year of the Duck," "Sunday Runners in the Rain" and "Strong-Man's Weak Child." He is now writing a new Gloucester-based play, "Fighting Over Beverly."

As a director, Mr. Horovitz has directed the world premiere productions of many of his plays.

Horovitz has written six original screenplays. The feature-film rights to "Strong-Man's Weak Child" have been purchased by Tri-Star Pictures and Horovitz has just completed the screenplay.

Horovitz has won numerous awards, including two Obies, the Emmy, Prix du Plaisir de Théâtre, Prix du Jury (Cannes Film Festival), the New York Drama Desk Award, an Award in Literature of The American Academy of Arts and Letters and The Eliot Norton Prize.

He is married to Gillian Adams, the former British National Marathon Champion. He is the father of five children, film-producer Rachael Horovitz, playwright/novelist Matthew Horovitz, Beastie Boys rock star/ actor Adam Horovitz and unemployed six-year-old twins, Hannah and Oliver Horovitz. The Horovitz family divides its time among homes in Gloucester, Massachusetts, New York's Greenwich Village and London's Dulwich Village.

—January 1992